FORENSIC PSYCHOLOGY

Forensic Psychology is the first practical and comprehensive guide to the practice of forensic psychology. It provides clear, detailed instructions on the basic skills, techniques and professional issues involved. It explains the history, development and application of forensic psychology, the sort of evidence that might be produced and how it can be applied. The authors cover topics such as offender profiling, psychometric testing, expert testimony, psychological autopsy and psycholinguistic techniques, and consider issues such as professional and ethical problems, and the need for training.

A handy reference tool and a practical guide, *Forensic Psychology* is an essential guide for forensic psychologists, clinical psychologists, lawyers and other professionals who need to understand the nature and application of psychological evidence in judicial proceedings. It will also be useful to students of forensic psychology, clinical psychology, forensic psychiatry or criminology.

G. H. Gudjonsson is a Reader in Forensic Psychology at the Institute of Psychiatry, University of London. His previous publications include *The Psychology of Interrogations, Confessions and Testimony* (1992) and *The Causes and Cures of Criminality* (1989) (with Hans Eysenck). He has testified in many high-profile cases in the UK.
L. R. C. Haward is Emeritus Professor of Clinical Psychology at the University of Surrey, and Honorary Consultant Psychologist to Chichester Health Trust. His previous publications include *Forensic Psychology* (Batsford 1981) and *A Dictionary of Forensic Psychology* (1990).

FORENSIC PSYCHOLOGY

A guide to practice

G. H. Gudjonsson and L. R. C. Haward

London and New York

First published 1998
by Routledge
11 New Fetter Lane, London EC4P 4EE

Simultaneously published in the USA and Canada
by Routledge
29 West 35th Street, New York, NY 10001

Reprinted 1999

© 1998 H. Gudjonsson and L. R. C. Haward

Typeset in Goudy by Routledge
Printed and bound in Great Britain by Redwood Books, Trowbridge, Wiltshire

British Library Cataloguing in Publication Data
A catalogue record for this book is available from the British Library

Library of Congress Cataloging in Publication Data
A catalogue record has been requested for this title

ISBN   0-415-13291-6 (pbk)
ISBN   0-415-13290-8 (hbk)

CONTENTS

ILLUSTRATIONS

Tables

Figures

PREFACE

Forensic psychology, defined in this book as that branch of applied psychology which is concerned with the collection, examination and presentation of evidence for judicial purposes, has in recent years gained increased recognition in the United Kingdom both in civil and criminal proceedings. This has been accompanied by a huge demand for specialised psychological services. Often psychologists are ill prepared for the type of work required and there is no up-to-date comprehensive text which they can refer to for advice and guidance. This is the basis for writing the book. The idea was to produce a practical and easily accessible handbook for psychologists engaged in court work. The emphasis throughout is on providing relevant background material on psychology and law, legal judgements, psychological principles, assessment techniques, professional and ethical behaviour, and guidance about the preparation of court reports and the presentation of oral testimony.

We have combined advice and guidance about current practice with brief accounts of historical developments relevant to forensic psychology. We believe this makes the book unique. One has to look back into the past in order to understand contemporary law, legal procedure and forensic psychology practice. Law is embedded within its own long history, and despite the rapid, sometimes premature, and occasionally ill-conceived legislation of the twentieth century, the judiciary interpret the law in a way which leans heavily upon historical precedent.

During the past decade there have been major developments in the use of psychology in the civil and criminal courts. The involvement of clinical psychologists in the arbitration of the 'test cases' concerning the Zeebrugge disaster is of historical and legal significance in relation to compensation being awarded for 'psychological damage'. On the criminal side, pioneering psychological research into psychological vulnerabilities and false confessions, accompanied by the application of psychological principles and techniques to major criminal cases where confession evidence was disputed, have been influential in a number of cases in the Court of Appeal, as well as improving police practice and social attitudes.

The authors are both experienced clinical and forensic psychologists with a previous background in law enforcement. Haward was the first forensic psychologist in the United Kingdom and over a period of three decades he pioneered the early principles and roles of forensic psychology. Prior to 1958 court work was dominated by members of the medical profession. The contribution of psychologists was incorporated into the medical colleague's report, often without proper acknowledgement. One of Haward's important contributions was to change this practice. In 1981 he produced the first English book on forensic psychology (Haward, 1981), which is now out of print. The present book overlaps very little with Haward's previous book.

Gudjonsson became actively involved in forensic psychology when he took up a forensic post at the Institute of Psychiatry in 1980. He took over from Haward as one of the most active forensic psychologists in the United Kingdom. Not only has Gudjonsson developed further the early work of Haward, he has broadened the field considerably and his evidence has been influential in a number of major cases in the Court of Appeal.

The authors' court work experiences have stimulated them to conduct relevant research in the field. It is active court case work, combined with extensive relevant research endeavour, which has the greatest potential impact on the courts, legal judgements, changes in legal practice, and the development and status of forensic psychology.

In this book the two authors combine their knowledge and experiences in the courts in order to produce a practical guide to other psychologists who are engaged in court work. The book will also be of value to other professionals who testify before the courts, including psychiatrists and social workers.

1

INTRODUCTION

A definition of forensic psychology

That great French scientist René Descartes (1596–1650) maintained that the only proper way for any scientific discourse to proceed was to 'define all terms and to prove all propositions'. Whilst we cannot hope to achieve such a depth of starting point as his *Cogito ergo sum*, we do deem it necessary to start with a definition of our subject.

The term 'forensic psychology' was first used in the UK by Haward (1953) in an address to the County Durham Psychology Group, later embodied into the Northern Branch of the British Psychological Society. In keeping with principles enunciated on that occasion, 'forensic psychology' is here defined as that branch of applied psychology which is concerned with the collection, examination and presentation of evidence for judicial purposes. Psychologists in the United Kingdom who assist the courts in specific cases are likely to agree that this statement adequately and appropriately defines their particular role on such occasions. It should be made clear that such psychologists are experts in their own right in some specified psychological speciality, and that it is only when applying their psychological skills for judicial purposes in a particular case, not necessarily appearing in court as an expert witness, that they can be said to be engaged in forensic psychology.

Not all psychologists agree with the above definition, however. In the USA especially, many psychologists appear to believe that activity at any one of the many interfaces between psychology and law merits the designation 'forensic psychology'. Perhaps the most extreme point of view is exemplified in a book edited by Cooke (1980), entitled: *The Role of the Forensic Psychologist*. His forty-two contributors – a mixed bag of interested parties which included lawyers, psychologists, mental patients, and prisoners, not least a 'lifer' who wrote his chapter and committed suicide – touch on almost every aspect of psychology remotely connected with law.

It should also be emphasised that the definition we adopted for this book centres upon *evidence*; it excludes professional involvement in a particular case which is not directly concerned with evidence as such. Thus Nietzel and Dillahay

1

(1986), in their eminently practical handbook *Psychological Consultation in the Courtroom*, describe ways in which psychological techniques are provided to the District Attorney or defence attorney to enable them to weigh down the scales of justice to favour their own side. In addition, activities recommended by Nietzel and Dillahay include training advocates in thespian skills together with special methods of ingratiating themselves with the jury; rehearsing the witnesses with videotapes and courtroom simulations, together with guidance on sartorial presentation; further courtroom simulations for the attorneys to try out their various ploys; social surveys to assess public reaction to the defence case; sampling views held by the public in population centres to find a venue for the trial possessing the strongest favourable bias; devising questionnaires for jurors designed to evoke significant attitudes of value during the jury challenge; and many more practical and potentially effective techniques.

Definitions produced by psychologists often prove contentious, and become established generally by agreement and usage. It is still too early for this to have happened with the term 'forensic psychology', and some justification for putting forward a specific definition seems desirable.

There is an etymological and semantic argument in its favour. The term forensic derives from the Latin *forensis*, meaning appertaining to the Forum, specifically the Imperial court of Rome, where matters in dispute were settled. *Court* and *dispute* are the two keywords: the first binds the term forensic to a legal setting, the second anchors it firmly to matters which are being disputed in court, namely, the facts in issue or *res gestae* in the case in support of which evidence is required or is disputed.

Our definition thus flows from this central theme of dispute in the context of individual legal proceedings, which is similarly apparent in the argument from tradition or long usage. Forensic pathology and forensic science are both concerned with the particular case. Forensic medicine developed in the same way, its relation to other aspects of law being more properly termed medical jurisprudence; in Scotland the term medicolegalism has been used. In forensic psychiatry, the primary function is clearly what we would regard as forensically diagnostic: however, since traditionally the purpose of diagnosis has been to determine treatment, the therapeutic role with offenders has developed naturally in the context of National Health Service provisions for forensic psychiatry units. This aspect of their expanded role is patently clinical rather than forensic, and it is noteworthy that the Prison Medical Service, which provides the physical counterpart to forensic psychiatry, has made no attempt to bolster its much-respected reputation by claiming a forensic appellation.

It is therefore apparent that in all professions adopting the adjective forensic in their title, with the exception of psychology, the expertise provided is directed solely or primarily towards the individual case.

Just why psychologists alone should want to adopt this nomenclature for their many diverse activities *vis-à-vis* the law is not easy to understand. Some years ago members of the nursing profession employed in forensic psychiatry units asked to be called forensic nurses, but as their direct experience of the work of forensic psychiatrists was purely clinical, the misapprehension on the nurses' part is perhaps understandable.

In contrast, members of the Criminological and Legal Division of the British Psychological Society (DCLP), many of whose members have never assisted in an ongoing court case, have succeeded after many years in their claim to be called 'Chartered Forensic Psychologists'. Their valuable contributions, both as a service within their own original speciality, as well in scientific research of high quality, has been applied to a wide variety of legal and law enforcement problems. These include the psychological factors involved in identification; jury processes; sentencing disparity and effectiveness; recidivism prediction, risk assessment, and offence typology. Such work has been timely, significant and practical, but these activities are traditionally those of the appropriate branches of applied psychology, and are not uniquely forensic. When the DCLP was founded twenty years ago, one of us (Haward) put forward vehemently the views expressed in this Introduction, and helped to persuade the founders not to call it the Division of Forensic Psychology: now that its members have achieved the appellation of chartered forensic psychologists, the next logical step will be to change the division's name to conform to their new status. Such a change may well have undesirable consequences for the profession itself, as Blackburn (1996), in his Inaugural Lecture entitled 'What is forensic psychology?', explains. This masterly analysis and erudite exposition of the practical and theoretical problems associated with the adoption of the title 'forensic' considers in some depth the implications which the use of the term has for the profession as a whole. It deserves serious study by anyone interested in the relations between psychology and law. Clearly, the concept of forensic psychology and its semantic nature is of theoretical interest; of more concern to the practitioner is that the label *forensic psychologist* has important implications for the development of career structures, for the public's perception of the psychologist's role in society, and especially for future relations between practising psychologists and their legal and law enforcement colleagues. Such issues are of such fundamental importance to professional psychology that in our view the term should not be employed, as Cranmer would have said, 'unadvisedly, lightly or wantonly', and echoes of these problems will be found in discussions in later chapters of this book.

A practical guide

This book is intended to be a practical handbook for forensic practitioners, in order to assist them with their preparation of court reports and presentation of evidence in court. The book is aimed primarily at psychologists, but other professionals who engage in court work, such as psychiatrists and social workers, will find the book helpful. We have attempted to include relevant forensic developments in other countries, including those in the USA and Europe, although the book is primarily aimed at UK practitioners.

There is a rapidly growing demand for specialist psychological expertise in civil and criminal cases. This reflects the broadening and expanding role of psychologists within the courts, the greater independence from medical colleagues, and the broadening of the criteria for admissibility of psychological evidence. Unfortunately, there is an insufficient number of suitably qualified experts available to cope with the demand. This has resulted in many inexperienced, ill-prepared and unsupervised psychologists being commissioned to prepare reports and appear before the courts. It is hoped that this book fulfils the need for a readily accessible practical guide, although it does not compensate for lack of training and experience, inadequate supervision, and unprofessional behaviour.

In Chapter 2 we provide a brief account of the relevant legal history in Europe, the USA and the UK. We draw attention to the key developments which have shaped the modern psychologist's application to legal problems and highlight some of the difficulties that were encountered by the early forensic psychologists. This is followed in Chapter 3 by a review of surveys which have been conducted into psychological evidence in court. This includes an early survey conducted in 1965 by Castell (1966) and further and more detailed surveys for the British Psychological Society (BPS) conducted in 1984 and 1995 by Gudjonsson (1985, 1996a). The three surveys provide a good insight into past and present practice of UK psychologists engaged in court work and show the important developments that have taken place during the past three decades.

Court work raises many ethical and professional issues. In view of their great importance to the administration of justice and the integrity of the profession as a whole, these are discussed in detail in Chapter 4. A description of current ethical codes is given, the types of ethical dilemmas sometimes encountered in practice are identified, and ways of dealing with ethical problems are discussed. In addition, the liability of forensic psychologists in civil proceedings is explained as well as the possible excuses which may be offered in defence.

In Chapter 5 the different roles of the forensic psychologist – clinical, experimental, actuarial and advisory – are discussed. In addition, the similarities and differences between psychological and psychiatric evidence are identified. The emphasis is upon collaboration and co-operation between the two disciplines, which possess complementary skills.

Chapters 6 and 7 focus upon the range of methods and techniques that are available to psychologists in their answers to legal issues and questions. Psychological testing, which is discussed in detail in Chapter 6, forms an important part of the forensic psychologist's assessment tools. Psychologists are in a unique position to apply reliable and valid tests to a range of human behaviour. In Chapter 7 a range of techniques in the use of psycholinguistics is discussed.

In Chapters 8 and 9 the contributions of psychologists are discussed within the framework of the English legal system for civil and criminal cases, respectively. Chapter 8 shows that civil law differs from criminal law in many respects, which has important implications for the forensic psychologist.

Chapter 9 illustrates how in criminal cases the psychologist can contribute at different stages of legal proceedings, which are comprised of pretrial, trial and sentencing issues. This chapter also highlights some important areas for the forensic psychologist, including the legal criteria for the admissibility of evidence in criminal cases, the assessment of disputed cases of confession evidence, offenders' attitude towards their offending, offender profiling, claims of amnesia, and recovered memories.

Chapter 10 provides psychologists with a practical framework for the preparation of court reports and presentation of oral evidence in court. The chapter begins by describing the initial contact between the psychologist and the referral agent and ends with practical advice about how to prepare for court and give evidence. It provides step-by-step advice about how to proceed from the time the psychologist receives the initial contact from the referral agent.

In Chapter 11 we draw together the main issues relevant to forensic psychology, including the origin, nature, development, contribution and scope of forensic psychology. Contemporary problems and the future of forensic psychology are highlighted.

2

HISTORICAL BACKGROUND

Introduction

Before solving the lawyer's problems psychologists have to translate them into their own language and scientific framework. To do this effectively, they first have to think like lawyers and see the problem in legal terms. Baker (1979) cites Professor Amos who, in 1831, addressed his law students by comparing them to the ancient god Janus with his two faces, one looking back into the past in order to understand contemporary law and legal procedure, and one looking forward to foresee the implications of contemporary legislation. Law itself has evolved over the past millenia, and the judiciary interpret the law in a way which leans heavily upon historical precedent.

This is especially the case in English common law, which remains in force and unchanged through the centuries until some particular offence or process is specifically updated into statute law or repealed. Modern law books still cite laws promulgated by Tudor kings alongside those of the present sovereign. An example of the staying power of ancient laws was Trial by Battle, which had been brought to England by the Normans in AD 1066. As late as the nineteenth century two litigants decided to settle their legal differences by this form of judicial combat, which at that time was unrepealed and therefore still a valid legal process (Ashford's case, 1819). Such a bloodthirsty usurpation of judge and jury was then quickly abolished by a bill rushed through Parliament. Today, there is still a substantial amount of contemporary behaviour which is proscribed by ancient statutes, and which, in theory at least, is still enforceable, although a special law reform committee has been convened to work through ancient laws and recommend those which could reasonably be repealed.

It is thus not surprising that some degree of historical perspective provides depth and a new dimension to the way the psychologist approaches a forensic problem. Similarly, the law never stands still. Since the present authors started their forensic practice, courts functioning for 800 years have been abolished, new ones have been created, and all manner of formerly lawful conduct have become criminal offences, many of them, such as those relating to data protection and computer usage, being inconceivable a decade or so ago. Legal processes and police powers have changed, and today's legislation becomes tomorrow's legal problems. The purpose of the present chapter is merely to outline briefly the history of forensic activities *vis-à-vis* the courts, and to trace some of the ways in which forensic psychology has developed in the UK. The history of law is covered by Walker (1968), Milsom (1969) and Baker (1979), among others, and the current position is described concisely by Darbyshire (1992) and Barker and Padfield (1996).

Pre-Victorian developments

Psychology has been intertwined with law since the dawn of recorded history, since both are concerned with human behaviour. The cuneiform tablets of Asia Minor, the papyri of ancient Egypt and the Greek and Latin scripts of early European civilisation bear witness to the interest shown in law by pre-nascent psychologists then called philosophers. The Decalogue which Moses brought down from the mountain contains offences which are still embodied in modern statute law, such as theft and murder, while other elements of the Old Testament still govern legal practice, such as the treatment of perjury in the law of equity, and that of corroboration in the law of evidence.

Later texts of the ancient world, Plato's *Republic*, for example, which is basically a search for the meaning of justice, have been studied in a continuing search to understand the psychological basis of legal concepts. Through the centuries of civilisation embryonic psychology has thus contributed unwittingly to the development of law.

Today psychology and law are so intertwined that some lawyers see the legal profession as a branch of applied psychology, while admitting that lawyers themselves make rather poor applied psychologists (Cromberg, 1994). However, it was not until medieval times that forensic activity, as such, appears when the Royal Courts recognised the need for experts to testify on matters beyond the general knowledge of judge and jury. By the twelfth century the two oldest forensic specialities – those of medicine and science – were being recognised.

Medicine and law

The use of forensic medicine came into being in England when moral pressures from ecclesiastic law halted the hanging of convicted women proved to be pregnant. To validate the pregnancy, a physician could be brought in if a prisoner 'pleaded her belly'. Forensic medicine was born. The first textbook on forensic medicine is said to have been published in China in 1247, and this seems to have served its purpose for 700 years, as the next edition did not appear until 1980.

Science and law

Circa AD 1124, Henry I employed investigators to detect unlawful tampering

7

with silver coinage. When irregularities were found and the perpetrators brought to court, the first 'expert evidence' by non-medical specialists, later to become forensic scientists, was placed on record.

English forensic psychology, as such, draws its expertise from both medicine and science, and can thus point to an unbroken line of service to the courts by its forbears during more than eight centuries. However, it was not until psychology itself emerged both as a distinct academic discipline and a profession that its forensic applications could be identified and separated from those of forensic medicine and forensic science.

Insanity and the law

The medieval use of expert witnesses in the English Plantagenet courts of law was only sporadic, and English jurisprudence lagged behind forensic practice elsewhere in Europe (Eigen and Andoll, 1983). There was, nevertheless, a slow but continuing change in the views about madness and its acceptance as negating criminal responsibility. Once this principle was adopted, the question of the accused counterfeiting madness became an issue.

The Wild Beast Test

Early notions of insanity were encapsulated in the Wild Beast Test, whereby only those exhibiting 'actions more like animal reflexes than moral choice' (Baker, 1979) were exempted from culpability. Most of the medieval lunatics, shackled and goaded beyond endurance, appeared to conform to this legal stereotype, which found explicit expression in Arnold's case (1724). From AD 1700 a gradual change in legal thinking about insanity can be detected. The Wild Beast Test surrendered to the belief that lunatics were not simply wild animals but humans, although the legal distinction between being mad or bad was still highly inconsistent.

Nineteenth-century developments

Simple rules for the plea of insanity enunciated in Arnold's case served forensic medicine until the M'Naghten Rules were introduced over a century later (M'Naghten's case, 1843; Daniel M'Naghten signed his name with at least six different spellings; lawyers prefer the M'Naghten version, which is therefore used here). The M'Naghten Rules proved more difficult to interpret and apply than those of Arnold, and during the intervening century a number of offenders, as in Hadfield's case (1800), who were sensibly declared insane, would have failed to qualify under the M'Naghten Rules. Although rationally based upon an explicitly psychological concept, that of cognition or 'knowing', the M'Naghten Rules still relied upon a notion of medical causation described as 'disease of the mind'. Hadfield suffered the delusion that he was a second

Christ, and must be legally executed in order to save the world: his otherwise motiveless attempted murder of an arbitrary victim and immediate surrender to the police was a logical means of procuring his execution. In the words of the later M'Naghten Rules 'he knew what he was doing, and knew that what he was doing was wrong' and under these Rules he could not have been declared insane. Fortunately for Hadfield he pre-dated M'Naghten, and the jury used its common sense and declared him to be guilty but insane.

In the M'Naghten Rules, the juxtaposition of two incompatible concepts, one subjective and the other a purely hypothetical construct, has often produced difficulties to psychologists when testifying on issues of insanity. Presented as 'medical' witnesses, they were forced to yield their scientific integrity to legal terminology.

With experience, the expert witness learns that lawyers share with psychologists the same meanings and understanding of critical concepts; in an ultra-conservative profession, they merely submit to the constraints and facade of archaic legal language, which retains its own linguistic form and continuity while adapting to contemporary changes in meaning. This is why some familiarity with the lawyers' interpretation of legal terms and concepts is so important to the forensic psychologist.

Later, the great Victorian reformers introduced a new caring attitude towards the mentally ill, supported by the psychological ideas of Janet and his followers. In addition to their impact upon notions of insanity, these ideas also influenced judgments in probate and divorce, and sowed the seeds for psychologists' participation in the appropriate special courts by the mid twentieth century. Elsewhere in Europe, unencumbered by M'Naghten and the necessary causation by mental disease, jurists were able to extend the psychological concepts to create a variety of other reasons for evading capital punishment, among which acute provocation, the irresistible impulse, and the *crime passionel* of the Code Napoleon were significant examples.

Forensic science

During these long gradual changes in forensic medicine, no similar development in forensic science is apparent. It was the Industrial Revolution which enabled forensic science to display its relevance, mainly in the civil law courts. In the Age of Steam there were numerous accidents involving mechanical devices, with which an agrarian population was unfamiliar, and engineers and industrial chemists found themselves increasingly adopting the role of forensic expert in compensation cases, laying a firm basis for forensic science and the later police laboratories.

Towards the end of the nineteenth century a reversal of attitudes began to take place. As psychiatrists moved away from the physical basis of medicine and embraced the more liberal 'moral' approach which would eventually lead to the practice of psychoanalysis and its many variants, psychologists themselves were forsaking their philosophical roots in favour of the experimental approach developed in applied science.

Leipzig: birthplace of forensic psychology

The world's first psychological laboratory was founded in Leipzig by Wilhelm Wundt (1832–1920), where sensory and behavioural phenomena were both measured and subjected to experimental manipulation. It was Ernst Weber, Professor of Comparative Anatomy at Leipzig University, who first introduced experimental psychophysics circa 1829 and discovered the JND (Just Noticeable Difference or 'threshold of sensation', Laming, 1987) – the first measure of subjective experience. More importantly, he devised the experimental methods which could be used to elucidate psychological problems.

Wundt fused the work of contemporary pioneers of psychological science with the statistical methods of Sir Francis Galton and developed experimental psychology in his laboratory with both theory-oriented and applied goals (Burt, 1962). Armed with Wundt's surprisingly refined techniques and the instruments he devised, students of Wundt spread through Europe demonstrating the applications of psychology to everyday life, not least in matters affecting the law. Other students came from the Old and New Worlds to study under Wundt, returning to make lasting contributions of relevance to jurists. Cattell (1895) examined experimentally the nature of testimony and revealed the effects of situational and individual differences, which are still being confirmed by more sophisticated methods a century later (Gudjonsson, 1992a). Bartol and Bartol (1987) argue that Cattell's early experimental work into human testimony in 1893 generated considerable interest among other researchers, including Binet (1900) who replicated Cattell's work in France. The work of Cattell and Binet was later to stimulate Stern's (1910) active research into testimony.

Another Leipzig student, Schrenck-Notzing (1897) is generally acknowledged as the first 'forensic psychologist' (in its modern restricted sense). Bavarian law enabled him to present in a Munich court in 1896 the details of laboratory experiments into suggestibility and errors of recall, which were both cogent and admissible in a case of murder. The salient issue which Schrenck-Notzing testified about was that witnesses in the case, due to pretrial publicity, had failed to distinguish between what they had seen happen and what had been reported by the press. The defendant was convicted, but expert testimony stimulated the interest of other psychologists (Hale, 1980).

Early-twentieth-century developments

Perhaps the greatest, though most controversial, luminary in Wundt's star-studded firmament was Hugo Munsterberg (1863–1916). In the case of the Flemish weavers, accused of delivering their wares in hues different to those ordered, Munsterberg called on the experimental work of both Wundt, and of the great colour physiologist Helmholtz himself, demonstrating to the court the apparent colour changes which occurred under the particular lighting conditions which differed between when the samples were viewed and when the material was later delivered.

Munsterberg followed Cattell back to the USA in 1892, where he set up a psychological laboratory at Harvard, and attempted to introduce applied psychology into the American courtrooms. There he found Anglo-Saxon rules of admissibility more constraining than in continental Europe: in the latter the inquisitorial system permitted anything relevant to be grist to the evidential mill, and the courts were unhampered by the limitations imposed by the adversarial system which the USA had been bequeathed by its early colonists from England. Reacting against legal opposition, Munsterberg (1908, 1909) wrote a popular account of what forensic psychology could offer the course of justice; this was both conjectural and controversial, and received with mixed feelings by lawyers and psychologists alike.

Despite this set-back, Munsterberg continued to advance the frontiers of forensic psychology, introducing hypnosis into the courtroom, and conducting experimental work directed at contemporary problems of evidence. His experimental work has stood the test of time: for example, one of his earliest experiments was concerned with the ability to discriminate between sounds occurring in close succession; his findings were referred to nearly sixty years later during the preparation of evidence for the trial of Oswald, accused of the assassination of President Kennedy, when the question was raised of how many shots had been fired.

Munsterberg, still a German citizen, was actively pro-German in the First World War: because of his political stance and openly critical attitude towards the Allies and possible American involvement, he became socially ostracised and professionally rejected and died in 1916 (Spillman and Spillman, 1993). His place in experimental psychology was taken by Judd, another but more circumspect pupil of Wundt's, who had also established a rival psychological laboratory at Yale soon after Munsterberg. Judd's principal and often overlooked contribution to forensic psychology was in the experimental techniques and associated instruments he devised (Judd, 1908). Most of these were still being used half a century later, and one was actually demonstrated at the British Psychological Society (BPS) Annual Conference at St Andrews in 1957 (Haward, 1958).

In 1911 another of Wundt's pupils, Professor Karl Marbe, created legal history by demonstrating in court the phenomenon of reaction time in a civil action, proving to the court's satisfaction that the engine driver assumed to be responsible for a railway accident could not have stopped the train in time to avert disaster (McCary, 1956). Marbe was the first psychologist to testify at a civil trial. He also testified in a criminal trial for the defence on the unreliability of testimony of child witnesses, who alleged that they had been sexually abused by their teacher (Bartol and Bartol, 1987).

The first published case where an American psychologist qualified as an expert witness was in 1921. The psychologist had been conducting research into juvenile delinquency and concluded that the 12 year old attempted rape victim in the case was a 'moron' and could not be believed. The psychologist's testimony was rejected by the court which noted, 'It is yet to be demonstrated that psychological and medical tests are practical, and will detect lies on the witness stand' (State v. Driver, p. 488, cited in Bartol and Bartol, 1987, pp. 11–12). This court's rejection of the psychological evidence may have discouraged other psychologists from testifying and it was not until the late 1940s or early 1950s that psychologists began to testify regularly in the American courts (Bartol and Bartol, 1987). However, according to Valciukas (1995), psychologists in the USA were not admitted as expert witnesses on mental disorder until 1962, and on issues of competency until two decades later.

Contributions from French pedagogues

Educational psychology had also become laboratory based. Alfred Binet (1857–1911) helped to found the first psychological laboratory in France at the Sorbonne, Paris in 1889. Having studied both medicine and law, he was well placed to apply psychology to legal problems, and his work (Binet, 1900) was not without influence in French legal thinking. Like Cattell, he became interested in the psychological nature of testimony, but later turned to the study of intellectual assessment for which he is better known (Gray, 1946). In collaboration with Theodore Simon he is credited with developing the world's first intelligence test as a psychometric instrument (Binet and Simon, 1905). This was designed specifically for identifying children of 'defective intelligence', a purpose which gained considerable forensic importance in the UK in the second half of the present century, as will be discussed later. The undoubted value of the Simon-Binet Test for many educational purposes created a widespread demand throughout the Western world and had wide-reaching forensic implications.

Of historical interest, Matarazzo (1990) dates the roots of psychological assessment independently to Ancient China and Greece, 2,000–2,500 years before the work of Binet and Simon. The ancient tests measured various aptitudes, such as literacy, verbal skills, writing and arithmetic, and are known to resemble current tests of abilities.

American contributions to psychometric assessment

An American version of the Simon-Binet test was prepared and issued as the Stanford-Binet, and later updated by Terman and Merrill (1937). Translated into many other languages, it became the standard test of juvenile intelligence until the introduction of the Wechsler Intelligence Scale for Children (WISC, Wechsler, 1955). The latter was based on a completely different system and was easier both to use and to explain to the juvenile courts, but in the UK, school medical officers continued to use the Terman-Merrill version of the Stanford-Binet Test in carrying out their legal responsibilities under the 1944 Education Act for several decades of the postwar period, over half a century after Binet conceived most of the test items.

During the First World War applied psychology blossomed on the clinical front in helping to deal with the many cases of shell-shock and post-traumatic amnesia which came flooding back from the Flanders trenches. At the time this work had no significant effect upon forensic psychology itself, but established a forensic role for clinical psychology which would come to fruition seventy years later when the concept of 'post-traumatic stress disorder' (PTSD) became legally recognised.

The advent of group testing

Another fall-out from the Great War occurred when the USA entered it in 1917. The usefulness of Binet-type psychometrics was now so well established that the American Psychological Association (APA) was asked to devise tests for use in recruiting for the armed forces (Gray, 1946). The result was the first group tests of intelligence, the Alpha for literates and the Beta for both illiterates and immigrants unable to understand the English language. The Alpha Test alone was used on nearly 2 million recruits, and retained for Army use postwar: the Alpha and Beta Tests were still being demonstrated in some UK undergraduate psychology courses as late as 1950.

Gray (1946) cites the many benefits which accrued to applied psychology from the use of the so-called Army Tests. They enabled the practical usefulness of psychological tests to become widely known to the general public. Because group testing was so economical compared with individual testing with the Simon-Binet, many of the private schools, smaller institutions, commercial companies, and other organisations could afford to adopt them for their own particular use. They initiated a rapid growth of new group tests, many devised by those who contributed to the original APA test items. The need for standardisation and validation of the new tests demanded new statistical techniques, and established statistics as a necessary subject in all psychology courses.

Although Munsterberg had introduced the first vocational test as early as 1910, it was the success of the Army Tests in selecting men and women for specific functions within the armed services which expanded group testing to traits, skills, aptitudes, etc. until almost every American teacher, personnel officer, vocational advisor and recruitment consultant, became objective-test conscious. Such a national test movement could not take place without even the judiciary becoming aware of it, making it possible in due course to introduce test results into the courtroom with an acceptance – at least in some States – that Munsterberg himself would have envied.

One other pioneer of forensic psychology deserves mention, namely, William Marston, who in 1922 became the first American professor of legal psychology. As a student of Munsterberg's, he maintained the tradition established by

Wundt and continued the latter's experimental work on the physiological effects of deception. This led to Marston's use of systolic blood pressure in lie detection, for which he claimed almost 100 per cent accuracy (Marston, 1917). Like his mentor, he presented his findings in an over-enthusiastic way, giving his 'lie-detector' an aura of validity which, despite its scientifically proven limitations, still persists today (Gale, 1988).

Forensic psychology in the armed services

During the interwar years no significant advance in Western forensic psychology appears to have taken place, but the Second World War created an unprecedented demand for applied psychologists, not only for selection programmes pioneered in the Great War, but in operational research. A special innovation was the development of military psychology, with inputs into the work of intelligence sections and service police units. Military psychologists in their functions in criminal investigation within the services, their concern with internal and external security, and later their role in the search for, and subsequent prosecution of, war criminals, provided an appropriate grounding in forensic skills, and enabled psychologists to make a new and useful contribution to this area of applied psychology (Cunningham, 1964; Gilbert, 1948; Haward, 1981; Meir, 1945). This wartime experience, noted by the many lawyers then in uniform and working for the Judge Advocate or Provost Marshal, made the courts more favourably inclined to see the relevance of psychological evidence.

Postwar developments in the UK

A much greater influence than military psychology upon the development of forensic psychology in the UK was the provision of a Treasury-funded career structure for applied psychologists, made possible by two statutes of profound social significance. These were the Education Act 1944 and the National Health Service Act 1946, which respectively provided school medical officers with the services of educational psychologists, and consultant psychiatrists with the services of clinical psychologists.

Since both types of medical practitioner had statutory duties regarding court proceedings, clinical and educational psychologists found themselves frequently providing evidence for courts, albeit vicariously, as part of their routine duties. The psychologist's quantitative data on persons appearing in court, commonly embodied in a subjective report by the medical witness, added a new dimension to the evidence on which judicial decisions were made.

Hearsay problems

Inevitably, human nature being what it is, medical reports tended to include only those facts selected from the psychologist's findings that supported the medical view of the case. When the findings in the two reports were consistent with each other, selection of the more significant findings from the psychological report was not especially objectionable, even though it might overplay the true position; but sometimes the psychological findings were inconsistent with medical opinion, and the final selective segments from the psychologist's report were a travesty of the conclusions drawn from the psychometric data as a whole.

This situation caused the psychologists much concern, and every effort was made to establish the principle that psychologists should make their reports separately to the court. The long-standing principle of ultimate medical responsibility, and the initial terms of employment which made the psychologist subservient to the direction of a medical practitioner, prevented these early attempts to achieve professional freedom from being successful. Many educational psychologists, as qualified teachers, had retained membership of their trade union, whose help they sought. Some clinical psychologists joined the Association of Scientific Workers, the only trade union prepared to accept them in those early days, hoping to solicit help in achieving a separation of psychological and psychiatric reports. Neither plan had any effect, mainly because such small numbers were involved compared with the overall union membership: at this time there were still counties without a single clinical psychologist within their boundaries.

One of us (Haward), failing to obtain any concessions from the medical staff for whom his court reports were prepared, and finding the Association of Scientific Workers impotent in this matter, supplicated the Attorney General, the Bar Council, the British Medical Association, the British Psychological Society, and the Whitley Council (which governed the qualifications, status, and indirectly the working conditions of clinical psychologists), and every other relevant organisation which might conceivably add weight to the psychologists' case, all to no avail.

The breakthrough finally came early in 1958, during a barrister's conference prior to a trial for attempted murder. The medical witness for the defence was Medical Superintendent of the County Mental Hospital where Haward was employed, and in a pretrial conference the QC asked the psychiatrist some searching questions about the psychological data embodied in the medical report. The psychiatrist was unable to answer these questions, and had to explain that this information had been derived from the psychologist who, at the former's request, had also interviewed the accused in prison. The barrister considered that reporting information derived from another person violated the Rule of Hearsay, and raised the matter with the Judge in Chambers, where the usual complication of the judge confusing psychology with psychiatry occurred. The judge confirmed that in his opinion the practice complained of was, indeed, an infringement of the Rule of Hearsay, and ruled that the psychologist should be called as a 'medical witness' in his own right.

The judge's ruling on hearsay referred only to the psychologist's findings included in the psychiatrist's report, but once established had wider implications.

Naturally Haward was not slow to broadcast this ruling within the profession, and later was requested by the English Division of Professional Psychologists of the British Psychological Society to prepare a substantive paper on the Rule of Hearsay in relation to psychological reports (Haward, 1965).

The medical profession, defending this assault upon their privileged position, riposted with the argument that their reports to the court often included data from other sources, for example, from reports by pathologists, radiographers and other specialists. Psychologists nevertheless stood their ground, pointing out that in all such examples the medical practitioner, by virtue of his medical training in all branches of medicine, was qualified to interpret such data. It was emphasised that psychometric data was unique and was not at that time part of medical education and that even though psychiatrists gained some familiarity with psychological tests in preparing for their Diploma of Psychological Medicine, their knowledge of test construction, validation and statistical underpinning was not sufficient for them to interpret test results with the necessary expertise required by law and provided by psychologists. Apart from applied experimental psychology, psychometrics is the only other completely unique contribution which applied psychology has to offer.

Other psychologists were quick to quote this precedential case when they wished to make their report independently to court, although many still preferred to avoid court appearances, especially if they were satisfied that their views were being fairly and accurately included in a medical report.

The ruling was explicitly endorsed in the English Exporters case (1973) where Mr Justice Megarry stated: 'The expert must not give hearsay evidence stating details of any transactions not within his personal knowledge in order to establish them as facts'. As Ward (1978) observes, this is precisely what psychiatrists do when psychological information is included in their reports and opinions. In the Meyer's case (1965), the House of Lords firmly rejected the Court of Appeal's acceptance of hearsay evidence, indicating that the common law could not properly be used to develop exceptions to the Hearsay Rule.

Because the Hearsay Rule has been a bedrock to British forensic psychology, recent trends to weaken this Rule are viewed with some misgiving. Civil law, explained in more detail in Chapter 8, possesses a more liberal attitude to evidence, and legislators have taken advantage of this to reduce the effectiveness of the Hearsay Rule in a succession of updating Civil Evidence Acts (1962, 1968 and 1995). The Civil Evidence Act 1968 weakened considerably the Hearsay Rule in civil proceedings by admitting certain types of hearsay evidence at the discretion of the judge. Statements by witnesses now deceased or who are incompetent to testify, and which were formerly inadmissible, can now be admitted under this statute, and the Morris case (1978) created the precedent in case law.

The most recent Civil Evidence Act (1995) goes even further, explicitly abolishing the Hearsay Rule for most civil proceedings, including those in administrative tribunals and formal arbitrations, but retaining it in the Coroner's Courts and the Court of Protection. Fagillon (1976) expresses concern that in civil cases at least, these changes in statute law create a loophole by which psychological data may be included in medical reports and tendered to the court as evidence.

It should be explained that an expert testifying on what the law conceives as being a medical problem was generally referred to as a 'medical witness'. As such there is no requirement to actually be medically qualified, and in the past a medical student, a pharmacist, and even a drug manufacturer, have been called as medical witnesses. There is thus no reason for a psychologist to demur at being thus addressed; an interesting reversal of roles occurred when a medical practitioner, called to give evidence for one of his patients with a damaged wrist, was refused recognition as a medical witness because the point at issue was held to demand orthopaedic experience which the general practitioner was deemed not to possess, whereas in another case, a postgraduate student undergoing clinical psychology training *was* admitted as a medical witness, since she possessed a psychology degree approved by the British Psychological Society and was therefore a qualified psychologist, and had already acquired relevant knowledge and experience of the matter at issue.

Modern forensic psychology, as a professional speciality devoted to the provision of expert testimony, has in its development during the past century been constrained and severely limited by the rules of admissibility in the adversarial system. We have seen how advances in psychological techniques, such as psychometrics and experimentation, came to provide material of relevance to the particular case, and how, in the UK, the Hearsay Rule finally allowed psychologists to present their evidence independently of their medical colleagues. The history of this modern phase of forensic psychology is therefore also the history of twentieth-century changes in the legal rules of admissibility.

There are two further rules of evidence regarding admissibility. The first of these is the Multiple Admissibility Rule, when evidence is admissible for one purpose but not for another. The Multiple Admissibility Rule was originally modified by precedential law in the Willis case (1882) to permit evidence to be admitted for multiple purposes in civil proceedings, although the rule still holds good in criminal trials.

The other admissibility rule is the Best Evidence Rule, laid down by Lord Hardwicke in 1745. This rule made, *inter alia*, copies of all original evidence inadmissible. It was strictly observed in the last century, to the extent that a large and heavy tombstone had to be manhandled from churchyard to court so that the inscription could be read to prove a relationship, because not even a certified copy, or a photograph, were admissible, being secondary rather than best evidence. The rule has gradually lost power as the need for court convenience, and judicial familiarity with typed carbon copies, and, more recently, photocopying, has led to a discretionary easing of the Best Evidence Rule. In the civil courts the rule is almost defunct, but still exists in criminal proceedings. In the Quinn case (1962), for example, the judge refused to admit a film of an indecent theatrical performance as prosecution evidence of an illegal act, because the film was not the best evidence. In recent years, even the stricter climate of the criminal court is mellowing to allow more liberal interpretations of the Best Evidence Rule. Nevertheless, the absence of 'best evidence' may be the subject of adverse judicial comment, and following the precedent laid down in the Francis case (1874) by Lord Coleridge, any secondary evidence may be slighted or ignored on the grounds that it lacks weight. It seems unlikely that a judge would publicly and explicitly express an adverse comment on a psychiatrist's report merely because it embodied a psychologist's findings. Fagillon (1976) very properly voices his concern that the changes in statute law are creating a loophole in civil law by which psychological data may be included in medical reports, and those of other professionals, and tendered to the court as evidence. It now seems that the threat to the psychologist's autonomy is also extending to the criminal law, and there is clearly a need for the profession to monitor legal practice in this area.

Changes in forensic psychology practice

The postwar years have seen a number of significant changes in forensic psychology practice, of which the expansion of forensic work, the introduction of specialised clinical and forensic training courses, the recognition of a career structure, and the effect of changes in law and legal attitudes are self-evident. Of particular professional significance, however, is the widening of the problems presented by particular cases and the techniques adopted in finding solutions for them. The last three decades have seen a number of forensic issues, which have exercised the minds of both lawyers and psychologists, come into prominence. These issues include problems arising from recovered memories of child sexual abuse, disputed confessions, and post-traumatic stress disorder (PTSD), which are all discussed later, while two other psycholegal issues and their sequelae are mentioned below.

The pornography phase

One of the best examples of a transitory sociolegal concern is that of pornography (Rembar, 1969; Haward, 1982). This was generally prosecuted under the Obscenity Acts, obscenity not being made a crime, either in the USA or the UK, until the nineteenth century and then applied infrequently and with manifest sexual prejudice; early cases included Eleanor Glyn's *Three Weeks*, where the offending passage merely described the heroine clad only in a dressing gown and lying on a rug with a rose stem between her teeth; the classical painting of Venus in the Dulwich Art Gallery, originally declared obscene but today legally on view; and Marie Stopes' booklet on contraception, a subject now commonly seen in teenage and women's magazines. The sexually permissive attitudes which evolved after the Second World War engendered less repressive public attitudes and a rapid increase in pornographic material. The ban on Boccaccio's *Decameron* was lifted, and Radclyffe Hall's *Well of Loneliness*, convicted earlier for its lesbian implications, became the BBC's *Book at Bedtime*. This trend in what some considered to be sexual laxity led to a backlash by moral campaigners which encouraged a crescendo of prosecutions under various statutes: the law was tightened up by the 1959 Obscenity Act, which made publication of obscene material (defined as possessing a tendency to corrupt) an indictable, and therefore more serious, offence, forbade prosecution under common law (with its more flexible processes and interpretations), and introduced search and destruction orders: a later Obscenity Act (1964) extended the offence to anyone in the trade who handled the books, including shop assistants, printers and bookbinders.

The proposition that explicit sexual material was corrupting was an *assumptio juris et de jure*, that is, unchallengeable in court, making any evidence to the contrary *inadmissible*. However, Parliament acknowledged that in some cases the assumed corruption could be mitigated by the material having some artistic, literary or scientific merit, or be of general concern for the public good. Effective use was made of this Section 4 defence in the Penguin Books case (1961), when twenty-three expert witnesses testified on the literary merits of *Lady Chatterley's Lover* and secured an acquittal. The 'public good' defence enabled psychologists to be brought in as expert witnesses; at first these were clinicians who, like one of us (Haward), used sexual materials therapeutically in special clinics for sexual disorders; later, psychological expertise was widened as more bases for the public good defence became apparent, and in the notorious Anderson's case (1971), popularly known as the OZ Trial and marked by a long procession to the Old Bailey of OZ supporters led by an elephant, a succession of academic, educational, paediatric and social psychologists took their place in the witness box. This was the largest number of UK psychologists ever to appear for the defence in one case, which proved to be the longest obscenity trial on record, and their evidence is well described by Palmer (1971).

The public good defence called for specialised psychological knowledge, which had to be presented in a way which did not relate to the real issue before the court, that is, whether or not the material before the court had, or had not, a tendency to corrupt those seeing it. The unscientific task of avoiding the central hypothesis and proving by implication taxed the ingenuity of psychologists, and the psychological defence of obscenity is explained in some detail by Haward (1975a, 1975b). In pornography cases the expert witnesses were faced with many problems, not least the sexual prejudices of the judiciary and jury. As Sir Norwood East (1955) points out, sexual conduct is generally regarded as perverse unless it conforms to one's own accustomed and restricted patterns of behaviour: sex offenders are notably more liable to be misjudged by prejudice and ignorance than other offenders. Perceptual prejudice was nowhere more apparent than in one case, where one of us (Haward) was asked to defend a large range of titles, among which he discovered *Rape Around the Coast* – a textbook on soil erosion; *Fun in Bed* – being games for sick children; and *Pornography* – Lord Longford's own diatribe against sexually explicit literature!

The public good defence enabled psychologists to dispel sexual ignorance, to some extent, by educating the court from the witness box, and the effective lowering of sexual prejudice did much to boost the acquittal rate. One persistent problem was the contamination of sexual content with violence and drug-taking, media presentations of which have recognised adverse consequences (Eysenck and Nias, 1978). Another problem was the paucity of hard scientific evidence on the effects of pornography on the user. The latter was helped by substantial US Treasury funding of extensive psychological research into the subject, the results of which were used by the Presidential Commission on Pornography, which summarised its findings in a 700-page report, supported by ten volumes of detailed research data (Lockhart, 1970).

The introduction of psychological testimony led to a long sequence of acquittals. The 'Establishment' responded with a series of counter-measures: these included: (1) pressure on Customs and Excise to confiscate all incoming sex books from abroad, especially those from Denmark, which had completely repealed its obscenity laws; (2) using the Post Office Acts rather than the Obscenity Acts where appropriate since convictions for *indecency* were easier to obtain than for *obscenity*; (3) confiscating complete stocks (instead of specimen samples) of sex magazines and books as 'evidence', which were then held for exceptionally long periods ostensibly awaiting court proceedings and then released without charges being brought, by which time the stock would be completely outdated and of little market value and which in some cases brought small traders to near bankruptcy; and (4) the use of forfeiture and destruction orders which prevented the accused from obtaining trial by jury, and caused loss of stock sometimes of five-figure value, magnifying by many times the maximum fine otherwise imposed for a conviction.

In addition, the courts began to interpret the law in a way which, despite the existence of the public good defence explicit in Section 4 of the Act, undermined and finally excluded effective psychological evidence. This involved two significant steps. First, the Maidenhead Rule was created (Haward, 1975b) which split the proceedings into two parts; part 1 excluded expert testimony until the court decided if the material was obscene and conviction appropriate, and only then, in part 2, admitted the expert evidence under Section 4. Even simple Aristotelian logic would predict that the probability of reversing a firmly established and explicit public decision was negligible, and this ploy proved successful in removing any impact the psychological evidence might have had. Finally, in Staniforth's case (1975) which eventually went on appeal to the House of Lords, it was decided that any evidence that pornography could be for the public good, even that which, for example, showed that contact with pornography lowered the sex crime rate (Ben-Veniste, 1970), was held to be inadmissible as it refuted the assumption that obscenity was *de facto* corrupting. The law does not allow scientific facts to get in the way of legal assumptions, at least until new legislation is brought in to take cognisance of such facts: twenty-two years later, psychologists are still waiting for this inconsistency within the Act to be remedied. Staniforth's case brought to an end the 'public good' contribution of sexological psychologists, although the Section 4 defence may still be used by psychologists whose expertise lies in the artistic, literary or scientific merits of the allegedly obscene article. However, after an initial spate of convictions following the Staniforth decision, public interest in suppressing pornography waned and became centred upon more topical concerns.

The phase of investigative hypnosis

Another transitory social concern centred upon the use of investigative hypnosis. Some clinicians, including one of us (Haward), had been using hypnosis routinely as part of their forensic activities since the early 1950s. In the beginning, a not uncommon request from medical practitioners was anxiety-reduction by hypnosis for impending witnesses requesting anxiolytic medication deemed inappropriate to their medical condition. This followed an already established practice of anxiety-reduction by hypnosis, using post-hypnotic suggestion, for candidates taking the driving test or other types of examination. From this developed the notion of using hypnosis with other witnesses to assist recall of significant facts, and this was later extended to victims, accused persons and parties to civil action. Bryan (1962) gives a general account of the use of forensic hypnosis, which aroused much controversy within the profession. At the peak of its popularity with the UK constabularies, circa 1980, Haward hypnotised seventeen potential witnesses in one week. Reiser (1980) and Udolf (1983) refer to a large number of USA cases which involved the use of hypnosis, and McConkey and Sheehan (1995) showed that there was a substantial increase in the use of hypnosis in Australia between 1981 and 1987.

By the late 1980s police interest in hypnosis had dissipated: this was due to a number of factors which came to prominence at about the same time. In the USA, evidence derived by hypnosis was being barred by its failure to meet the Frye Rule (in Frye's case, 1923), which stated that evidence derived from scientific tests are inadmissible unless generally recognised as reliable for the purpose by the appropriate scientific community: hypnosis is not generally recognised as a reliable means of retrieving information (Gudjonsson, 1992a). More importantly, the use of hypnosis has in the USA resulted in a number of cases of miscarriage of justice, which led to many States prohibiting its use for evidential purposes (Gibson, 1995). In the UK, the Home Office issued guidelines concerning the use of hypnosis by the police which effectively discouraged its use by constabularies; Wagstaff (1988) gives a well-reasoned discussion of the Home Office Circular. More recently, McConkey and Sheehan (1995) discuss some of the dangers of using hypnosis in police investigations and provide detailed and helpful guidelines for practitioners about its use. A consistent view among the scientific community is that hypnosis should only be practised by clinical psychologists and medical practitioners, who, in addition to their professional qualifications, have had specific training and experience in the use of hypnosis and are knowledgeable about police procedures and investigative interviewing.

For formal investigations and enquiries where those involved are not required to testify in a criminal court, less objection to the use of investigative hypnosis has been made, and the technique has proved to be of value in selected cases, although the forensic application of hypnosis is limited (Laurence and Perry, 1988; McConkey and Sheehan, 1995).

During the past decade, new interviewing techniques have been developed which overcome the legal and practical problems encountered with investigative hypnosis. Known as the 'Cognitive Interview' (Fisher and Geiselman, 1992), the techniques can also be used with children and persons with learning disability (Milne and Bull, 1996), which is a considerable advantage over the use of investigative hypnosis. The Cognitive Interview is now commonly being used by police forces in the UK to elicit memory recall of witnesses and victims, and on occasions co-operative suspects (CPTU, 1992). There are fewer objections to police officers utilising the technique than has been the case with hypnosis. It is likely that in the future the Cognitive Interview will replace the need for investigative hypnosis, except in cases of psychogenic amnesia, and forensic psychologists may be increasingly called upon to train police officers in Cognitive Interview techniques. In complicated cases, they may be requested by the police to conduct the interview themselves.

Conclusions

Current law is embedded in history, because universally recognised crimes were formulated in pre-Christian times. It is therefore necessary, in understanding contemporary legal thinking, to have some sense of law's historical development. This chapter has provided a brief survey of just one pathway through legal history, drawing attention to a few key developments which have shaped modern psychology's application to legal problems.

Forensic psychology has two historical roots which stretch back into the distant past. One develops from the ancient philosophers' interest in the role of law in civilised society and the notion of justice; the other stems from the need to differentiate and identify, for sociopolitical purposes, individuals and groups in terms of their behaviour. The first is theoretical and leads from notions of strict liability for offences, to the idea of degrees of responsibility and the mitigation of punishment for cases where the offender is no longer a rational human being but an irrational one, to whom the term mad has been applied. Along this line of development, we therefore see first the distinction emerging between being bad or mad, and later the latter dividing itself between insanity (legally presumed to be temporary) and the more permanent state of idiocy. The present century has seen the concept of insanity refined to provide further defences, such as those of diminished responsibility and automatism. Some European countries have extended the mental element in crime further to include such states as acute provocation and crimes of passion. In world law, there is a marked cleavage in law between those countries whose principal law-makers were Christian, such as the British Commonwealth, Europe and the Americas, and those countries who legislated from substantially different moral codes. This difference is important to those forensic psychologists of today who have an international clientele, or whose nation changes dramatically from one type of jurisdiction to another, as in Hong Kong or in newly independent third world states.

The second historical root of forensic psychology is more practical than theoretical: it also comes from the pre-Christian era, and traces the behavioural differences between human groups and between individual people. This has led to behavioural mensuration and what we now call psychometrics, both of which combine to provide psychology's unique contribution to science. The forensic psychologist's expertise in quantifying both mental and behavioural concepts is perhaps the best justification for his or her presence in the legal arena in those cases when the issues would otherwise be the sole province of the psychiatrist or other medical specialist.

More importantly, the emergence of psychology as a recognised science, and the entrepreneurial driving force of the Leipzig school, enabled psychology to contribute to legal proceedings in a completely original way by drawing attention to the rules governing *normal* behaviour which were not apparent to the ordinary man, and indeed often ran counter to his beliefs about behaviour and its motivations.

The last hundred years has seen a fusing of these two roots into a forensic expertise which stands with its feet in the two camps of forensic medicine and forensic science, but is distinct from both. The strength of forensic psychology lies not only in its unique function, but in its firm scientific foundations which are consistently upgraded by continuing research.

The closing part of this chapter demonstrates that psychology, in addition to its work in traditional areas of law, is also at the forefront of new legal developments and the social issues which create the need to bring them into effect.

3

SURVEYS INTO PSYCHOLOGICAL EVIDENCE IN COURT

Introduction

It is forty-four years since Haward first discussed the scope and role of psychology in legal proceedings in the UK. He argued that psychologists had a considerable contribution to make and proposed a number of ways in which this could be achieved (Haward, 1953, 1959, 1961). Haward's innovative proposals were not accepted by another early forensic psychologist, Cunningham (1964), who believed that Haward's proposals were 'too sweeping and far reaching to gain a hearing from the judiciary' (p. 8). In contrast to Haward, Cunningham (1964) believed that the forensic psychologist had most to offer in relation to police work and the solving of crime, that is, in the area of offender profiling.

In an early survey among clinical and educational psychologists in the UK, Castell (1966) found that few psychologists were actively engaged in court work. This finding appeared to support Cunningham's (1964) early scepticism about the role of psychologists in civil and criminal proceedings. Those who were involved in court work most commonly had referrals from psychiatrist colleagues where the psychologist's findings were incorporated into the psychiatrist's report. At that time Haward (1965) raised concern about this practice, which apparently was often done without the knowledge of the psychologist involved.

There is currently little information available about the court work of psychologists in the UK and in other countries. Loftus (1986) has provided an important account of her own experiences as an expert witness in the USA, where her evidence has been primarily concerned with the research on human perception, memory and eyewitness accounts. In the UK, Haward (1981) and Gudjonsson (1996b) have provided detailed accounts of their own civil and criminal cases, which show that there is an increasing demand for the services of clinical psychologists. Whereas Loftus typically gives evidence on general research findings in experimental psychology, Haward and Gudjonsson have emphasised the use of tailor-made experiments for the specific case.

Since Castell's survey there have been two further studies conducted for the British Psychological Society (BPS) into psychological evidence in court, which

24

are referred to as the 'BPS surveys'. The first survey was conducted by Gudjonsson in 1984 and the second by the same author in 1995. The results of the two surveys will be discussed in detail, along with Castell's survey. In addition, Edmondson (1995) has recently completed a survey among prison psychologists into expert evidence before Discretionary Lifer Panels. Prison psychologists nowadays often complete risk assessments on discretionary lifers and they are now increasingly having to testify before the Panels and be cross-examined on their findings and opinions.

These four surveys are important in establishing the extent to which psychologists in the UK are involved in court and tribunal work, the nature of their involvement, the professional issues concerned, and the changes that have taken place over the years.

Castell's 1965 survey

In a survey carried out in 1965 for the English Division of Professional Psychologists, Castell (1966) sent out a questionnaire about court reports and evidence in court to members of the English and Scottish Divisions of the BPS. In total, 113 replies were received, with sixty-one and forty-nine of the respondents being educational and clinical psychologists, respectively. This represented a response rate of about one quarter of the members of the combined Divisions of the BPS. It is not known how many of the non-respondents had given written or oral evidence.

Of the 113 subjects who responded to the survey, ninety-seven (86 per cent) had produced written reports and of these forty-seven (48 per cent) had given oral evidence in court. Of those who had produced reports, fifty-five (57 per cent) were educational psychologists and forty-two (43 per cent) were clinical psychologists. This survey did not include any academic or occupational psychologists who may have contributed to court work. With respect to testifying orally in court, twenty-six (55 per cent) were educational psychologists and twenty-one (45 per cent) were clinical psychologists. Of the educational and clinical psychologists who had testified, twenty in each group had given oral evidence only once per annum. This means that 77 per cent of the educational psychologists and 95 per cent of the clinical psychologists testified in court only once per annum. On the basis of this data, Castell concluded that educational psychologists produce more written reports than clinical psychologists, whereas clinical psychologists proportionally more often give oral evidence in court.

Although some of the psychologists were accepting referral of cases privately directly from solicitors, the majority were collaborating with their medical colleagues. The most common arrangement, which was reported by fifty-five (57 per cent) of the psychologists, was for the psychologist's findings to be incorporated into the medical report. Only forty-one (42 per cent) of the psychologists claimed to submit independent reports to the solicitor or court. There were no differences found between the educational and clinical psychologists in this

25

respect. Fewer than half of the psychologists were receiving fees for their court work.

Castell classified the types of question the psychologist was asked to address in the report into three groups: (1) 'Assessment of intelligence, abilities, attainment'; (2) 'Differential diagnosis, assessment of impairment, disability, etc'; (3) 'Disposal, prognosis'. Educational and clinical psychologists were commonly asked to address intellectual assessment issues, with twenty-five (45 per cent) and thirteen (31 per cent) of the two professional groups having been asked to address this issue, respectively. As far as diagnostic issues are concerned, twenty-two (52 per cent) of the clinical psychologists and five (9 per cent) of the educational psychologists had fulfilled this function. Disposal issues were more commonly requested from the educational (64 per cent) than clinical (14 per cent) psychologists. The results indicate that clinical psychologists were most commonly asked to address diagnostic issues, whereas educational psychologists were much more often concerned with disposal and prognosis. This appears to reflect the nature of their respective employment and day-to-day work.

The educational psychologists most commonly gave evidence in the juvenile court, whereas the clinical psychologists more commonly gave evidence in the higher civil and the higher criminal courts.

The respondents were asked to describe the kinds of difficulties they had experienced in relation to court work. The most common problem, which was reported by eighteen (19 per cent) of the respondents, related to the psychologists being unhappy about psychiatrists inappropriately attempting to interpret the psychologist's findings in court. Here the question of hearsay evidence is important as well as the role and independence of the psychologist.

The second most common problem, which was reported by eleven (11 per cent) respondents, was difficulties with communicating effectively to the court the technical aspects of the psychological assessment. Eight (8 per cent) psychologists complained about the lack of feedback about the outcome of cases.

The majority (58 per cent) of the respondents emphasised the importance of formal training in forensic psychology.

The 1984 BPS survey

The primary stimulus for the 1984 BPS survey was the publication in the *Bulletin of the British Psychological Society* of an article by Tunstall *et al.* (1982). The article discussed in detail the psychological assessment by, and evidence of, a number of psychologists who testified in a major fraud trial at the Old Bailey. The article raised a number of concerns about the negative attitude of the court to psychologists acting as expert witnesses and about the disclosure in open court about confidential test material.

The Professional Affairs Board of the BPS became concerned about test disclosure in open court (Newman, 1983) and wanted to know: (1) how many psychologists were involved in presenting evidence in court or before a tribunal;

and (2) how commonly psychologists were required to disclose in open court details about psychological tests beyond the overall test findings. For this reason the Division of Criminological and Legal Psychology (DCLP) commissioned a survey into psychological evidence in court, the results of which were published (Gudjonsson, 1985).

A twenty-item questionnaire was constructed and sent to all members of the different Divisions. Only those psychologists who had given evidence in court or at a tribunal during the previous five years were asked to complete the questionnaire. Of the 190 psychologists who responded to the survey, 127 (67 per cent) were male and sixty-three (33 per cent) were female. Five of the respondents had not actually given oral evidence, but had completed the questionnaire with regard to having written court reports. An additional four questionnaires were completed by psychologists who were employed outside the UK. Therefore, 181 of the questionnaires were completed by UK psychologists who had given oral evidence. The great majority of the respondents were clinical (71 per cent) and educational (22 per cent) psychologists.

The number of reports submitted by the respondents varied considerably. Over half (57 per cent) had submitted ten or fewer reports during the previous five years, the range being 1–500. Only nine psychologists (5 per cent) had produced more than 100 reports. Only 17 per cent had produced tribunal reports, the range being 1–150. The psychologists received their referrals from solicitors (86 per cent), medical colleagues (68 per cent), social services (46 per cent), probation service (31 per cent), law enforcement agencies (12 per cent), Reporter in Scotland (8 per cent), and Procurator Fiscal in Scotland (3 per cent).

Out of the 181 UK psychologists, ninety-two (51 per cent) had given evidence in civil cases (e.g., compensation, matrimonial, child care and custody proceedings) and ninety-one (50 per cent) in criminal cases. The mean number of appearances were 3.95 (range 1–4) and 3.78 (range 1–27) for the civil and criminal cases, respectively. The psychologists had most commonly testified in the Magistrates' Court (46 per cent), Crown Court (22 per cent), Juvenile Court (18 per cent) and High Court (9 per cent).

The great majority (67 per cent) of the psychologists had given evidence only once or twice. Six (3 per cent) had appeared more than ten times in civil cases and eight (4 per cent) in criminal cases. Only fourteen (8 per cent) had given evidence in person to a tribunal, the mean number being 2.6 (range 1–10). Seventeen (9 per cent) had given evidence at a Children's Hearing in Scotland (mean = 10.2, range 1–40).

The psychologists were asked to indicate what tests and instruments they generally used when preparing court and tribunal reports. A small minority (4 per cent) stated that they did not use any psychometric tests. For the remaining respondents, the most commonly used tests were the WAIS and WISC and a range of neuropsychological tests. Only a minority (9 per cent) stated that they most commonly relied on personality tests, the MMPI, the EPQ and the 16 PF being the personality tests most commonly used.

The respondents indicated on what their evidence in court was generally based. The results showed that the psychologists most commonly relied on behavioural assessments/interview data (46 per cent) and cognitive test results (39 per cent).

Over half (56 per cent) of the psychologists reported that they were generally 'extensively' cross-examined in court on their evidence. Fifty (28 per cent) had been asked to disclose detailed information about the psychometric tests beyond the overall test findings. This sometimes involved an item-to-item analysis of the test items and scoring in open court. Test disclosure most commonly occurred in relation to intellectual and neuropsychological tests and happened both in civil and criminal cases. It was noted that some psychologists had successfully declined to carry out item-to-item analysis of tests in open court. Judges were apparently sometimes sympathetic to the psychologists' need to protect confidentiality and validity of psychometric tests.

The great majority (95 per cent) of the respondents said that generally the courts favourably accepted their evidence. Only eight (4 per cent) psychologists had found the courts generally critical of their evidence. Only a minority (22 per cent) had found themselves presenting a case whilst another psychologist did so for the 'other side'.

In general, the psychologists were more positive about preparing reports than testifying orally in court. Over 20 per cent of the respondents said they felt 'negative' about appearing as an expert witness whilst about half felt 'positive' about it. This showed the varied attitude of the sample. Many psychologists found giving evidence in court stressful and reported feeling inadequately informed and trained for the role of an expert witness.

On the basis of the results obtained from the survey, Gudjonsson estimated that psychologists testify in only about one or two cases out of every ten where they have submitted reports. The survey did not separate civil from criminal cases with respect to frequency of testifying. This has been done in the 1995 BPS survey and highlights some important differences between civil and criminal cases, which are discussed in the next section of this chapter.

The 1995 BPS survey

The purpose of this survey was to obtain up-to-date information on the court and tribunal work of psychologists in the UK (Gudjonsson, 1996a). The questionnaire used was similar to the one used in the 1984 survey in order to make it possible to compare changes between the two periods. The questionnaire used in this survey was more detailed and obtained information which had not been collected previously. This included information about the types of legal issue addressed in the report, details of the court where the psychologist had testified, and whether or not the psychologist had been asked by the referral agent to alter the report in order to make it more favourable. The issue of compromised reports arose from Gudjonsson's (1992a, 1994a) concern about psychologists being pressured by defence solicitors to delete unfavourable evidence from their reports.

The 1984 survey was only completed by those psychologists who during the previous five years had appeared in person as an expert witness in either a court or tribunal. In contrast, the 1995 survey was aimed at all psychologists who had prepared a court or tribunal report during the previous five years, irrespective of whether or not they had testified in person.

The questionnaire was circulated to all UK members of the different divisions of the BPS in March 1995 and by the end of August 525 completed questionnaires had been returned. Most of the respondents, 415 (80 per cent), were clinical psychologists and sixty-three (12 per cent) were educational psychologists. The remaining respondents included academic (6 per cent), occupational (4 per cent) and counselling (3 per cent) psychologists. There was some overlap between the categories because a few psychologists reported belonging to more than one of the groups (e.g. being a clinical and an academic psychologist).

The total number of reports prepared during the previous five years as reported by 498 respondents was 16,881. About two-thirds (65 per cent) of the respondents reported having prepared ten or fewer reports, the range being 1–2,000. Only twenty-nine psychologists (6 per cent) had prepared more than 100 reports.

Most reports were prepared for civil proceedings, the total number of reports for this purpose being 9,354. This comprises 55 per cent of the total number of reports for different types of proceeding. The second largest group of reports was produced in family, juvenile or matrimonial proceedings, the total number of reports was 3,794. This represents 22 per cent of the total number of reports in the survey. Concerning criminal proceedings, 2,541 reports had been produced, which represents 15 per cent of the total number of reports produced. The total number of tribunal reports was 710.

Ninety-six (19 per cent) of the psychologists had produced reports for some other types of court proceedings, which included Sheriffs Court and Children's Panels in Scotland, Court of Protection, Criminal Compensation Board, and General Medical Council.

As far as the source of referral is concerned, 453 (87 per cent) of the psychologists reported that they had accepted a referral from solicitors, which is identical to the figure obtained in the 1984 BPS survey. This was followed by referrals from the social services (39 per cent) and medical colleagues (32 per cent). The single most common source of referrals was that of solicitors and then the social services (73 and 11 per cent of those who responded to the question, respectively). It was very rare for the psychologists to state that they most commonly had referrals from medical colleagues (5 per cent), Probation Service (2 per cent), and Crown Prosecution Service (<1 per cent).

The respondents were asked to indicate the number of reports that they had produced during the previous five years addressing the issues given in Table 3.1.

The results indicate that over half of the respondents had produced reports concerned with post-traumatic stress disorder (PTSD) and other compensation issues, such as head injury. This was followed by issues concerned with child care proceedings, which was reported by 47 per cent of the psychologists. A quarter of the respondents reported having produced reports for mitigation purposes, either with or without treatment being offered. Legal issues concerned with fitness to plead or stand trial, diminished responsibility or insanity defence, and the reliability of witness or confession statements were reported by a minority (9–14 per cent) of the psychologists.

The psychologists were asked if they had been asked to alter or delete parts of the report to favour the side instructing them. Out of 514 psychologists who replied to this question, 139 (27 per cent) reported that they had been asked to modify their reports, primarily (87 per cent) by solicitors. Forty-nine psychologists (36 per cent) said that they had refused the request, seventy-five (56 per cent) had complied, and ten (7 per cent) said that what they did depended on the circumstances and the type of request made. A request to change the wording of a sentence or to elaborate a point had been requested from forty-four of the psychologists and of those thirty-seven (84 per cent) had complied. Thirty-two psychologists had been asked to alter the opinion or the conclusion

Table 3.1 The main issue addressed in the psychological report [a]

The isssue	N[b]	%	Sum[c]	Range
PTSD	288	55	3,944	1-1,000
Other compensation	264	51	5,537	1-1,000
Childcare	245	47	2,551	1-400
Sentencing/disposal (treatment)	129	25	1,950	1-800
Mitigation (no treatment)	123	24	670	1-100
Fitness to plead/stand trial	72	14	231	1-50
Reliability of witness statements	71	14	250	1-26
Diminished responsibility/insanity	50	10	151	1-22
Disputed confession	49	9	527	1-192

Notes:
[a] This table was adapted from Gudjonsson (1996a).
[b] This represents the number of respondents who had produced at least one report.
[c] These figures are a slight underestimate because eighteen respondents did not indicate how many reports they had produced in each category.

in the report. Seven (22 per cent) of these respondents had complied with this request. A request to remove unfavourable findings, such as unfavourable test or interview material, from the report was reported by forty-four psychologists and of those eighteen (41 per cent) had complied with the request. Removing a reference to a document seen, including previous psychological reports, had been requested from nineteen of the psychologists and fourteen (74 per cent) had complied with this.

Only 290 (56 per cent) of the 522 psychologists who responded to the survey reported that during the previous five years they had given oral evidence in court or tribunal. The range was one to eighty-two court appearances. Of those who had given evidence, the majority (51 per cent) had appeared in court only once or twice and only forty-four (15 per cent) had given evidence on more than ten occasions.

Out of a total of 1,936 court appearances, 1,316 (68 per cent) were attended by forty-four (15 per cent) of the 290 psychologists. This indicates that most of the psychologists had given evidence very infrequently, whilst a small minority gave evidence on a regular basis.

Table 3.2 gives the type of Court where the psychologists gave evidence. Most commonly the psychologists gave evidence in the Crown Court (43 per cent), Magistrates' Court (40 per cent), and in Family, Juvenile and Matrimonial proceedings (39 per cent). Some of the evidence given in Family, Juvenile and Matrimonial proceedings is presented in the Magistrates' Court, but in the present survey this was kept separate from criminal cases heard in the Magistrates' Court. Sixty-eight (23 per cent) of the psychologists reported having given evidence in the Civil Division of the High Court, where civil cases concerning compensation are most commonly heard. A number of psychologists were active in the Scottish Courts. Five psychologists reported having given evidence in the County Court, three in the Court of Session (Scotland), two at Official Inquiries, two at Arbitration, and one at a Lifer Review Panel. Surprisingly, no psychologist reported giving evidence at a tribunal, not even at a Mental Health Tribunal which are very commonly attended by psychiatrists.

It appears from the survey that those psychologists who produced reports in compensation cases testify very rarely whereas it is common for psychologists to testify in criminal proceedings.

The number of cases where psychologists had to testify in Court can be worked out as a proportion of the number of reports produced. This was done for the three main areas Civil (compensation and commercial); Criminal; and Family, Juvenile and Matrimonial. Only those psychologists who had produced twenty or more reports in the respective areas were included in this analysis in order to avoid bias in the figures due to a low number of reports.

The results indicated that psychologists in compensation cases testified in no more than 2 per cent of the cases where they had produced a report. The corresponding figure in Family, Juvenile and Matrimonial proceedings was 10 per cent.

Table 3.2 The type of court where the oral evidence was given[a]

Court	N[b]	Sum[c]	Range
Crown Court	125	409	1-40
Family/Youth/Matrimonial	113	553	1-80
Magistrates Court	116	292	1-20
High Court (Civil Division)	68	224	1-20
Tribunals	36	173	1-50
Sheriffs Court (Scotland)	23	137	1-50
Children's Hearing (Scotland)	12	83	1-50
Coroner's Court	7	9	1-3
Court of Appeal (Criminal Division)	3	5	1-3
Court Martial	3	3	1
Other types of court	14	48	1-10

Notes:
[a] This table was adapted from Gudjonsson (1996a).
[b] This represents the number of respondents who had given evidence at least once.
[c] These figures are a slight underestimate because six respondents did not indicate how many times they had given evidence in different types of court.

In criminal cases they had to testify in 20 per cent of the cases where they had produced reports.

Provided with the following options, the psychologists indicated what their evidence is generally based on:

a   interview of client;
b   behavioural assessment (e.g., functional analysis);
c   psychometric testing;
d   studying documents;
e   interviewing informants (e.g. relatives);
f   other.

Interviewing the client, studying documents and administering psychometric tests were most commonly endorsed, with 97, 87 and 85 per cent of the respondents ticking these categories respectively. A large proportion of the psychologists (79 per cent) reported that their evidence was also generally based on interviewing informants. The findings indicate that when psychologists give evidence in court they often base their evidence on a combination of material obtained from interviews, psychometric tests and by studying the relevant documents in the case.

The psychologists were asked if it was common for them to be *'extensively'* cross-examined on their evidence. Out of the 290 respondents, 129 (44 per cent) reported that they were usually extensively cross-examined on their evidence. The 44 per cent figure is significantly different to the 56 per cent reported in the 1984 survey and indicates that the psychologists in the 1995 survey were generally less extensively cross-examined than those who took part in the survey in 1984. This could be due to the UK courts being more accepting of psychological evidence than they were in the early 1980s.

As far as disclosure of psychological tests in open court is concerned, ninety-eight (34 per cent) of the psychologists reported that they had been asked to disclose detailed information about psychological tests beyond the overall test findings. This is similar to the 28 per cent from the 1984 survey. A request for disclosure of test material most commonly occurred in relation to intellectual and neuropsychological assessments.

The psychologists indicated how accepting they thought the court was of their evidence. Almost half (48 per cent) said the court had been very accepting of their evidence. A further 49 per cent said the court had been quite accepting of their evidence. Only 3 per cent of the psychologists said they had found the court generally critical of their evidence.

Almost half (44 per cent) of the psychologists had found themselves presenting evidence whilst another psychologist did so for the 'other side'. The corresponding percentage in the 1984 survey was 22, which indicates that there has been a significant increase in the number of cases where evidence is presented by both sides in the legal dispute. This indicates that in recent years there has been an increase in the incidence of a 'battle of experts' in the courts.

The Edmondson survey

Edmondson (1995) noted that with the introduction of Discretionary Lifer Panels in October 1992, which resulted in these Panels having the power to direct the Home Secretary to release a discretionary lifer, there had been a marked change in the work of some prison psychologists in the UK. Previously prison psychologists had contributed to the assessment of life sentence prisoners and their reports were commonly used to assist the Parole Board without their having to testify orally at the hearings. However, since the introduction of Discretionary Lifer Panels the evidence provided by Prison Service employees can be more readily challenged by the lifer and his or her legal advisers. This has resulted in prison psychologists who have written reports on discretionary lifers having to testify and defend their reports at the Discretionary Lifer Panel hearings.

Edmondson sent out a total of 104 questionnaires to prison psychologists who had been identified as being involved in the Discretionary Lifer Panels process.

Of the eighty-nine (86 per cent) psychologists who replied to the questionnaire, forty-two (47 per cent) had written reports on lifers for a Discretionary Lifer Panel. The number of reports submitted ranged from one to twenty-four, and half of the forty-two psychologists had testified in person. Out of a total of 151 cases, the psychologists gave evidence on forty-seven occasions, which means that the psychologist had to testify in about one-third of the cases. It was evident that some psychologists were called to testify much more frequently than others. The author could not give a reason for this difference. Over half of the psychologists were called to give evidence by the lifer or the legal representative. The main reason for their being called to testify was to support the findings and opinions expressed in the report. They were also commonly called because of the psychologist's specialist knowledge of the prisoner.

As far as the oral evidence was concerned, the psychologists were most commonly cross-examined on the treatment given, the changes that had occurred in the prisoner, and predictions about future behaviour (i.e. risk assessment). About two-thirds of the psychologists reported having been treated fairly during the hearing. A number of psychologists reported feeling disadvantaged because they had not been given sufficient prior warning that they were to attend as a witness. This situation can cause a great deal of stress among expert witnesses.

Of ninety-two cases where the recommendations of the psychologist and Panel were known, there was an agreement in seventy-one (77 per cent) of cases. This indicates that the Panels were generally in agreement with the psychologist's findings and opinions.

More than half of the participants in the survey had received specialised training in risk assessment, whilst about one-third had received training in expert witness skills. In spite of this, many of the psychologists felt in great need of training in report writing and presenting oral expert evidence. Edmondson suggests that prison psychologists may lack the confidence rather than the skills in acting as expert witnesses in risk assessments.

Edmondson concluded that many psychologists are apprehensive about preparing reports for Discretionary Lifer Panels, but in spite of this the majority of those who had testified had found the experience rewarding.

Conclusions

The evidence presented in this chapter indicates that many psychologists in the UK are preparing reports for a court or a tribunal. The demand for their services seems to have increased steadily since the early 1960s and their roles have broadened considerably. Currently, psychologists most commonly prepare reports in civil cases concerning compensation, but they only testify in court in about 2 per cent of the cases. In contrast, psychologists who prepare reports in criminal cases have to testify in about one in every five of their cases.

Psychologists generally base their evidence on a combination of material from interviewing the client, psychometric testing, studying documents and previous reports, and from interviewing informants. This broad-based assessment approach represents an important step in producing comprehensive reports (Gudjonsson, 1994a) and will be discussed in detail in subsequent chapters.

Psychologists are commonly asked by solicitors to alter their reports in order to make the findings more favourable to their client. Often psychologists comply with such requests, which raises a number of ethical and professional issues. These will be discussed in detail in Chapter 4.

4

ETHICAL AND PROFESSIONAL ISSUES

Introduction

Scientific and professional organisations are increasingly developing formal standards of behaviour for their members. These are normally presented in the form of a code, which outlines the kind of behaviours that are consistent with those professional standards and those that violate the code. Lindsay (1996) argues that an ethical code has two distinct purposes. First, it is intended to regulate inappropriate behaviour, which is concerned with minimum or mandatory professional standards and it typically gives descriptions of behaviours that are unacceptable and are likely to justify a complaint. Secondly, the aim is to promote optimal or aspirational behaviour through the use of guidelines about good practice. Therefore, a good professional code should help psychologists to stay out of trouble and hopefully also improves their professionalism and good practice.

According to Lindsay (1996), psychology has experienced a particular difficulty in devising an ethical code because it is both a scientific and applied discipline, comprising several distinct fields of professional activity, such as those of educational, occupational, clinical and criminological psychology. Each may raise its own ethical concerns. Another problem is that for many ethical issues there are varied opinions within psychology about what exactly constitutes unethical behaviour (Lindsay, 1996). Pfeifer and Brigham (1993) raise concern about the increasing number of non-clinical forensic experts, such as academics, and the additional ethical dilemmas they face due to conflict over the blurred distinction between their role as an advocator versus an educator without having any recognised standards or guidelines.

Psychological associations in different countries have each produced their own code of Conduct. Lindsay (1996) has reviewed the codes used in the USA, Canada and European countries, including the UK. There is a considerable overlap in terms of content and areas of ethical concern, but differences exist in terms of style, length and specificity. The European Federation of Professional Psychologists' Associations (EFPPA) has produced a 'meta-code' which sets standards for all associations which are members of the EFPPA (Lindsay, 1996).

The American Psychological Association (APA) and the British Psychological Society (BPS) have both produced a code for their members. These apply to both academics and practitioners. The BPS Code of Conduct does not specifically address forensic work and it was not until 1994 that the APA 'Ethics Code' did so (Canter *et al.* 1994).

The purpose of this chapter is to discuss professional standards in psychology and the ethical issues that sometimes arise when psychologists engage in forensic work. A brief review will be presented of the APA and BPS Ethics Codes and the types of ethical problem that arise in forensic practice and ways of dealing with them.

The BPS code of conduct

The BPS is required under its Royal Charter to maintain a code of conduct. The Society had created an Ethical Committee shortly after both the Education Act 1944 and the National Health Service Act 1946 introduced an extensive career structure for applied psychologists. The committee considered some basic ethical principles which later provided the milieu for the development of a code of conduct. The background to the code is given as follows:

> In 1985 the Society adopted a code of conduct prior to the introduction of the Register of Chartered Psychologists with provision for an Investigatory Committee and Disciplinary Board to consider complaints of professional misconduct against members of the Society. In the light of experience in dealing with several dozen allegations of misconduct these committees recommended some amendments to the code. After extensive consultations the following revised code of conduct was approved by the Council in February 1993 and adopted forthwith.
>
> (British Psychological Society, 1995a, p. 452)

The code sets out some minimum standards for professional behaviour with which psychologists are required to comply. Guidelines to good practice are produced by specialist subsystems (divisions) within the BPS.

The code sets out in broad terms the following professional standards:

1 *General* In all their work psychologists shall conduct themselves in a manner that does not bring into disrepute the discipline and the profession of psychology. They shall value integrity, impartiality and respect for persons and evidence and shall seek to establish the highest ethical standards in their work.

2 *Competence* Psychologists shall endeavour to maintain and develop their professional competence, to recognise and work within its limits, and to identify and ameliorate factors that restrict it.

(p. 452)

The code emphasises the need for psychologists to recognise the boundaries and limitations of their own competence and to refrain from claiming competence in specialised areas of psychology where they have had insufficient training and experience.

3   *Obtaining Consent*   Psychologists shall normally carry out investigations or interventions only with the valid consent of participants, having taken all reasonable steps to ensure that they have adequately understood the nature of the investigation or intervention and its anticipated consequences.

4   *Confidentiality*   Psychologists shall maintain adequate records, but they shall take all reasonable steps to preserve the confidentiality of information acquired through their professional practice or research and to protect the privacy of individuals or organisations about whom information is collected or held.

(pp. 452–3)

Subsection 4.3 of the code is particularly relevant to forensic psychology, because it deals with possible breach of confidentiality where public safety is at stake. It states:

'In exceptional circumstances, where there is sufficient evidence to raise serious concern about the safety or interest of recipients of services, or about others who may be threatened by the recipient's behaviour, take such steps as are judged necessary to inform appropriate third parties without consent after first consulting an experienced and disinterested colleague, unless the delay caused by seeking this advice would involve a significant risk to life or health.'

(p. 453)

5   *Personal Conduct*   'Psychologists shall conduct themselves in their professional activities in a way that does not damage the interest of the recipients of their services or participants in research and does not inappropriately undermine public confidence in their ability or that of other psychologists and members of other professions to carry out their professional duties.'

(p. 453)

Recently, the Division of Criminological and Legal Psychology (DCLP) have produced ethical guidelines on forensic psychology. These are very much based on the Guidelines of the APA, discussed below (British Psychological Society, 1997).

American Psychological Association (APA) Ethics Code

Canter *et al.* (1994) provide a detailed account of the background to the APA 'Ethics Code'. The first formal ethical standards were published by the APA in 1953. These standards were based on descriptions given by their members of situations where they were faced with ethical dilemmas. Many revisions have been made to the code since 1953 by the APA Ethics Committees. Canter *et al.* give the most up-to-date and comprehensive version of the code. This includes a detailed specification of the standards set by the APA. The current APA Code is much more comprehensive than the BPS Code and provides better guidelines for professional practice. It is particularly effective in warning psychologists to take preventive action where potential ethical problems may arise in practice and there is a major section on the resolution of ethical violations. This is undoubtedly due to the fact that in the USA the risk of litigation in professional practice is much higher that it is in the UK. The APA ethical code is subject to periodic revisions as new practices and ethical issues develop.

In the current APA Code there are six general principles and 102 mandatory ethical standards. The general principles form the basis for good professional standards and practice. They are aspirational and not directly enforceable and comprise the following areas: (1) Competence; (2) Integrity; (3) Professional and Scientific Responsibility; (4) Respect for People's Rights and Dignity; (5) Concern for Others' Welfare; and (6) Social Responsibility.

The 102 ethical standards are divided into eight sections and cover different aspects of psychology in addition to twenty-seven general standards that are potentially are applicable to all practising psychologists. Canter *et al.* (1994) devote an entire chapter to the ethical issues that are specifically relevant to forensic and related activities. These are included in the APA Code for the first time. The recommendations that they make are relevant to 'all psychologists who are performing forensic or potentially forensically relevant functions' (p. 145). This broad scope of forensic psychology grew out 'of the fact that although some psychologists routinely provide services in forensic settings, many others may unexpectedly find themselves subpoenaed to produce records, having to submit to depositions, or being required to testify in court regarding a current or former student, client, or patient' (p. 145).

The adversarial nature of legal proceedings places forensic psychologists under pressure to assume the role of an advocate for the side instructing them. The results of such pressures are clearly evident from the BPS 1995 survey.

In the USA and UK a distinction is made between ordinary witnesses and expert witnesses. Expert witnesses differ in three major ways from other witnesses. First, they are allowed to give an opinion based on their special knowledge and expertise and are allowed to draw inferences from data. Secondly, they can, at the discretion of the court, remain in court while other witnesses give evidence. Thirdly, they may be asked to comment on the testimony of other witnesses.

There are six mandatory standards specifically applicable to forensic activities in the APA Code. These are as follows:

1   *Professionalism*   [In addition to complying with all other provisions of the APA Ethics Code as relevant to their activities, psychologists should base their forensic work on appropriate knowledge of and competence in the areas underlying such work, including specialised knowledge concerning special populations.

2   *Forensic Assessments*   Psychologists' forensic assessments, recommendations, and reports are based on information and techniques (including personal interviews of the individual, when appropriate) sufficient to provide appropriate substantiation for their finding.

3   *Clarification of Role*   In most circumstances psychologists avoid performing multiple and potentially conflicting roles in forensic matters. When psychologists may be called on to serve in more than one role in a legal proceeding – for example, as consultant or expert for one party or for the court and as a fact witness – they clarify role expectations and the extent of confidentiality in advance to the extent feasible . . .

4   *Truthfulness and Candor*   In forensic testimony and reports, psychologists testify truthfully, honestly, and candidly and, consistently with applicable legal procedures, describe fairly the bases for their testimony and conclusions.

5   *Prior Relationships*   A prior professional relationship with a party does not preclude psychologists from testifying as fact witnesses or from testifying to their services to the extent permitted by applicable law. Psychologists appropriately take into account ways in which the prior relationship might affect their professional objectivity or opinions and disclose the potential conflict to the relevant parties.

6   *Compliance With Law and Rules*   In performing forensic roles, psychologists are reasonably familiar with the rules governing their roles. Psychologists are aware of the occasionally competing demands placed upon them by these principles and the requirements of the court system, and attempt to resolve these conflicts by making known their commitment to this Ethics Code and taking steps to resolve the conflict in a responsible manner.

(pp. 146–54)

Canter *et al.* (1994) discuss in some detail the various steps that psychologists should take when engaging in ethical decision making. These steps are also relevant to UK psychologists and are in broad and adapted form as follows:

Know the professional ethics code   It is important that psychologists are fully familiar with and understand the ethical code of their profession. Ignorance of the code is no defence if the psychologist is in breach of those recommended standards. If there is a formal complaint of a breach of the minimum standards then the professional Society will have to investigate the complaint and disciplinary proceedings may follow.

Know the applicable laws and regulations   Psychologists should be well acquainted with current and relevant (state and federal) laws and regulations. In forensic practice in the UK this would include mental health legislation, such as the Mental Health Act 1983, Data Protection Acts, and the Police and Criminal Evidence Act (PACE) and its Codes of Practice.

Psychologists who are advising the police in the investigation of criminal cases should be careful not to recommend procedures that are in breach of the Police Codes of Practice. For example, in one English murder case a psychologist was advising the police about how to obtain a confession from a suspect and recommended to the police manipulative and coercive techniques which were against the spirit of their own Codes of Practice. The psychologist concerned did not appear to be at all familiar with the Police Codes of Practice.

Know the rules, regulations and policies of the institution where you work   Many scientific and professional organisations have internal rules, regulations and policies, which all employees are expected to be familiar with and follow as appropriate. Organisations may have vastly different rules and policies depending on their function, setting and location. Differences may involve such areas as confidentiality, security, ethical approval in research and clinical practice, the sanctioning of and conditions concerning private work, and the wearing of identification cards.

Engage in continuing education in ethics   Even when psychologists are well familiar with their own professional ethical code it is important that they broaden their knowledge about ethical principles and dilemmas by keeping reasonably up-to-date with the scientific and professional literature on ethics and by attending workshops as appropriate.

Identify when there is a potential ethical problem   Psychologists should be vigilant to detect potential ethical issues that may arise in their work. Being aware of one's weaknesses, possible prejudices, and limitations is important. For example, within an adversarial legal framework psychologists may sometimes try to please the referral agent to the extent that their integrity is compromised. Allowing oneself to be manipulated into unprofessional conduct by forceful legal advocates can easily happen to psychologists if they are inexperienced or naive as to the implications of their conduct.

Learn a method for analysing ethical obligations in often complex situations   Canter *et al.* (1994) state that there are a number of systems or strategies available for analysing and tackling ethical problems, but they do not provide the reader with a description of any of them. Instead, they point the interested reader to some key references (Haas and Malouf, 1989; Keith-Spiegel and Koocher, 1985).

Consult with professionals knowledgeable about ethics It is recommended that psychologists consult well informed colleagues or other professionals when faced with difficult ethical dilemmas. Talking through the ethical problem with a colleague may help, particularly if that person is knowledgeable about ethics. On occasions professional bodies may be consulted, such as the Law Society when psychologists are being pressured by lawyers to produced compromised evidence.

Notes, test material and documents

Psychologists should keep detailed notes of their assessment and treatment of clients. These, along with test forms and documents in the case, must be stored in a safe and secure place. In hospital settings these should normally go into the patient's hospital notes. As far as court cases are concerned, some psychologists are in the practice of destroying their notes and test material after a few years. This is very unwise, because sometimes cases reappear several years later and the previous records may be of vital importance at a future date. There have been a number of cases involving miscarriages of justice which went back to the Court of Appeal a decade or more after the original conviction. In one case, detailed notes kept by a psychologist of the assessment were of major importance to the case twenty years after the original assessment.

Problems arise when psychologists retire from practice or die without having made provisions for their confidential case material to be disposed of. In one case a psychologist instructed by a defence solicitor died in a drowning accident before the case went to court, but after he had completed his assessment. The psychologist's father, noting the official Witness Statements in the case file, unwisely took the case material to the nearest police station, which resulted in the instructing solicitors making a formal complaint about breach of confidentiality.

The BPS Investigatory Committee

Most detailed codes of conduct present desirable standards of professional conduct from which practitioners tend to fall short. One of the enduring problems with those charged with administering the code is deciding the extent to which the shortfall is morally insignificant, or at which point disciplinary action is justified, and where one draws the line between the increasing sanctions which may be imposed. The BPS has an Investigatory Committee which scrutinises complaints of professional misconduct brought to the Society. The Investigatory Committee provides regular reports of their concern in *The Psychologist*. Many of the allegations may be ill-founded or brought by mentally disturbed patients – a common concern among psychiatrists and nurses. Where the evidence is sufficient to justify further action, the case is sent to the Disciplinary Committee for a decision. Minor infringements are dismissed with a warning and advice, and the more serious malfeasances are dealt with by suspension of membership for various periods of time, usually one or two years, the final sanction is to be struck off the membership register, which can lead to termination of a professional career in the public services. In addition to professional sanctions taken against a psychologist, some allegations of professional misconduct may also lead to criminal or civil proceedings against the psychologist and a number of cases of this type are on record. Among the concerns expressed by the Investigatory Committee arising from formal complaints made against members, are the following:

1 *Practising beyond present competence*, which exposed the psychologist to legal action (dealt with later in this chapter). This conduct can be detrimental to the client or patient.
2 *Submitting to pressure* by employers to undertake work for which competence, training or qualifications are inadequate.
3 *Failing to provide* adequate supervision of junior staff, to the potential detriment of the client and/or public, and putting the employer and junior at risk of civil action by the client or third parties.
4 *Using outdated techniques*, which while appropriate in the past, have now been revised and improved, found to be no longer scientifically acceptable, or are regarded by the profession as undesirable by reason of discriminatory or other content.
5 *Failing to obtain* explicit consent of patient or client consent where necessary. Note that legally, consent is required before touching a patient or client, e.g. when attaching sensors for monitoring psychophysiological variables.
6 *Failing to take action* regarding physical or psychological health problems which could interfere with professional practice.
7 *Using language* in reports and other communications which is undiplomatic, or could cause personal offence, or contravene statutory prohibitions regarding race or sex discrimination.
8 *Making personal criticisms* of colleagues, as distinct from pointing out factual errors or disagreeing with their conclusions.
9 *Failing to observe* confidentiality.
10 *Failing to comply* with instructions for test administration and scoring procedures; the Committee noted that psychological tests are often scored incorrectly.
11 *Ignoring evidence* from contemporary research, which should have affected advice, disposal or treatment decisions.
12 *Failure to use up-to-date test material*; the Committee draws attention to the need for continued professional development and the use of up-to-date test material when assessing clients.
13 *Inaccurate and misleading information* provided to court and tribunals; the

Committee sometimes receives complaints about psychologists providing inaccurate, incomplete or misleading information to the courts.

Recent surveys into ethical dilemmas

Members of the APA, the BPS and the Swedish Psychological Association (SPA) have been asked about the types of ethical dilemmas they have encountered in their work. We briefly discuss the three surveys.

Pope and Vetter (1992) sent out a survey form to 1,319 members of the APA about examples of ethical dilemmas that they encountered in their work. The APA members were selected at random and 679 replied, which gave a response rate of 51 per cent; out of that number 134 respondents indicated that they had not encountered any ethical problem in their work in the past year or two. The remaining respondents provided a total of 703 ethically troubling incidents, which the authors grouped into twenty-three categories. The eleven most commonly reported ethical dilemmas are shown in Table 4.1.

The most commonly reported ethical dilemmas concern confidentiality. This represented 18 per cent of the total number of incidents and often centred around potential risks to third parties, child sexual abuse incidents and indiscretions by colleagues.

Table 4.1 Categories of ethically troubling incidents from three surveys[a]

Category of incident	APA (%)	BPS (%)	SPS (%)
Confidentiality	18	17	30
Blurred, dual or conflictual relationhips	17	3	18
Payment sources, plans, settings and methods	14	3	4
Academic, teaching and training dilemmas	8	3	0.6
Forensic psychology	5	2	0.6
Research	4	10	1.8
Conduct of colleagues	4	7	8
Sexual issues	4	6	0.6
Assessment	4	6	1.2
Questionable or harmful interventions	3	8	8
Competence	3	3	3

Note:
[a] This table is adapted from that of Pope and Vetter (1992) in the American (APA) survey. The British Psychological Society (BPS) and Swedish Psychological Society (SPS) surveys were conducted by Lindsay and Colley (1995) and Colnerud (1997), respectively.

The second most commonly reported ethical dilemmas relate to the boundaries around the professional relationship with a client. This may take different forms, such as friendships with clients, romantic attraction, and treating people whom psychologists already know on a personal basis.

Payment issues represented the third most commonly reported ethical dilemmas. This included inadequate insurance cover for treating patients, requesting payments for failure to keep appointments, adjusting fees according to the means of the client, and patients giving their therapist gifts.

For the remaining ethical dilemmas, two types of dilemma, 'forensic psychology' and 'assessment', are particularly relevant to forensic psychology. The main concerns with regard to the former were the willingness of some psychologists to provide biased and compromised testimony for the side instructing them, giving in to pressures and inducements from solicitors to present compromised evidence, and presenting opinions which are not based on data or scientific principles. As far as 'assessment' is concerned, dilemmas centred around psychometric tests and computerised interpretations being available to mental health professionals who are inadequately trained in their use, the practice of some psychologists of using only some of the subtests of intelligence tests (e.g. the WAIS-R and the WISC-R) without indicating that this is the case, basing conclusions on inadequate data, and ignoring other sources of data.

Lindsay and Colley (1995) conducted a survey on ethical dilemmas among 1,000 members of the different divisions of the BPS, chosen at random. The survey asked the psychologists to 'describe in a few words, or more detail, an incident that you or a colleague have faced in the past year or two that was ethically troubling to you' (p. 449). The psychologists were requested to reply to the survey even if they had not experienced any ethically troubling incidents. A total of 284 (28.4 per cent) replies were received. Of those 105 (37 per cent) said they had no ethical dilemmas to report. Out of the remaining 179 psychologists, a total of 163 ethically troubling incidents were reported.

The results of the BPS survey are in many ways similar to those obtained from the APA survey (see Table 4.1). Confidentiality was the single most commonly reported problem. It comprised 17 per cent of the total number of incidents, which is remarkably similar to the 18 per cent in the APA survey. The main types of confidentiality dilemma mentioned by the BPS members were: (1) risks to third parties, including the reporting of sexual abuse, incest, disclosure of crimes, and threatened violence; (2) disclosure of information withheld by others, such as relatives, authorities, and colleagues; (3) inappropriate or careless disclosure by others; and (4) access to confidential records by others.

Dual relationship problems, payment matters and forensic issues comprised a minority (2–3 per cent) of the ethically troubling incidents. A dual relationship is where the psychologist is acting in another role besides a professional one. Ethical problems may arise when there is a conflict of interest regarding the dual relationship, such as testifying as an expert witness for a close friend or a member of one's family.

Colnerud (1997) conducted a study of ethical dilemmas among members of the Swedish Psychological Association (SPA), using a translation of the questionnaire developed by Pope and Vetter (1992). The questionnaire was sent to 300 (5 per cent) of the 6,000 SPA members, selected at random, and 184 (61.3 per cent) replied. Overall, the findings are similar to those found in the other two surveys (see Table 4.1), with the exception that confidentiality was much more commonly reported in the Swedish survey as a problem than the other two surveys.

Contractual duties

Most forensic psychologists in the UK are in full-time employment and their private medico-legal work has to fit around their contractual duties, as in the case of other experts. This may cause a delay in reports being prepared and is of concern to the Law Society (1996).

The BPS surveys, discussed in Chapter 3, indicate that the two main fields of application as far as court work is concerned are clinical and educational psychology. In the case of educational psychologists, preparing reports which subsequently become relevant to possible civil or criminal litigation is a part of their existing contractual duties (Gudjonsson, 1996a). A similar situation exists in clinical psychology where the psychologist is asked to testify about a current or past patient either at a tribunal or in court proceedings. Here the original report produced for educational or clinical purposes may find itself incorporated into evidence in judicial proceedings. This can be a very unsatisfactory situation, because a report prepared for one purpose becomes used for another, and often a very different, purpose. A solution to this problem, which sometimes happens in practice, is that the patient's solicitor requests an up-to-date report from the psychologist specifically for the purpose of the pending legal proceedings. This has the advantage of the report being focused upon the relevant issues and used for the purpose for which it is intended.

In most instances psychologists engage in court work on a private basis and the work needs to be organised around their contractual duties. It is important that psychologists are clear about the boundaries between their private and contractual duties. The psychologists need to negotiate with their employer about the use of facilities, such as the use of consulting rooms for assessments, telephones and fax machines, test material, stationery, secretarial support, and time away from contractual duties. In some institutions the psychologist refunds his or her employer an agreed amount for the use of facilities.

The main disruptions to contractual duties typically occur with regard to court attendance. It may be easy for psychologists to organise assessments and preparation of the report to fit in with their contractual duties, but to set aside a few days for court attendance which may be cancelled at a very short notice or be substantially delayed can cause considerable disruption to one's work schedule. This may raise professional difficulties and an ethical issue. For example, Gunn

(1991) argues, from the point of view of a psychiatrist, that it is ethically wrong of mental health professionals to devote excessive amounts of time to court work at the expense of providing much-needed treatment to patients.

Confidentiality

In clinical and forensic work confidentiality is one of the most frequently reported ethical dilemmas. Bromley (1981) distinguishes between four different models of confidentiality in clinical settings, which are referred to as: (1) 'absolute confidentiality' (everything communicated by the client is totally confidential); (2) 'limited confidentiality' (what is disclosed depends on the type of information and to whom it is disclosed); (3) 'contractual confidentiality' (the clinician and client negotiate any disclosure); and (4) 'discretionary confidentiality' (the clinician determines the limits of confidentiality).

Communication between a lawyer and a client is 'privileged', which means that it is protected from disclosure in evidence in legal proceedings. In the UK no such privilege applies to expert witnesses, although it exists for state-registered psychologists in some States of the USA. In forensic work in the UK, 'absolute confidentiality' does not apply and no medical and paramedical professional has a legal privilege which enables them to refuse to answer a question as a witness in court or to disclose clinical notes (Finch, 1984). Psychologists may be served with a subpoena to act as a witness in a civil or criminal case. They may also be subpoenaed to disclose and bring along relevant documents, such as case notes and test forms. If the psychologist perceives ethical problems about handing over records a consultation with a colleague or lawyer may prove helpful. On occasions a court order may need to be questioned or challenged. Under such circumstances judges may be sympathetic to a practitioner who is unwilling to disclose material on grounds of professional conscience.

Thelen et al. (1994) describe a survey of a large number of psychologists with regard to their beliefs concerning confidentiality in cases of suicide, homicide and child abuse. They found that psychologists relate to their own personal code when deciding whether or not to breach confidentiality, and that approximately 25 per cent of the respondents believed in absolute confidentiality. The authors discuss the possible conflicts and stress to which those conforming to a code of absolute confidentiality are liable, in the light of legal and APA mandates.

In the broader aspects of forensic work, such as the assessment and treatment of offenders in out-patient clinics or concerning in-patients in secure units, relevant information is typically shared by the members of the multi-disciplinary team. Similarly, as far as the preparation of court reports is concerned, confidentiality is also of the 'limited' variety. Here certain persons, typically the referral agent or the client's lawyers, will be provided with the forensic report and the relevant information pertaining to the assessment requested.

Forensic cases pose a potentially serious problem with respect to confidentiality in a number of different ways. The main ones are as follows:

Obtaining information from third parties   When conducting a forensic assessment, informants, such as relatives, spouse, friends or colleagues may need to be consulted. In addition, it may be important to obtain access to medical records, school reports and other confidential records. This requires the consent of the client being assessed or that written permission can be obtained through the client's solicitor. Psychologists need to be very careful when approaching third parties for information without the client's written consent, because the mere request for information requires some kind of an explanation to the third party which must be handled very delicately. In addition, the information obtained from a third party may well be subject to confidentiality requiring formal written consent before it can be disclosed.

To whom the report should be disclosed   When preparing court reports only the referral agent and the client are entitled to a copy of the report. The report should not be disclosed to other parties without the consent of the client or the lawyer involved. This principle includes colleagues commissioned by the other side who request a copy of the report.

Reports prepared for the prosecution   When psychologists conduct assessments for the prosecution it is very important to explain to defendants that anything they say which is relevant to the assessment will be forwarded to the Crown Prosecution Service and may be used against them in court. The position is different when the report is commissioned by the defence, because if the findings are not favourable then the report need not be disclosed to the prosecution. Solicitors sometimes ask to be present when assessments are conducted on behalf of the prosecution, or request that their defence expert is present. Some psychologists are in the practice of refusing such requests without a satisfactory explanation. Our view is that solicitors, their legal representatives, and defence experts should be allowed to sit in on the assessment if this is requested. There are no reasonable grounds on which such a request can be declined unless that third party interferes inappropriately with the assessment. Indeed, when confessions are made to the expert witness it is particularly helpful when the defendant's solicitor is present at the time (Gudjonsson, 1994a).

Admissions of crime or other sensitive information   Psychologists have an ethical duty not to disclose information about the criminal acts of a patient, although the BPS certainly recognises that there are circumstances where there may be an overriding social obligation to disclose it to a third party, such as the social services or the police. In the UK there is no legal obligation for psychologists or other professionals to disclose voluntarily to the police the crimes they know or suspect have been committed by their patients. However, the Children Act 1989 (Bridge *et al.*, 1990), and the accompanying guidance for doctors working with child protection agencies, make it clear that mental health professionals must not withhold information which may place a child at risk of ill-treatment or neglect. Indeed, knowledge or belief of abuse will usually justify a mental health professional making a disclosure to an appropriate, responsible person or officer of a statutory agency. In addition, the deliberate concealment of a crime during an investigation may be interpreted as an unlawful obstruction of an officer in the execution of his duty.

During a forensic assessment clients sometimes request that some of the information provided by them is not disclosed in the expert's report. This may include sensitive material which is not always relevant to the legal issues to the case, such as a history of having had an abortion or been the victim of a sexual assault. In many instances this kind of sensitive information need not be disclosed, unless it is directly relevant to the issues being addressed in the report or might become important in terms of mitigation in the event of the client being convicted of the offence with which he or she is currently charged.

Disclosure of test material   Following item-to-item analysis of tests in court, the BPS became concerned about the lack of confidentiality of psychological test material (Tunstall *et al.* 1982). Lawyers may try to discredit the validity of psychological tests in a number of different ways, including challenging the face validity of the tests and marginalising their importance and relevance to the legal issues. Test forms and manuals may be produced as exhibits in court and circulated among a number of people. This can undermine the validity of tests in future cases. In some well-publicised court cases in England judges have been sympathetic to the request of psychologists to protect sensitive test material from being disclosed in open court. Psychologists should be aware of the need to protect test confidentiality and should attempt to minimise any risk of disclosure which may undermine the validity of the tests that they are using. Any ethical dilemmas about test disclosure can be discussed with the trial judge and a reasonable compromise can often be reached (i.e. providing the jury with as much information about the test as is necessary for their deliberation whilst not revealing subtle details which may compromise the test's validity).

Psychologists should be aware that their court reports may be distributed to a large number of people, professional and non-professional. Often the clients themselves are provided with a copy of the report. This can cause difficulties in conducting the forensic assessment. First, once the client has read the expert's report and conclusions it may prove difficult for the expert for the other side to conduct a neutral assessment. The client may also have discussed the report with a number of people, including his or her solicitor, family and friends, which could influence his or her performance on further testing. Secondly, some psychologists give an unnecessarily detailed description of tests in their report, which may compromise the validity of the tests in future use. For example, some tests are subtle in nature and client's detailed familiarity with the tests, as well as public knowledge about them, makes it more likely that the answers given are going to be influenced by self-serving factors and deliberate faking. When tests are used in order to detect possible faking, either in terms of clients' giving a favourable account of themselves or malingering (e.g. faking intellectual deficits, memory problems, mental illness), revealing details about these instruments and procedures in court reports or in oral evidence can seriously undermine the validity of these tests for future use. Even if the clients in question know nothing about the tests, lawyers acting for the other party are sometimes quick to use the idea of public knowledge of psychological tests as a way of discrediting the test results in a given case. The issue of test disclosure will become an increasing problem as information becomes easier to access through the internet. Ready access to scientific knowledge increases the likelihood of abuse. It is worth remembering that some defendants in criminal cases are highly motivated to seek out information for their defence and they may be surprisingly well informed about certain test procedures.

General guidance on disclosure of raw test scores to other experts has been published by the BPS (Professional Affairs Board, 1997). When raw test scores are requested by an expert instructed by the 'other side', psychologists should note the following. It may be difficult for psychologists to evaluate another psychologist's report without details of the raw scores. Psychologists should disclose raw test scores when appropriate. However, raw scores, like other information from the report, should not be disclosed without the instructing agent's consent. Preferably this consent should be in writing. The disclosure of the raw test material should not take place unless the report has been properly disclosed to the 'other side' and the instructed psychologist has received a copy of it. Psychologists can refuse to disclose raw test material to experts who they do not believe have the expertise to interpret the scores satisfactorily. For example, one of us (Gudjonsson) refused to disclose the raw scores to a psychiatrist, who had been instructed by the opposing side, due to his lack of familiarity with the psychometric tests. The opposing lawyers instructed a chartered clinical psychologist to whom the raw scores were disclosed.

Roles and emotional conflicts

Some writers (e.g. Sadoff, 1988; Shuman, 1993) have expressed concern about mental health professionals testifying about a patient that they are currently treating. The disadvantage is that the therapist may be less objective and dispassionate in his or her evidence than a more neutral expert witness. Even when the therapist is totally objective he or she may still be construed by the court as being biased in favour of the patient. Another point raised by Shuman (1993) is that the court assessment may adversely affect the subsequent therapeutic relationship between the therapist and the client. Shuman strongly argues for separate assessment and therapeutic functions in both civil and criminal cases irrespective of whether the psychiatrist or psychologist is court-appointed or privately retained.

The argument in favour of the therapist testifying is that he or she probably knows the patient better than an independent doctor called in specifically for the forensic assessment. Gunn and Taylor (1993) strongly argue in favour of service providers being able to testify on behalf of their patient and see no reason why they could not be fully objective in their evidence.

Arcaya (1987) discusses the ethical dilemmas of psychologists when they experience conflicts between their therapeutic role and feelings of repulsion and disgust over the offender's criminal deeds. Many offenders have committed horrific crimes which may raise intense emotions in the expert witness and result in a bias which is unfavourable to the client. Arcaya suggests that under those circumstances clinicians should carefully weigh all the evidence for and against the client's culpability in their head and provide separate sections in their report for contradictory perspectives on their client. In contrast, Cornell (1987) argues against such a single solution to the problem and emphasises the importance of considering the context and circumstances in which the report is being prepared.

In many cases psychologists are asked to prepare reports where the defendant's guilt is being disputed. In such cases psychologists should avoid forming assumptions about the defendant's guilt or innocence. It is always best to focus on the relevant legal and psychological issues with an open mind. Once the psychologist has formed assumptions of guilt or innocence then it tends to bias the assessment in favour of their assumption. For example, there have been cases of miscarriage of justice where psychiatrists providing psychological explanations for the defendant's denial of guilt proved instrumental in convicting him.

Making assumptions about the defendant's guilt and moral culpability raises important ethical problems among expert witnesses and the bias it may cause (Pfeifer and Brigham, 1993). The well-known American academic psychologist Elizabeth Loftus gives an excellent illustration of this type of bias: 'If I believe a defendant is innocent, if I believe in his innocence with all my heart and soul, then I probably can't help but become an advocate of sorts' (Loftus and Ketcham, 1991, p. 238).

Impartiality

When preparing court and tribunal reports it is important that experts are impartial in their written and oral evidence. Lack of impartiality raises very important ethical issues for expert witnesses and these should not be ignored. Partiality implies potential bias in the expert witness's evidence, which may seriously mislead the court. Such bias may be unintentional or deliberate. On occasions it arises out of naivety as in a case of a psychologist who commented after being criticised by a colleague for producing a biased report, 'I thought if you were instructed by the defence you only included in the report findings that are favourable to the client.'

In *Access to Justice*, Lord Woolf (1996) emphasises the importance of impartiality in the expert evidence. He states:

> There is wide agreement that the expert's role should be that of an independent adviser to the court, and that lack of objectivity can be a

serious problem. This may sometimes arise because of improper pressure on experts from solicitors, as was found in a survey of clinical and educational psychologists, results of which were reported in the May 1995 issue of *The Psychologist*.

(p. 143)

Lord Woolf is here referring to the results of the 1996 BPS survey (Gudjonsson, 1996a). He believes that the current system has the effect of exaggerating the adversarial role of experts and this helps neither the court nor the parties concerned. He quotes a recent remark made in judgment at the Court of Appeal: 'For whatever reason, and whether conscious or unconsciously, the fact is that expert witnesses instructed on behalf of parties to litigation often tend . . . to espouse the cause of those instructing them to a greater or lesser extent, on occasion becoming more partisan than the parties' (Woolf, 1996, p. 143).

Lord Woolf makes a number of recommendations concerning expert witnesses, including courts being able to appoint their own experts and assessors as required, that the duty of the expert should be to the court and not to the expert's client, that experts from different sides meet at the discretion of the court and reach an agreement on the salient issues and if possible produce a joint report (if experts fail to reach an agreement the reasons for it must be specified), and that the expert should end the report by declaring that the report includes everything which is relevant to the validity of his or her conclusions.

Lord Woolf's *Final Report to the Lord Chancellor* is specifically on the civil justice system in England and Wales. However, the importance of impartiality and Lord Woolf's recommendations are also applicable to criminal proceedings.

Biased evidence

There are a number of reasons why an expert witness's report and oral evidence may be biased. These include the eagerness to please the referral agent, as well as giving in to pressure from third parties, such as solicitors, barristers, social services or clients. Another reason which is commonly overlooked, but can have devastating consequences concerning the outcome of a case, is the expert's prior assumption of guilt or innocence, which may influence the nature of the assessment and the conclusions reached.

Eagerness to please

In his 'Lund Lecture', delivered at the British Academy of Forensic Science in November 1994, Lord Chief Justice Taylor focused on expert witnesses and gave a critique of their role in civil and criminal cases (Taylor, 1995). He was clearly concerned about the eagerness of some experts to produce a report that was favourable to the party who commissioned it. He states:

There is, for the reasons I have already given, a fear that expert opinion is partial to the party who commissioned it. I hope this relates only to a minority but there exists a suspicion that some 'experts' will ask their instructing lawyer what they want to hear from them before giving their opinion. I have myself when at the Bar, been asked more than once in conference with an expert 'What do you want me to say?' It is extremely important for all the professions involved to find an effective means of countering this abuse which does considerable damage not only to the reputation of the profession to which the witness belongs, but also to our system of justice.

(p. 5)

The above quotation emphasises how important it is for expert witnesses to give a genuine opinion and not be influenced by a desire to please the person who commissioned the report. We do not know how often this eagerness to please seriously misleads the court. Even if the expert does not testify orally in court, the biased report, and also sometimes the physical presence of the expert in court, is commonly used in the bargaining process in the hope that it will favour the outcome of the case for the party who commissioned the report. In criminal cases the result may be that the Crown Prosecution Service decides to offer no evidence against the defendant and the case is dismissed.

Experts being asked to produce a modified report

The 1995 BPS survey into psychological evidence in court, the results of which were discussed in Chapter 3, showed that many psychologists report being pressured to alter a report in such a way as to make it more favourable to the side instructing them.

On the basis of the survey and our extensive forensic experience, it is evident that psychologists, and undoubtedly also other expert witnesses, are sometimes asked to modify the report. This may include requests for the following:

Improving clarity, consistency and correcting factual errors   It is not uncommon for experts to make factual and typographical errors in their reports. If not corrected these could mislead the court, and may cause an embarrassment to the expert if he or she is asked to testify or if an expert from the other side is asked to comment on the report and identifies the errors. It would be quite legitimate for the party who commissioned the report to ask for these to be corrected before the report is served on the other side. Similarly, lack of clarity is sometimes a major problem in experts' reports. As Lord Chief Justice Taylor pointed out in his 'Lund Lecture' (Taylor, 1995), expert witnesses must make their specialist evidence comprehensible to the ordinary lay person and they should avoid using scientific jargon. The instructing solicitor may justifiably request that the report be modified to make it more comprehensible. Thirdly, experts are sometimes inconsistent in what they say in the report and this may need to be corrected. For example, a psychologist described a defendant in one part of the court report as 'being suggestible' and in another as 'scoring low on suggestibility'.

Deleting a reference to documents provided When the psychologist is commissioned to prepare a report the referral agent provides him or her with all the relevant documents in the case. These will be need to be listed in the report (see Chapter 10) so that the court will know what documents were seen prior to the preparation of the report. As will be discussed in Chapter 10, the documents seen will depend upon the nature and purpose of the assessment, but they may include such material as the client's 'proof of evidence' and previous psychological or psychiatric reports. Sometimes solicitors do not want the expert to refer to these documents, because they may then need to be disclosed to the other party, which could be to the client's disadvantage. This may include something that the client told his solicitor which may be construed as unfavourable to his case, such as a confession, or that a previous expert's report contains unfavourable material. The solicitor may ask at the beginning of the assessment that no reference is made in the report to certain documents because they are 'privileged material' and should only be used as 'background material'. Alternatively, the solicitor may ask the psychologist to delete any reference to the documents after the report has been completed.

Whether or not to comply with the solicitor's request raises important ethical considerations. The client's proof of evidence is a privileged document and this is the argument that solicitors typically use when they want experts to delete a reference to the document from their report. However, the legal privilege lies between the client and his or her solicitor. Solicitors may or may not obtain their client's permission before disclosing the proof of evidence to the expert. Once the expert has been provided with the document it is very difficult for him or her to ignore the fact that they have seen it, particularly when the information obtained from the document is pertinent to the issues being addressed in the report. For example, sometimes the account the client gives the expert of his background and behaviours is in great contrast to that given to the solicitor when the proof was taken. This discrepancy may be very important when assessing the client and may influence the opinions given by the expert.

Even when the proof of evidence is provided it may not be the only proof taken by the solicitor. The following case is an example. In a murder case involving a disputed confession, the proof of evidence, which was undated, showed that the defendant was denying any responsibility for the offence. The implication was that from the beginning of the solicitor's involvement in the case his client was denying the offence. During the psychological assessment the defendant told the psychologist that for some months after the offence he was admitting the offence and gave the solicitor details of the crime. He then decided to retract the confession and new proof of evidence was taken. The expert contacted the solicitor who freely admitted that a previous proof had been taken but it was not disclosed to the expert since it incriminated his client. It is difficult to avoid the thought that in this case the solicitor was trying to mislead the expert into providing a report which was incomplete.

A similar problem may arise in the case of omitting a reference to other experts' reports or findings. For example, omitting a reference to a previous psychological report, where extensive psychometric testing was undertaken, could be embarrassing to the psychologist if he is required to give evidence in court and has to admit that he was aware of the previous findings but had failed to acknowledge these in his report because doing so might prove unfavourable to his client's case. More importantly, not being able to refer to the previous findings may give a misleading picture of any subsequent test results. For example, in one case a psychologist was asked to assess a defendant who had been extensively assessed intellectually a few weeks previously, but the client's solicitors did not want the previous report mentioned in the current report due to other test findings which were not favourable to the defence. During the current assessment the IQ scores were markedly higher than those obtained previously, particularly on the Performance subtests which indicated the likelihood of practice effects. In view of the solicitor's instructions, the psychologist could not mention the likelihood of practice effects in the interpretation of the findings. Therefore, the court might have been left with the impression that the defendant was somewhat brighter than he actually was, which was not in the client's interest.

Our view is that it is very unwise of psychologists to acquiesce in requests to exclude mention of relevant documents which could have substantial bearing on the expert's interpretations, opinions and conclusions. There is a move in civil proceedings for letters of instruction to be disclosed to the court and these commonly list the documents sent to the expert for his or her consideration. Perhaps a similar change should also apply to criminal cases, which would reduce the pressure placed on experts and the ethical dilemmas that accompany such practice.

Not mentioning unfavourable test findings   There have been a number of cases when on psychometric tests some of the findings are favourable to the defence whilst others are unfavourable. There may be a number of reasons for this including the low correlation commonly found between tests, even when measuring similar constructs, and the complexity of human behaviour. For example, even though persons of low intelligence commonly perform poorly on tests of memory, and tend to be more suggestible than their brighter contemporaries, there are some intellectually impaired persons who do not follow this expected pattern. When this happens solicitors may ask the psychologist to delete any reference in the report of the memory and suggestibility tests and then use the low IQ scores to imply high suggestibility. Psychologists should not comply with such practice, because it can seriously mislead the court and in addition undermines the integrity of the psychologist and the profession. The following case illustrates the disastrous consequences that can happen when psychologists give in to the pressure of solicitors to delete unfavourable findings.

Mr M. was charged with serious criminal offences after making a confession to the police during interrogation. In court the defence disputed the confession and argued that the man was of low intelligence, had possible brain damage, and as a result might be sufficiently suggestible to render his confession unreliable (invalid). When cross-examined in court the psychologist denied having assessed the defendant's suggestibility (i.e. he said he had not administered any tests of suggestibility). The defendant was then seen by a crown psychologist and his suggestibility was assessed by the use of the Gudjonsson Suggestibility Scale. The defendant told the crown psychologist that the defence psychologist had administered the same test when assessed by him. The psychologist had to go to court and explain why he had misled the court. It appears he had given in to pressure from a solicitor to delete a reference to the suggestibility scale and when cross-examined in court he was too embarrassed to admit to it.

Omitting a reference to a confession made to the expert   In cases of disputed confessions defendants sometimes fully admit the offence when assessed by the defence or crown psychologist, even when they have denied it to their solicitor. Gudjonsson (1994a) discusses such cases and the ethical issues that may arise as a result. Another growing problem is that defendants are increasingly disputing the reliability of their confession to the police, even when they have never actually retracted or denied it to their solicitor. That is, the defendant fully accepts that he committed the offence, but the defendant pleads not guilty and the defence want the crown to prove the case. They then instruct a psychologist to identify if there are any psychological vulnerabilities which may render the confession inadmissible, such as a significant intellectual impairment or learning disability. In such cases the solicitor may not provide the psychologist with the defendant's proof of evidence and hope that he or she does not ask the defendant any questions about the offence. In other cases solicitors have specifically asked psychologists not to ask the defendant any questions about the offence. The more narrowly focused the psychological assessment is, the greater the risk that the psychologist will overlook relevant and salient matters, a consequence which could cause an embarrassment to the psychologist if he or she is required to testify in court (Gudjonsson, 1994a).

When a psychologist refuses to alter the psychological report the solicitor may instruct another psychologist to do a more focused assessment, where he or she focuses only on the tests that revealed favourable outcomes in the previous assessment. The solicitor may therefore be able successfully to control the conclusion in the report by giving the expert very specific instructions. Psychologists should avoid colluding with this practice because it could result in serious ethical dilemmas for the psychologist and possibly cause a miscarriage of justice.

The following case illustrates the point.

Mr C was in his early thirties. During police interviewing he confessed to seriously sexually assaulting a young boy, which included an offence of buggery. He later retracted his confession and a psychological assessment was commissioned to establish if he possessed any psychological vulnerabilities which were relevant to disputing the confession. During the psychological assessment the defendant made a detailed confession to the psychologist, which corroborated fully the confession he had made to the police. When the report was completed the defendant's solicitors asked the psychologist to delete the reference to the confession, which he declined to do on the basis that it was relevant to the assessment. The solicitor commissioned another psychological report, and specifically instructed the psychologist not to ask about the offence and focus only on the defendant's intelligence and suggestibility. No reference was made in the second psychological report about the previous assessment. The Crown Prosecution Service was persuaded, on the basis of the new psychological assessment, not to offer any evidence to the charge of buggery, but the defendant pleaded guilty to a lesser charge of indecent assault.

A multiplicity of ethical codes

The professional psychologist is subject to a number of different ethical codes which are not always congruent. This chapter has been so far largely concerned with the ethical code laid down by the psychologist's governing professional body, breaches of which expose the offender to professional sanctions. Mention has also been made of the psychologist's personal code of ethics; this arises during early development as a result of explicit moral training by parents and teachers, incidental learning and role-acquisition. As Thelen *et al.* (1994) found in their survey, most psychologists faced with an ethical dilemma use their personal code as the primary context for reaching a decision.

Yet another code comes from indoctrinated religion, and is usually derived from holy scripts. Breaches of a religious code may be subject to punishment by the religious authorities or the community; the more serious offences may lead to the death penalty, as in the Muslim Fatwah imposed upon Salman Rushdie. Not surprisingly, conflicts between the various codes arise and exacerbate the ethical dilemmas which the psychologist encounters. The 'white lie', a deception practised in the assumed interests of the second party is frequently faced by the physician and relatives of a terminally ill patient who may lose all vestige of hope if faced with the truth. Research psychologists have long been faced with the white lie dilemma when the experiment requires ignorance of its purpose to remain valid. The forensic psychologist faces similar dilemmas in respect of certain assessment tests and techniques where the validity relies upon test naivety.

Professional liability

Beyond these ethical codes, there are, however, two legal codes, civil and criminal, with which the psychologist must comply. Breaches of legal codes, such as refusing to answer questions from the witness box which would break confidentiality, can lead to imprisonment for contempt of court, a sentence which has been imposed upon at least one psychiatrist who refused to reveal facts about a patient, present in court, which he believed would be seriously detrimental to his patient's mental health.

The three areas of law in which professional conduct has led to legal proceedings are breach of contract, tort, and criminal offences. These are discussed by Haward (1983) and the article on professional indemnity insurance and legal advice for psychologists by Clark *et al.* (1987) is particularly relevant, giving examples of the types of risk and liabilities involved. We live in an increasingly litigious society, encouraged by an emphasis on 'rights' rather than responsibilities, by contingency fees in the USA, and by the availability of legal aid in the UK, sometimes in the context of greed replacing human concern. Professional psychologists with only private practice income and inadequate professional liability insurance could be bankrupted by damages awarded against them in a civil law suit. Hill (1987) reported that in the USA some doctors were paying out over 30 per cent of their gross income on insurance: if the present rate of increase in litigation continues, insurance premiums would become higher than the average salary within the foreseeable future. Guidance for chartered psychologists on public liability insurance, which is still relatively modest, is given by the Professional Affairs Board (1995); with allegations of misconduct by psychologists in the UK already running into three figures annually, a 24 per cent increase over the previous year (Prestige, 1997), forensic psychologists would do well to re-examine their professional indemnity cover and the nature of the current risks. The following notes provide a simple outline of likely risks to which UK forensic psychologists are exposed in undertaking professional services, and more detail will be found in the many available books on contract and tort available, some of which are mentioned below. Professional liability is a complex area of law with differences between different jurisdictions; Markesinis and Deakin (1994) give useful insights into foreign law.

Law of contract

A legal contract, with special exceptions, requires each party to exchange something the other wants, known as the 'consideration': the psychologist exchanges his professional services for a fee. Qualifying clauses and disclaimers may be built into the contract, but may not be enforceable if the courts decides the conditions specified in the contract are exceptionally onerous, or offend statutory regulations, such as those on consumer protection. Penalties for breach of contract, such as failing to comply with the conditions, may be written into the contract by the psychologist and enforceable at law.

Some contracts may be oral or even implied, but such contracts are difficult to prove in court unless there are convincing witnesses to the exchange. Written contracts are therefore preferred whenever professional protection is required. For example, in order to claim for payment of fees and out-of-pocket expenses it is advisable to provide a watertight contract which itemises all the conditions attaching to the contract, such as expenses chargeable, overall fee (if fixed) or rate per unit time. If fees are time-rated, it is important to keep accurate and meticulous timesheets, as well as all relevant receipts for all disbursements as these may have to be justified.

Legal problems regarding contracts have increased, both because more forensic psychologists are entering private practice, either as individuals, in partnership with colleagues, or as contracting consultants to a group operating as a limited liability company.

Law of tort

Tortious acts, and subsequent claims for compensation, form a significant part of the forensic psychologists' workload, and this aspect is dealt with in Chapter 8. Occasionally psychologists find themselves in court as the tortfeasor, required to defend their professional behaviour against a civil suit brought by a client as plaintiff. Unlike common law crimes, where the necessary intent has to be proved, civil law is concerned primarily with the act itself: the aim of the civil court is to recompense the victim, not to punish the offender. The nature of torts varies with time and the progress of civilisation, and new torts are created in consequence of social change. For example, compensation legally claimable for post-traumatic stress disorder had to await the introduction and establishment of this diagnostic concept before being legally recognised as a tort. Other new torts which have appeared within recent years include, invasion of privacy, breach of confidence, abuse of statutory powers, infringement of status, and those offences created in the European Community known as Eurotorts (Heuston and Buckley, 1992). Most new torts are still based on principles which have been established during past centuries, but some reflect significant changes in social perceptions and the developing complexity of modern civilisation. The torts most likely to be committed by the forensic psychologist are trespass, defamation and negligence.

In addition to the chapter by Haward (1983), a general introduction to torts committed by psychologists is also given by Schwitzgebel and Schwitzgebel (1980), but any legal textbook on tort will provide a comprehensive understanding of the potential for committing torts without intent in forensic psychological practice.

Trespass

Trespass, from the Latin trans-pass – to go beyond a private limit – occurs when a person is aggrieved at having his rights unlawfully infringed. There are three types of trespass – to the person, to land, and to goods. Trespass to the person is itself in three stages, namely assault, battery, and mayhem, although the latter term is now archaic.

Unlike criminal assault, tortious assault is committed without touching the person; its definition, remaining unchanged since the Middle Ages, is any act, short of physical contact, which a reasonable person could construe as likely to cause harm. The victim need not actually experience fear, but must be in some expectation of hurt (for example, Bruce's case, 1966). Producing electrodes for electrodermal monitoring during an interview, or a penile plethysmograph sensor for assessing impotence as a defence in a rape case, are examples of a potential trespass. Words alone are usually insufficient to be tortious, but when accompanying an act, such as holding out a sensor connected by wire to an apparatus and saying 'I'm going to clip this electrode to your ear' may be enough to pass beyond the client's limit of acceptability if frightened of electricity. However, if the words alone cause hurt, such as a state of stress, the utterance becomes a tort in its own right, following the precedent in Wilkinson's case (1897). First-time accused persons often feel extremely vulnerable and forensic psychologists will have no difficulty in bringing to mind examples of casual statements they have made which could have aggrieved the more sensitive or more litigious client.

Battery, as a tort, is defined as touching a person against his will. It has nothing to do with battering, as in criminal law, although the tort of battery may lead to criminal proceedings, as did an unwanted kiss in the Chief Constable of Devon and Cornwall's case (1982) and is merely an affront to the victim's dignity. In the case of the unwanted kiss the affront is self-evident. Unlike assault, the victim need not feel in fear of being harmed. Putting a comforting arm round the shoulders of a weeping client is potentially tortious. In one case even brushing past a person was declared tortious by the court: social perceptions having changed significantly in the intervening years, a contemporary court would be unlikely to find this tortious. In contrast, projecting heat or light upon a person may be construed as battery, as when a camera flashlight is used.

Mayhem is battery leading to physical hurt. One psychologist nearly became a defendant in a mayhem suit when the paranoid client he was escorting down the stairs tripped and fell, and claimed that the psychologist had pushed him. Had the client's solicitor not refused to take action the psychologist could have found himself as defendant in court. Aversion therapy created many tortious problems of this sort: in the USA it led to a long and complicated series of cases extending between 1971 and 1973, from which emerged the Wyatt-Stickney Rules which have since governed the practice of this form of behaviour therapy. Today, torts formerly based on mayhem are treated as cases of professional negligence, discussed later.

Torts causing emotional rather than physical damage, which historically were also classed as mayhem, are now generally referred to in the UK as innominate torts, and in the USA as the Prima Facie Tort Doctrine (Heuston and Buckley, 1992). The most common form of this tort, which affects psychologists as potential tortfeasors, is the distress caused in revealing to clients their psychiatric diagnosis, such as schizophrenia, which has serious social connotations. Another source of innominate tort is the termination of a regular meeting between psychologist and client. In these cases, the contact between the two will have filled some psychological need of the client over and above the professional relationship. Sometimes the need exists within the psychologist, who consciously or unconsciously encourages a transitory relationship which makes it emotionally more difficult for the client to accept its termination. This is a common hazard in psychological treatment, affecting professionals of either sex, and at least one female psychologist has been successfully sued for what the judge referred to as 'predatory psychotherapy'. The fact that the psychologist later married the client was deemed to aggravate rather than mitigate the offence. This tort can occur in any professional relationship, and usually requires more contacts than occur in forensic practice, but as some compensation cases have taken up to twelve years to be resolved, and may require repeat testing and lead to the client requesting sessions for advice and reassurance, the forensic psychologist is not immune to this form of client-dependence.

The final trespass to the person which has involved psychologists is any constraint imposed upon the freedom of the client. False imprisonment (in this context false means erroneous or wrongful) is committed whenever the client is 'deprived of the liberty to go where he pleases' (Spicer's case, 1977). One psychologist locked up his department having interviewed a client after the other staff had left earlier, not realising that the client was still in the toilet; had the client been falsely imprisoned all night the damages awarded in a subsequent suit could have been heavy. As it was, the psychologist noted that the client's car was still outside and returned to find the client still in the toilet and unaware of his false imprisonment, but it is important to appreciate that the tort is committed even when clients are unaware that they are not free to leave (Meering's case, 1919). Knowledge of the constraint increases the severity of the tort and the subsequent damages. 'Time-out' procedures come under this heading. False imprisonment can actually take place in the open air where no physical barriers exist, as in some desensitisation programmes. This tort does not apply to clients who are already in legal custody, or compulsorily detained in hospital under the Mental Health Act.

Torts to third parties

In English law, torts are regarded as private wrongs between two parties, and third parties are not legally recognised, being joined together with other injured persons as second parties. In the USA, however, the courts have recognised a legal duty to third parties since the Tarasoff case (1976). The tortfeasor in this case was a psychologist, employed by the University of California, whose client he assessed as being dangerous. Because Tarasoff had no contractual duty to inform his employer of details of client's case histories, which were already protected by professional confidentiality, the psychologist kept his client's perceived dangerousness to himself. The client then murdered a student, whose parents discovered the clinical facts in the subsequent investigation, and sued both the psychologist and his employer as joint tortfeasors. The court concluded that the privilege of professional confidentiality ends where public peril begins, and upheld the parent's claim. In Ramona's case (1989) the professional duty to third party was clarified, bringing the conflict between confidentiality and the duty to protect third parties from the ethical to the legal arena. Beck (1990) gives a comprehensive discussion on this subject, while Appelbaum and Zoltek-Jick (1996) discuss the US legal situation since the Ramona case. The Tarasoff duty is not recognised in the UK, which has no separate and distinct law of privacy, and the US has developed one from English case law which can be raised in defence of breaches of duty to third parties. To protect privacy, the UK lawyers use the innominate tort, discussed above, as well as trespass to land, explained in the next section, to deal with media snoopers and photographers who invade privacy. The European Convention of Human Rights also protects certain rights to privacy.

Defamation

Whatever the various duties of a forensic psychologist may be, one duty usually involves communicating information about the client to a third party. In doing so, the competent and caring psychologist will want to be honest and diplomatic, but it is not always possible to be both at the same time. Some statement in the psychologist's reports may be construed by the client as personally offensive, and litigation against the psychologist may be taken if the client is aggrieved at losing the case for which forensic expertise was originally commissioned. Defamation is a trespass against reputation: of the two kinds of defamation, slander is spoken and therefore a transitory tort, while libel is written and remains tortious throughout its existence. Slander is a tort only, but libel (in English law but not in Scottish or USA law) is also a crime because it can cause a breach of the peace. For this reason, criminal libel requires the involvement of only two persons, the defamer and the defamed, whereas libel as a tort requires three persons, including a third party to whom the defamed suffers a loss of reputation. Another difference is that in tort, truth is a good defence, for then the defamed are deemed to deserve their ill reputation, but in criminal libel the rule is 'the greater the truth, the greater the libel' because the defamed are then more outraged by public exposure and thus more likely to breach the peace. Defamation is a common law offence codified by various statutes such as the Defamation Act 1952, and is defined as any statement which exposes a person to hatred, ridicule or contempt, or causes the person identified to be shunned and avoided. Anything said in court is privileged, so the sometimes slanderous statements addressed to expert witnesses, or used to describe them to the jury by a denigrating counsel, are beyond remedy. Some barristers, when unable to fault the expert testimony, denigrate the witness and thus, by implication, the evidence they have offered. In one pornography case, the prosecuting counsel, having elicited the fact that the witness had had venereal disease, told the jury that this was nothing to be proud of, and asked them if they would be happy to see the witness married to their daughter, adding; 'Would you welcome Mr- as the putative father-in-law of yourself or your son?' In the same case, a distinguished psychologist was described to the jury as 'a person of Dutch extraction who affirmed rather than took the oath', spoken in a manner which implied that little credence should be given to the evidence of such a foreign infidel.

Most libel is written, but need not be verbal; photographs, cartoons, films and waxworks have been held to be libellous. Proof of any damage caused by the libel is not required, but the court requires proof that it was libellous, that it was published to at least one person other than the defamed, and that it identified the plaintiff, if only by implication. The judge decides whether there is a prima facie case, using Lord Aitken's Test, that is: 'would the words tend to lower the plaintiff in the estimation of right-thinking members of society' (Sim's case, 1936): if so, the case continues and the jury decides whether or not the three necessary facts have been proved.

Authors of books and papers are directly liable for any defamatory statements in their text. Criticism in reviewing, even opinions, have been the source of defamatory actions; Prokop (1974) was a psychologist who criticised a textbook and was sued by its author. Editors are under a special duty to ascertain the nature of the text with which they are concerned. Defamation is said to run against the defamer, so if a justifiable statement about a client innocently identifies another person of whom it is untrue, the latter has a valid claim against the psychologist for defamation.

Negligence

Negligence is a tort in its own right, as well as an ingredient in many other torts. Professional negligence emerged in AD 1534, and involved surgeons during the Wars of the Roses. Because damages are generally greater in cases of negligence, especially professional negligence, the plaintiff's legal advisor will usually try to formulate the offence in terms of negligence rather than the more obvious tort which has been committed.

In criminal law, negligence exists as criminal negligence, and occurs in those cases where the client suffers substantially and the defendant is clearly lacking in care for the client or concern for the consequences of his conduct. Under the Health and Safety at Work Act, 1975, forensic psychologists in charge of departments or with responsibility for subordinate staff are liable for negligence as a breach of statutory duty, and can face two years' imprisonment and an unlimited fine for negligence, which under this Act automatically becomes a crime.

When the defence realises that a case of negligence is likely to succeed, an attempt is made to claim contributory negligence by the plaintiff. In Scane's case (1959) for example, the driver who had knocked a boy off his cycle claimed contributory negligence on the grounds that the boy had been ascertained as 'educationally subnormal' and the defence claimed that he could be assumed to have below average cycling skill. Contributory negligence based upon such common-sense assumptions are commonly successful and can substantially reduce the damages awarded. In this case, the assumption was shown to be unwarranted by a field experiment showing boys of the plaintiff's intelligence were not significantly different in cycling skill, at the site of the accident, than boys of average intelligence.

Defences in tort

Although forensic psychologists are exposed to potential torts in most of their professional activities, there exists a range of recognised defences which protect them in most civil suits provided they have behaved prudently and without malice within the limits of the professional ethical codes which apply to them. Examples of both special defences, which apply to one type of tort, and general defences in tort are provided by Haward (1983); this is a complex subject beyond the scope of this volume, and reference should be made to specialised legal texts on torts such as Carter-Ruck *et al.* (1992) and Markesinis and Deakin (1994).

Consent is the most important legal defence of all. The rule is: 'One who consents cannot claim for injury', and obtaining written consent for any professional procedures from which aggrievement might follow should be an essential part of a forensic psychologist's routine. The need for explicit consent is obvious in all psychologist–client interactions, remembering that mere words can create an innominate tort, and assessment techniques sometimes involve touching the patient. It is particularly important when psychologist and client are of the opposite sex, since body contact by even casual touch can cause offence.

There are two forms of consent, explicit and implied. Implied consent is when the client, by his compliant behaviour and absence of protest, agrees to follow instructions or co-operate in some procedure. When a client holds out his hand for Galvanic Skin Response (GSR) electrodes to be clipped on, he is implicitly consenting to electro-dermal monitoring, although the consent is not 'informed' unless a prior explanation has been given. 'Informed consent' is an American term embodied in USA regulations; in English law the term used is 'real consent' (Gunn and Taylor, 1993). It is important that the client understands, and is competent to understand, to what he is consenting. Consent lasts only for as long as the client remains in agreement and may be withdrawn at any time. Many forensic psychologists may feel safer using forms which detail and describe the measures to be carried out; such forms provide evidence of exactly what has been agreed to by the client.

The best defence of all

The special and general defences against litigation under the law of tort described briefly above are all retrospective. They come into consideration only after the plaintiff has obtained legal advice and the defendant is made aware that his client is aggrieved by some act on the part of the defendant and civil proceedings may be, or have been, instituted. Prevention, however, is always better than cure. Good psychologist–client relations form the bedrock of professional practice, and should be developed as first priority from the time referral takes place. In the context of friendly relations and mutual respect, it is difficult for the client to feel aggrieved by any action on the part of the psychologist which has been adequately explained beforehand, has the client's consent, and has been performed to the best of the psychologist's ability and with the appropriate level of competence which the profession would expect from the particular status of this member. Developing the degree of positive relationship advocated here goes beyond that required by either legal or ethical codes, but is essential if the psychologist wishes to avoid recriminations, formal complaints, or serious litigation.

Crimes

It is unlikely that a psychologist would unwittingly commit any criminal offence as part of his professional conduct. The question of whether perquisites are lawfully permitted by the employer or unlawfully taken by members of staff is a thorny one: the unlawful taking of perks could be treated as either the tort of trespass against goods or as the crime of theft. This is a grey area in so far as perquisites are rarely specified in an employment contract or company regulations, and while most employers turn a blind eye to perks taken on a small scale, the line they draw between perks and theft is not made explicit and differs between employers.

A more serious situation can arise when UK psychologists are invited to assist in cases being tried in foreign jurisdictions. In a trial in one former British colony, the psychologist interviewed and assessed the accused in prison and prepared a report. This was examined and found unacceptable by the government prosecutor, and the psychologist was asked to repeat the assessment. It was not known what had happened to the accused meanwhile, but on the second testing occasion he was rigid, unduly polite, uncommunicative and produced a significantly different score. This second session had been recorded clandestinely and unknown to the psychologist, and was produced at the trial to contradict the original assessment. The psychologist was immediately arrested on a charge of conspiring to pervert the course of justice. His psychiatric colleague, whose evidence agreed with the earlier report, had meanwhile managed to catch an earlier plane back to the UK. The charges were eventually dropped, but not before the psychologist had suffered for some time the indignities of a local prison.

Conclusions

Psychologists should always act professionally and ethically. They should not engage in any practice which carries the risk of misleading the court and bringing their profession into disrepute. Unethical behaviour not only undermines the integrity of the expert concerned, it reflects badly on the entire profession. It has taken many years for psychology to be respected by the courts and to be seen as an independent profession which has something unique to contribute to legal proceedings.

This chapter has focused on ethical codes and the types of ethical dilemmas that are particularly relevant to forensic practice, and has suggested ways of dealing with some of the ethical dilemmas commonly encountered. Of course, membership of a professional organisation is voluntary and psychologists can avoid having to comply with the ethical codes by not being members of the professional organisation. This difficulty is easily overcome by solicitors referring clients only to chartered psychologists in the UK and to state-registered psychologists elsewhere. This will ensure that the psychologist is covered by a disciplinary-enforced ethical code.

In addition, the liability of the forensic psychologist in civil proceedings has been briefly explained, with a note of the possible excuses which may be offered in defence. The most important defence which can be offered is evidence that the client consented to the actions undertaken by the forensic psychologist in preparing evidence on his behalf, but good professional–client relations will generally prevent litigation against the individual psychologist, and is an essential part of good forensic practice.

5

THE ROLES OF THE FORENSIC PSYCHOLOGIST

Introduction

The English legal system requires the expert to qualify as an expert every time he testifies as an expert witness. This makes sense, as although there are necessary qualifications which are common to every psychological problem facing the court, each particular case presents differences in the evidence which may be important to the expert testimony. In a road traffic accident which leads to a claim in tort for compensation, for example, the essential problem in one case may be whether brain damage following a closed head injury is actually present at all: in a similar case, the existence and degree of brain injury in the plaintiff may be accepted by both sides, and the disagreement may centre upon the plaintiff's subsequent earning power. In the first case clinical training in neuropsychology is clearly a *sine qua non*, whereas in the latter case an occupational psychologist experienced in the cognitive requirements of the many grades of work in industry and commerce may be the more relevant expert to call upon.

Each discipline is likely to offer different solutions to the same problem, and be able to offer solutions to problems beyond the competence of experts in a different discipline. It often happens that the expert in one discipline has a special interest and expertise in a second discipline, and can offer the court the benefit of this secondary expertise when the problem in the case calls for it. For example, some medical practitioners develop specialised interests and knowledge of relevant areas of psychology. Similarly, some psychologists have developed a specialised knowledge in areas of mental disorder (Murphy and Clare, 1995). Indeed, there is often a considerable overlap between the contribution of psychologists and psychiatrists in judicial proceedings. This is particularly true with regard to a clinical assessment.

One of the difficulties produced by the concept of 'The Compleat Forensic Psychologist', an expert purporting to be all things to all lawyers, is that psychology's corpus of knowledge is now too great to be claimed by any one person. Sub-specialities have developed within psychology, each with its own vocabulary, each requiring different skills in its social applications and providing a different gamut of experience. The modern lawyer would generally be able to differentiate between a psychologist and a psychiatrist, but may have no inkling that an expert in one psychological speciality is likely to have only rudimentary knowledge of another speciality. Clearly justice demands that *expert* evidence be tendered by an expert from the relevant speciality. The danger is that the full-time forensic psychologist is assumed to be a forensic specialist, when the role is more that of the general practitioner: when called as an expert witness he could be expected to answer questions in psychological areas which are beyond his professional competence. Some expert witnesses may attempt to answer such questions, believing themselves to be adequately competent to do so, or that by expressing professional ignorance on the matter in question, they think they would negate the acceptability of other parts of their evidence and possibly undermine the client's case.

The practice of forensic psychology calls for different types of approach or 'roles' depending on the nature of the case being assessed. Haward (1981) identified four discrete roles, designated clinical, experimental, actuarial and advisory. These are discussed below before highlighting some of the main differences between psychological and psychiatric evidence.

Clinical (assessment) role

The clinical role, as described elsewhere by Haward (1981), is somewhat of a misnomer, since it refers to two separate classes of activity. Both involve the psychologist in an interpersonal relationship with one of the parties, and involve some form of objective personal assessment, usually within a psychometric framework, but only one of these activities is strictly clinical in nature. This role was originally referred to as *clinical* because it was one almost exclusively occupied by clinical psychologists. Clinical, an adjective derived from *klinik*, the Greek word for bed, clearly refers to a role which deals exclusively with what the law regards historically as *medical* problems. Today many conditions which were viewed as being exclusively medical in nature have become more appropriately the province of abnormal or clinical psychology, and a long way from the 'clinic' or bedside: nevertheless, they are the immediate concern of the clinical psychologist working within the medical framework of the NHS, or of the clinically trained educational psychologist concerned with behavioural rather than strictly educational problems. Both specialities frequently come together in the youth court to speak on child abuse cases, and to support or challenge protection or custody orders requested by local authorities, or to deal with fostering or adoption problems. Harnett (1995) argues that family court work has become a highly specialised area of clinical psychology.

The clinical role therefore refers to those problems of evidence where the mental state or mental abnormality of one of the parties is relevant to the legal issue, but also includes neuropsychological problems such as those incurring in traumatic brain damage, as well as physical disabilities which may have a psychological concomitant, or impair earning power, career prospects, or the fulfilment of educational potential. Other important clinical areas are the involvement of psychologists in the assessment of post-traumatic stress disorder (PTSD) and neuropsychological status (Gudjonsson, 1996a). It is our view that the term 'clinical role' should be restricted to this strictly clinical usage.

A related role, which has also been labelled 'clinical' because it involves personal interaction with one of the parties in the case, is, in fact, non-clinical and deals with normal cognition and behaviour of the sort which do not normally come within the province of the clinical psychologist. For example, in one case where the accused was alleged to have hurled a brick through the windscreen of a police car, the defence held that this would not have been possible, given the position of the accused at the time and the fact that he was left-handed. It was therefore necessary to prove to the court that the accused was, indeed, left-handed, and that the predicted trajectory from a left-handed throw was significantly different from the actual trajectory of the missile that was used. A full range of laterality tests was given, and these showed acceptable inter-test reliability, while a number of witnesses to fact were available to testify as to the consistency with which the accused used his left hand. Although on this occasion it was a clinical psychologist who gave the expert testimony, a psychologist from any speciality who had made a study of laterality and was conversant with the appropriate tests could have undertaken this role. Other cases where non-clinical but formal psychometric assessment has been required for evidence include the measurement of manual skill when the cause of an accident from either clumsiness or inadequate machine safety is in question; and the measurement of manual speed and dexterity when the rate for the job is legally challenged.

While from the theoretical point of view, it would be reasonable to separate these two assessment specialities, in practice, in either case, the potential expert witness must pose the question: 'Does this evidential problem require me to adopt an assessment role, and if so, is my knowledge, experience, and skill relating to the appropriate psychometrics adequate for this purpose?' Well-standardised cognitive and personality tests are generally useful in many assessments, but occasionally the situation calls for a familiarity with industrial practices with which only an occupational psychologist with relevant experience is competent to deal. Often the expert finds that the assessment requires the use of test instruments which need restandardisation on a sample more appropriate to the subject, or which need suitable modification (with subsequent reliability/validity testing) to provide the special information sought by the court. One of us (Haward), for example, has made extensive use of specially devised Thematic Apperception Test (TAT) pictures, producing scenes by line-and-wash illustrations or photographs which are relevant to the problem or the case history of the subject concerned. The 'Forensic TAT' can be a powerful instrument in eliciting motivation and emotion-generating situations, especially when used in conjunction with electrodermal responsivity (Haward, 1964, 1969, 1981).

The characteristics of the assessment role described above are that it necessitates (1) a personal interaction with someone connected to the case – the accused, the plaintiff or defendant in a civil hearing, or sometimes even a witness, and (2) making a formal assessment, using objective psychometric measurements, subjective scales and questionnaires, and information from other sources. This role is one commonly adopted by clinical, educational and occupational psychologists, and demands a sound knowledge of test construction, the logic and mathematical understanding of its statistical basis, and the relevance of its reliability, validity and significance to the problem in hand. It should be remembered that to win a case in a civil court, one party has only to show a *preponderance* of proof to win the case. With only a 51 per cent weight of evidence required, discarding test evidence because it just misses the 5 per cent probability may well defeat the ends of justice merely because of obsessional adherence to what is after all a purely arbitrary choice, yet this is a far from uncommon practice. The jury are quite capable of making up their own minds in a common-sense way on test probabilities, provided that these are put to them in a simple way. It is in the assessment role that psychologists really comes into their own, for this has been their principal function unique to their profession. At a time when all their therapeutic techniques – including behaviour therapy, as well as counselling, vocational guidance, management advisory services, and so on – have been taken over and shared by other professions as well as untrained entrepreneurs, the current fashion of denigrating psychometrics is illogical, short-sighted and damaging to the profession.

The experimental role

If sophistication in psychometric assessment is psychology's only genuine *raison d'être*, the special emphasis placed in undergraduate training on the experimental method is the second strongest card in the forensic psychologist's hand. The experimental role is an impersonal one in the sense that the expert witness adopting this role will not normally see the party for whom the experimental work is undertaken unless and until they go into court to testify. Experiments are useful ways of both obtaining facts and extracting them in a situation which is both relevant and meaningful to a jury. In some cases, they are necessary because there is no other source of data which the forensic psychologist believes are necessary for him to form the expert opinion which the court requires.

For instance, a prison officer testified that he overheard a prisoner giving to his visitor details of the crime which pointed conclusively to the guilt of a named person. The prisoner averred that the prison officer had misheard what he said. Left at this stage, a jury would have to decide which of the two was telling the truth, and their subsequent judgment would be based upon which person they believed to be the most honest. No one could doubt that the odds favoured the prison officer. But the problem involved more than the veracity of the two; it also involved the plausibility of the explanation. How probable was it that a significant part of the conversation could be misheard during a visiting session in prison? By making an audiotape recording of the conversational hum in the prison visiting room, and superimposing the essential part of the prisoner's alleged conversation at the usual sotto voce level which obtains in such environments, it was possible to provide the auditory stimulus which an experimental group could be asked to interpret. Needless to say, the results confirmed the well-known misperception of vocal communication. Such results could not prove the truth of the prisoner's explanation, but did show that mishearing in the particular situation was more likely than not, and provided relevant data on which the court could come to a more informed decision.

In many cases the type of experiment required is obvious from the circumstances, although of course there are usually a number of different ways of going about it. Time and expense are obvious constraints, especially within a legally aided case, but Home Office regulations and other legal impediments may also limit the choice of alternative ways of obtaining the required data. Within its bureaucratic limitations, the prison service has been very co-operative in providing facilities for the forensic psychologist, and police constabularies are especially helpful when the experimental work is undertaken for the prosecution. There is a natural absence of enthusiasm for professional activities perceived as enabling the accused to evade the long arm of the law, but even when the psychologist is attempting to undermine police perceptual testimony, as being honest but mistaken, the higher echelons of the constabulary have co-operated in providing such data as visual acuity norms within a given police division, as in Hawley's case (1964).

In civil cases heard before the High Court, pre-hearing experimental work is often useful, since in many actions for tort involving working conditions in commerce or industry, decisions made upon guesswork or presupposition can be immeasurably improved by recreating or simulating the conditions which obtained at the time of the incident which is central to the res gestae. We cannot emphasise too strongly the importance of the sound training in experimental psychology provided in the undergraduate courses of Oxbridge and the older red-brick universities, and the experimental methodology developed further in a sound doctorate programme. Thus equipped, both applied and academic psychologists are well able to devise unique, innovative experiments which answer directly some of the questions which the forensic psychologist has translated from the solicitor's original request. One of us (Haward) has devised experiments for forensic purposes undertaken in aircraft in flight, on the bridge of a ship at sea, in a supermarket, cotton mill, hospital laboratory and at the subterranean coalface in the deepest colliery in the north (Haward, 1981): the other (Gudjonsson) has explored the frontiers of psychophysiology and used laboratory-based techniques to answer forensic problems (Gudjonsson, 1979, 1992a; Gudjonsson and Haward, 1982; Gudjonsson and Sartory, 1983).

The actuarial role

The actuary is a mathematician who studies the incidence of a given human event in an appropriate sample of the population, and calculates from its base rate the probability of its future occurrence. This enables insurance companies to predict fairly accurately how often insured events – from loss of property to loss of life – will occur. The actuarial role is therefore one in which the forensic psychologist presents evidence of the probability of some event; such information is obtained in two ways, by a search of the literature where such data is likely to have been reported, or by fieldwork in which the data is gathered *ab initio*.

For the literature search, 'Psychological Abstracts' is always a good starting point. Computerised searches, while rapid, are sometimes too shallow in coverage, and one may need to go back to the interwar years to obtain the information desired which has not yet been absorbed into the computer archives. In one case, an important element of the identification of the accused was the fact that the offender had the habit of frequently pulling the lobe of one ear. But was this a common habit? Going back half a century, a study by a social psychologist had found that this habit had a base rate of 1 in 2,500 of the sample studied, and this strengthened the belief in this particular case that correct identification had been made.

Sometimes the search needs to go back even further. When Lee Harvey Oswald was brought to trial for the assassination of President J.F. Kennedy, one of the problems was whether one rifle shot (allegedly by Oswald) or two shots had been fired almost simultaneously, introducing the possibility of a second assassin, and raising the question whether it was the Oswald bullet which had actually killed the President. The question of how closely the ear can differentiate between two sounds became relevant to the forensic enquiry, and was answered by some early research undertaken and published at the turn of the century by Munsterberg, whom we discussed earlier in Chapter 2.

Psychological literature is not the only source of actuarial data, of course. In clinical problems the medical literature may be more relevant, and journals of sociology can yield a rich harvest on occasion. Medico-legal, criminological and forensic science journals are often particularly relevant, while the annual statistical tables published by the Home Office and other government ministries are especially good for up-to-date base rates. Average earnings, when related to IQ scores, specific skills, or disablement, have proved invaluable in compensation cases when plaintiffs are no longer able to pursue their former occupation and loss of future earnings needs to be realistically predicted (see Table 8.1 in Chapter 8).

When a literature search has thrown up nothing of relevance, the required information has to be obtained by direct investigation in the field. Sometimes this can be completed by careful sampling and the use of questionnaires, but where feasible the use of direct observation in the field may be necessary. In one case, two offenders committing a robbery were identified as a black man and a white blonde girl with a ponytail hairstyle, who escaped in a yellow automobile. Shortly afterwards, two people answering this description driving a yellow automobile were stopped in another part of the city. Because witnesses saw only the back of the offenders and failed to note the registration marks of the vehicle, positive identification could not be made. Observers conducted a census of yellow cars driven by mixed-colour couples within the city which gave an actuarial probability of there being two vehicles containing such a couple present on the same day as being what the defence colourfully described as one in the entire population of Australia. This satisfied the jury who convicted the two offenders. The fact that later the conviction was overturned by the evidence of mathematical and statistical experts, who criticised the details of the data, is a salutary lesson that, like all roles mentioned, they should not be adopted unless the psychologist has the appropriate level of competence in this role.

The use of statistics and probabilistic reasoning are increasingly being applied to the solution of problems in judicial proceedings. Bring and Aitken (1996) argue that there are a number of reasons for this change, which include theoretical developments about the use of statistics in court, increased availability of data, the availability of more powerful computers, and technical developments in forensic science. The 'likelihood ratio', which is an important principle for evaluating the weight of the evidence for and against the defendant, is particularly important in evaluating scientific evidence in the courtroom (Robertson and Vignaux, 1995).

The advisory role

Additional to the roles already mentioned, a fourth role has come into greater prominence during the past decade. This is the role in which forensic psychologists examine the evidence put forward by another expert, usually but not always of their own profession. This has been termed the advisory role because the experts asked to assess the evidence of another professional are not providing new evidence to the court, but are advising the side engaging their services on possible weaknesses in the other expert's report, and how best to undermine the latter's evidence when he or she is testifying in court. It is the least stressful of the various roles, because the psychologists as advisors do not have to justify their own conclusions and opinions, do not have to face cross-examination, and do not have to undertake all the work necessary in providing psychological evidence in the first place (see Tunstall et al., 1982, for an important case example of this role). However, sometimes advisors are required to testify and be cross-examined about their opinion. It is an increasingly common practice for psychologists to sit in court while their colleague for the other side testifies. They may advise counsel what kinds of question to ask of the psychologist for the opposing side, who may also have conducted his or her own clinical assessment of the client.

By the very nature of court procedure and the adversary system, the advisory role is a destructive one: unlike assessors of professional publications, who are expected to be *constructively* critical, pointing out both strengths and weaknesses in the author's position, and suggesting ways in which the presentation can be improved, the counsel uses the advisor to concentrate only on the weak parts of the expert evidence, with the aim of denigrating the competence of the expert and devaluing the evidence itself. Elsewhere in Europe, where the inquisitorial system reigns, such a role has no meaning. Psychologists may tender opposing opinions, which the judge may accept or reject, wholly or in part, but no opportunity exists for one expert to publicly belittle another in court. Some psychologists see an ethical problem here and eschew the advisory role, preferring not to demean a fellow professional, or believing that the so-called 'battle of the experts' and the sometimes unwarranted negation of an expert's competence renders a disservice to the profession.

On the other hand, it must be said that some psychological evidence offered in court is of very poor quality (Gudjonsson, 1993), and that every psychologist should be prepared to defend his statements at the bar of professionalism. On one occasion testimony that a person was socially competent, on the basis of the Vineland Maturity Scale completed by the patient himself, was contradicted by photographs produced in court showing the person to be living in filth, squalor and personal neglect. This is not the best way to enhance the reputation of the psychologist or his profession. The advisory role is therefore an important safeguard in maintaining standards in forensic psychology, and the ethical considerations against adopting this role can be met; after all, the advisor is able to exercise his own judgment and discretion as to the form his critique should take, and as to the questions he should prompt his counsel to ask the other expert.

There are two separate functions in this role. The first and more common one is to receive, assess and report back to the lawyer engaging the advisor, a report submitted by an expert for the opposing side. This is usually by a member of the advisor's own profession, but occasionally a psychologist is asked to advise on a report by an expert from a different discipline, for example a school medical officer reporting results of tests which they administered themselves, a psychiatrist reporting on parental personality in a child-abuse case, a personnel officer justifying at an industrial tribunal the discharge of an employee on psychological grounds. In such cases, the advisor evaluates the validity of the data and the logic and cogency of the opinions, and submits a report which may be used by counsel when the expert is being cross-examined.

The second function is undertaken in court. The advisor is usually seated with the solicitor and behind the counsel, and listens to the other expert testifying. Weaknesses in the latter's evidence will usually have been discussed prior to testifying, in a counsel's conference, when the advisor will have been asked for some critical questions which could be asked which would be likely to reveal the testifying expert's errors or omissions. Questions put to the expert in the witness box, either in the examination-in-chief or cross-examination, may also elicit new evidence or opinions that were not included in the original report, and the advisor then comments on these, and suggests further questions, by writing notes which the solicitor passes to counsel.

The advisor may not escape from this one-sided task entirely scot-free, and apart from the possibility of being called to testify and be cross-examined about the bases for the advisor's own opinions, the differences of professional opinion between advisor and witness(es) may be aired later in public, leading to sometimes acrimonious debate within the profession, at annual conferences or in the pages of learned journals. In one notorious case, four experienced clinical psychologists, including two professors and an expert on test dissimulation, together with an educational psychologist of professorial level, agreed that the accused was functioning at the borderline level of intelligence. A university lecturer who had made a study of intelligence, especially among graduates, was called as advisor to the prosecution, and on the basis of observing the accused in court, and despite the consistent psychometric findings and supportive case history, believed the accused to be of average intelligence and to have misled all the defence psychologists as well as his previous teachers. Under cross-examination by prosecuting counsel, the test evidence was ridiculed, item by item. The advisor, by working unseen through cross-examining counsel, can have a highly significant impact on the jury's perception and understanding of expert evidence, and psychologists adopting the advisory role should be aware of the impact which undertaking this role can have upon colleagues and upon the profession as a whole. Of course, scientific integrity must be maintained at all times, and the psychologist has a duty to assist the course of justice by drawing to the court's attention expert opinion which is clearly unsound. To take up a partisan position and encourage denigration of those of opposite opinion, particularly through lawyers' unfair and illogical criticism of acceptable well-standardised tests such as those of Wechsler, may prove to be a gross disservice both to psychology and to justice.

Psychological versus psychiatric evidence

Unlike the varied contribution of the forensic psychologist, the principal role of the forensic psychiatrist involves a mental state examination of persons suspected to be suffering from mental disorder and the provision of appropriate treatment. Gunn and Taylor (1993) define forensic psychiatry as 'the prevention, amelioration and treatment of victimization which is associated with mental disease' (p. 2). This definition is based on a medical model of diseases and emphasises the importance of *mental disorder* in the practice of forensic psychiatry. The traditional function of psychiatrists is the mental state examination and the observations of signs and symptoms of mental disorder. Without mental disorder there would be no forensic psychiatry. In contrast, Haward (1981) defines forensic psychology as 'that branch of applied psychology which is concerned with the collection, examination and presentation of evidence for judicial purposes' (p. 21). According to Haward's definition, there is no need for the existence of mental disorder. Indeed, in contrast to forensic psychiatry, forensic psychology would exist in the absence of mental disorder. The reason for this is that forensic psychology arose historically from psychology's focus on understanding human behaviour generally, rather than specifically in relation to mental disorder, which is fundamental to psychiatry.

Grisso (1993) argues that both forensic psychology and forensic psychiatry are at risk of losing credibility within the courts due to adverse publicity in relation to some recent cases. Two factors appear to have contributed to the problem. Firstly, both disciplines have a rather weak scientific base. It is not sufficient for their credibility that forensic psychiatry has gathered much clinical and research data on mental disorder and that forensic psychologists 'can borrow from knowledge accumulated across decades of controlled, empirical research on human behavior in the basic fields of developmental, personality, cognitive, social and abnormal psychology' (p. 135). The second problem is the lack of quality control over the practices of both professions, which has resulted in inadequate and unethical practices by some experts. We discussed in Chapter 4 how this can undermine the credibility of psychology in the courtroom.

Grisso states four important differences between psychiatrists and psychologists. First, there are fundamental differences in the *content* of their contribution to individual cases. Psychiatrists are specifically trained to deal with biological, medical and psychopharmacological questions. In contrast, psychologists are better trained to deal with issues that go beyond mental disorder, such as describing the person's functional abilities, personality, behaviour and coping strategies. Although psychologists are sometimes able to comment on the effects of medication, expertise in this field lies predominantly within the province of psychiatry.

Second, the two disciplines use different *methods* in their assessment of individual cases. Psychiatrists rely principally on interviews and observation for their assessment. In contrast, psychologists commonly use standardised and qualitative assessment methods (e.g., IQ tests, personality tests) in addition to interviews of clients and informants. Many of the tests available are based on recognised scientific principles.

Third, there is an *epistemological* difference between the research of psychologists and psychiatrists. Psychiatrists more commonly base their research on observations of large clinical samples, whereas psychologists are likely to conduct controlled experiments. This difference relates mainly to the fact that the psychologists' training in general psychology requires them to be able to design and perform controlled experimental studies on a variety of psychological issues. This makes psychologists particularly suitable to perform Haward's experimental role. In spite of this, American forensic psychologists appear to focus predominantly on the clinical role and their work overlaps considerably with that of forensic psychiatrists (Bartol and Bartol, 1987; Shapiro, 1990). Their contribution to the experimental role, focusing on issues in a particular case, is completely lacking, although the research data they have provided, which is pertinent to forensic problems in general, is substantial.

Fourth, the two professions use different *mentoring* systems. Forensic psychiatry training more often makes use of teaching hospital departments and residency training, whereas graduate programmes in psychology are based within the psychology departments of universities.

There is one further fundamental difference between psychologists and psychiatrists, which is not discussed by Grisso, but it is of great importance, at least for clinicians practising in the UK. Unlike forensic psychologists, forensic psychiatrists have to be approved for the purpose of Section 12 of the Mental Health Act 1983 by the Secretary of State as having special experience in the diagnosis and treatment of mental disorder. The Mental Health Act 1983 controls the involuntary hospital detention and treatment of mentally disordered patients and provides doctors with special powers and responsibilities (Bluglass, 1990a). In addition, psychiatrists have special responsibilities with regard to mentally disordered patients in community settings, which includes the statutory supervision of restricted patients (Barry et al., 1993). There is indeed a heavy clinical, legal and moral burden on those practitioners who have to manage the potentially dangerous patient (Webster et al., 1994; Baker, 1997). Shapiro (1990) makes the valuable point that it is the failure to conduct a reasonable and competent evaluation that may result in legal liability rather than the failure to predict accurately future violence.

The main implication of the differences between psychologists and psychiatrists is that they have different skills and apply different methods to the assessment, which when used jointly can be employed to the maximum benefit of the case.

Grisso argues that the potential loss of credibility of the two disciplines can be overcome by them collaborating in three distinct areas: (1) working jointly on cases, where appropriate; (2) working together to improve the quality of forensic practice, for example by conducting joint seminars and workshops; and (3) improved clinical and research training programmes for psychologists and psychiatrists.

It seems from Grisso's (1993) review that forensic psychologists and psychiatrists do not commonly work together on cases. This also seems to be the case in the UK. However, psychologists and psychiatrists clearly have complementary skills and their individual contributions can jointly maximise the understanding of some cases. Over the years one of us (Gudjonsson) has worked jointly on several cases with psychiatrists, which has proved very effective in a number of major criminal cases (Gudjonsson and Gunn, 1982; Gudjonsson, 1992a, 1996c; Gudjonsson and MacKeith, 1997). To illustrate the importance of joint psychological and psychiatric contributions, Gudjonsson (1996c) discusses one well-publicised case, 'The Guildford Four', where the reports on Carole Richardson influenced the Home Secretary's decision to refer the case back to the Court of Appeal (Gudjonsson and MacKeith, 1997).

Conclusions

We have argued that the roles adopted for producing psychological evidence and testifying in court can be classified into four groups. The first group consisted of a role which required personal interaction with a party to the case, and involved either clinical or non-clinical assessment: the strictly clinical role required competence in clinical assessment and often overlaps with the contribution of the forensic psychiatrist, while the non-clinical assessment demanded competence in specialised assessment, usually but not exclusively educational or occupational.

The experimental role typically involves experiments in the field or laboratory and is concerned with testing an hypothesis derived from the problem presented to the psychologist. The methodology used may be based on an individual case study design or on the collection of extensive field or experimental data. In view of the psychologist's training in experimental methodology this role presents him or her with a unique opportunity to contribute to the solution of some legal issues. It is a role that is seldom fulfilled by forensic psychiatrists.

The actuarial role is concerned with the incidence of specific human behaviour patterns and the probability of their occurrence in a particular setting or environment. This can be achieved by either analysing data from other investigators' research or collecting data *de novo*. The actuarial role is of growing importance in the forensic sciences and has advanced immensely in recent years. It is not a commonly practised role within psychology.

The advisory role has become increasingly common in recent years. At its best it provides an important and objective peer review of another expert's report. This can be extended to the psychologists sitting in court and advising the opposing side on the questions to ask during the cross-examination. On occasions, the advising psychologist has conducted his or her own assessment of the client and may give evidence in court. It is important to recognise that in a given case the psychologist may perform more than one role. For example, the clinical and advisory roles are commonly practised at different times in the same case.

Irrespective of their role, in forensic applications, psychologists should generally conduct the necessary bibliographic research relevant to their enquiry, and then proceed to assessments or experiments by which they hope to answer outstanding questions.

There are some similarities and differences between psychological and psychiatric evidence. Both share a rather weak scientific base, which is readily open to criticism during cross-examination. Differences between the two disciplines relate to content, method, epistemology, mentoring and clinical responsibilities of their respective contributions. There is much scope for improved co-operation between the two disciplines in judicial proceedings.

6

PSYCHOLOGICAL TESTING

Introduction

The main purpose of the psychological assessment in judicial proceedings is to perform a specific evaluation of an individual's relevant strengths (potential, capacities, healthy features) and weaknesses (deficits, problems, pathological features) in order to assist the judge and jury in their decision making. For this purpose psychologists may employ different psychological principles, procedures and methods. With the exception of offender profiling, document analyses, and experimental work conducted in the absence of the client, these require direct access to the individual, who would normally be assessed individually rather than in a group. The methods used will depend upon the nature of the assessment, the theoretical orientation, training and experience of the examiner, and the types of legal issue to be addressed. In Chapter 3 it was noted that when psychologists conduct an evaluation of a case in judicial proceedings they commonly employ a combination of methods, including interviewing, behavioural observations and psychological testing.

Psychological testing can be applied to many different functions and behaviours which are relevant to civil and criminal legal issues. These include: intellectual abilities (Wechsler, 1981); social functioning (Doll, 1965; Sparrow et al., 1984); neuropsychological status (Lezak, 1995; Martell, 1992); personality (Eysenck and Eysenck, 1991; Pope et al. 1993); post-traumatic stress disorder (Stone, 1993); the prediction of dangerousness (Monahan, 1981, 1984, 1988) and risk assessment (Towl and Crighton, 1996); psychopathy (Cooke et al. (1996); moral development and reasoning (Kohlberg, 1976; Kohlberg and Candee, 1984); sexual problems (Salter, 1988); anxiety, depression and anger problems (Spielberger, 1983; Beck and Steer, 1987; Novaco, 1975); the attitudes of offenders towards their crime (Gudjonsson, 1984a; Gudjonsson and Singh, 1988, 1989); the competence and reliability of a witness in a criminal trial (Gudjonsson and Gunn, 1982); various legal competencies (Grisso, 1986a); interrogative suggestibility and compliance (Gudjonsson, 1997a); and malingering (Gudjonsson and Shackleton, 1986; Rogers, 1988; Pollock, 1996).

The testimony about psychological tests generally occurs under two different circumstances (Weiner, 1995). First, the psychologist testifies as a specialist concerning a particular test, such as the MMPI-2 or WAIS-R, and does so in isolation from other sources of information in the case. Here the interpretation of the score is based entirely on a normative frame of reference and knowledge of the relevant literature. Secondly, the psychologist serves a more extensive interpretative function where he or she applies psychological tests only as a part of the overall assessment and then interprets the test findings in conjunction with other sources of information. In practice, the second function is by far more common and it is the fundamental basis for a comprehensive evaluation of the client.

Irrespective of which of these two functions the expert witness fulfils, the psychologist should have good basic knowledge of the tests which he or she uses. In this chapter the essential knowledge of the basic principles of psychological testing and the nature of psychometric tests are discussed. Anastasi and Urbina (1996), Cronbach (1984) and Klein (1992, 1995) provide important background information about the development and use of psychological tests and these are cited where appropriate. Of crucial importance here is the standardisation of tests, their reliability and validity, and the interpretation of test scores.

Grisso (1986b), Matarazzo (1990) and Heilbrun (1992) offer general guidelines for the use of psychological testing in legal contexts. These are discussed in some detail in this chapter in view of their importance to the forensic assessment. How psychological testing is applied to specific legal issues in criminal and civil cases is discussed in Chapters 8 and 9.

Concepts and principles of psychological testing

There are various ways of defining the word 'test'. In a broad sense, a psychological test comprises a standardised or systematic form of examination (e.g., being required to respond to set questions, statements or other stimuli), in order to determine the presence or absence of a particular skill, knowledge or characteristic. Most tests are made up of a number of individual items, to which the examinee's responses are aggregated and presented on a numerical scale. The nature, form, content, administration and scoring of the tests vary considerably. The word 'psychometrics' is used to refer to the application of statistical techniques to psychological testing. This includes a structured design, formal procedure which everybody has to follow, numerical scoring with established 'error of measurement' and confidence intervals, and validation.

In contrast, projective tests, as traditionally used, rely on psychodynamic models of understanding, which in forensic work can provide an important basis for formulating clinical hypotheses. They are now used less frequently in the UK for forensic assessments than they were formerly, but they are still favoured by many psychologists with a psychodynamic orientation, especially in America and Europe. Indeed, Brown (1988) takes a fellow psychologist to task for using only quantitative cognitive measures. Objective quantitative versions of standard projective tests have been derived which meet some of the criticisms raised against the original versions, and these derivations have been used in court. For example, Gazono and Meloy (1994) confirm the value of the Rorschach in assessing psychopaths and aggressive offenders for the courts, and Timsit (1992) emphasises the forensic value which French psychologists place on this technique. Sakhova (1986) states that psychologists have a unique role in forensic work in identifying the motivations of the accused, and Heilbrun (1992) makes the point that projective tests can overcome some of the factors, such as defensiveness, evasiveness, denial and malingering, which lower the validity of cognitive tests. The subordination of UK law to European Community law means that psychologists in the UK may encounter evidence based on projective tests put forward by their opposite number in some European court. Projective tests have used pictorial, verbal, auditory and tactile stimuli, but only the first medium is in general use.

One particular value of thematic apperception is that the stimuli enable subjects to displace their concerns and project them on to the character on the card. In this way, they can express their immediate problems without explicitly identifying themselves with them, and so release to the examiner ideas associated with guilt, shame, or other emotions which might otherwise remain unexpressed. With this in mind, a forensic technique has been devised using specially drawn pictures illustrating significant situations relating to the forensic problem. The technique is described by Haward (1964), and examples of line drawings specially created by the author for use in official inquiries appear in Haward (1969).

In spite of their forensic potential, projective tests, with few exceptions, suffer from poor inter-scorer reliability, lack validity and are influenced by a number of contextual factors which are difficult to control (Klein, 1992). Their application in forensic practice is therefore not generally recommended, except as a way of generating hypotheses which can be further tested.

The concept of 'trait' was introduced by Allport (1931) and refers to 'a generalized response-unit in which resides the distinctive quality of behavior that reflects personality' (p. 369). A 'trait' may reflect individual differences in both 'personality' and 'abilities'. However, the term 'personality' is used in different ways in the literature. Some authors use the term 'personality' to refer to both 'temperament' and 'abilities' (Eysenck and Gudjonsson, 1989), whereas others restrict it to the measurement of non-intellectual aspects of behaviour, such as emotional adjustment, interpersonal relations, motives, attitudes, and interests (Anastasi and Urbina, 1996). Winter (1996) makes a further distinction by arguing that traits or temperament (the non-intellectual aspects of personality) should be considered as being distinct from 'motives' and 'cognitions' (attitudes and beliefs). For the purposes of this book, the term 'personality' is used in accordance with that recommended above by Anastasi and Urbina (1996). Psychological tests refer to the measurement of both personality and abilities. The term 'abilities', as used in this book, incorporates various intellectual aspects of behaviour and includes instruments used to assess various legal competencies (Grisso, 1986a). The assessment of both personality and abilities is important in the forensic evaluation; their respective importance depends on the legal issue that the psychologist is addressing in a given case (see Chapters 8 and 9).

Personality and abilities can be measured either 'idiographically' or 'nomothetically' (Allport, 1937). The 'idiographic' approach involves exploring traits (including abilities) within the individual person and how these are integrated. In contrast, the 'nomothetic' approach involves the development of scales, questionnaires, and inventories, whose purpose is to determine how the scores obtained are distributed in a particular population. Psychometric tests employ the nomothetic approach of enquiry, whereas projective tests and clinical interviews are idiographic in nature and depend more upon the skills of the examiner than on the standardised format of nomothetic tests (Klein, 1992). Idiographic methods may provide important clinical insights and a wealth of data on an individual, which can be helpful in terms of diagnosis and prognosis in forensic settings (Theilgaard, 1996).

The standardised format of psychometric tests has the advantage of providing robust and objective data, but such tests are quite circumscribed in terms of what they measure and they do not allow for idiosyncratic variations in terms of administration and scoring. In some cases this lack of flexibility and the apparent crudeness of some psychometric tests may reduce the psychological value of psychometric tests.

The purpose of psychological tests

At the most basic level, the purpose of psychological tests is to obtain information about an individual in a standardised and valid way. As far as psychometric testing is concerned, there are two main functions. First, to measure differences between individuals in relation to particular abilities (e.g., intellect, literacy, memory, neuropsychological functions), personality traits (e.g., extraversion, emotional stability, conscientiousness, openness, suggestibility, compliance), or clinical problems (e.g., anxiety, depression, paranoia, bizarre or unusual thinking). This is the essence of the measurement of individual differences. The second function is to measure differences in the reactions of the same individual on separate occasions. There are a number of reasons why individuals may need to be tested on more than one occasion. These include monitoring changes in cognitive and personality functioning as a result of treatment intervention (Sigurdsson *et al.*, 1994), situational variations ('transitory states') in mood and anxiety that need to be objectively monitored (Spielberger, 1983), studying the effects of trauma, such as a head injury or a major psychological trauma, on psychological functioning, and repeated testing to investigate possible malingering.

Normative scores

Standardisation is an essential part of psychometric test construction and development. It implies a uniform procedure in terms of administration and scoring. The nature of the test and its administration and scoring are provided in the manual of newly developed tests. The process of standardisation involves the test being administered to a representative sample of people for whom the test was developed. Standardised tests sometimes provide norms for several different populations (e.g., persons in the general population, psychiatric patients, persons with learning disabilities, offenders). When scores are dependent upon the gender and age of the participants then separate norms need to be provided for these. For example, scores on intelligence tests are strongly influenced by the age of the examinee. For this reason some tests (e.g., the WAIS-R; Wechsler, 1981; the EPQ-R; Eysenck and Eysenck, 1991) provide age bands for the normative scores.

Another factor to be aware of is that tests commonly have to be restandardised over time as the population on which they are based changes (Pope et al., 1993), or, as in the case of IQ tests, there are major gains in scores over generations which make the individual scores artificially inflated if they remain uncorrected (Flynn, 1987). Problems may exist with the norms of some intelligence tests, such as Raven's Standard Progressive Matrices, which undermine their forensic value (Gudjonsson, 1995a).

The normative scores of a test are used to evaluate the individual's performance in relation to a particular reference group (e.g., contemporaries from the general population). Without this normative frame of reference, a test score cannot be properly interpreted. Psychometric test scores are interpreted with reference to an appropriate comparative sample. This indicates how much the score obtained falls above or below the mean for the normative sample. The actual scores obtained on a test can be expressed in various ways. These are discussed in detail by Anastasi and Urbina (1996), Cronbach (1984) and Klein (1992) and will only be briefly discussed here.

The direct numerical count from a test is known as the 'raw score'. The raw score needs to be converted to either a *standard score* or a *percentile score* in order to know how it compares with other raw scores. The standard score is derived from the 'mean' and 'standard deviation' scores of the normative sample. The mean (M) represents the average score for normative sample, while the standard deviation (SD) score is a statistical measure of the spread of scores around the mean. The standard score for a given individual expresses the number of standard deviations below or above the mean at which the score falls. It is calculated by subtracting the difference between the individual's raw or scaled score (X) from the normative mean (M) and dividing the difference by the normative group's standard deviation (SD).

A simple illustration of obtaining the standard score is as follows. John obtained a Full Scale IQ score of 75 on the WAIS-R. The mean and standard deviation scores for the WAIS-R are 100 and 15, respectively. The difference between the individual score (75) and mean score (100) is 25 IQ points, which when divided by the SD of the normative sample (15) gives a standard score of −1.65 (or 1.65 standard deviations below the mean).

Another way of expressing the significance of raw scores (or 'scaled scores' as on the WAIS-R) is to convert them into percentile ranks. Percentile scores are expressed in terms of the percentage of persons in the standardisation groups who fall below or above a given raw score. A percentile score of 50 represents the median (i.e., central tendency). A test score above 50 represents a score above average, whereas a score below 50 falls below average. A score may be said to fall outside the normal range (i.e., it is abnormal) when found in fewer than 5 per cent or more than 95 per cent of the normative population, respectively. This corresponds to the 5th and 95th percentile rank. When placed within the normal distribution it is equivalent to a standard score of 1.65 (i.e., 1.65 standard deviation below or above the mean, respectively). For example, an IQ score of 75 represents the bottom 5 per cent of the general population (5th percentile rank), whereas an IQ score of 125 represents the top 5 per cent of the population (95th percentile rank). An IQ score of 70 falls in the 2nd percentile rank (i.e., performance in the bottom two percent of the population) and it is equivalent to a standard score of −2.00.

Anastasi and Urbina (1996) and Cronbach (1984) discuss in detail the advantages and disadvantages of the two methods of interpreting test scores. The main advantages with the standard score are that it is directly and precisely proportionate to the raw score and it is readily accessible to statistical analysis. However, difficulties arise when the distribution comprising the norms is skewed, because this makes the interpretation of the individual test score more difficult. The other problem is that standard scores are difficult to interpret for persons unfamiliar with statistical analysis. The main advantages of using percentile scores, for an appropriate reference group, in court reports is that they are easy to explain and understand, are much more meaningful to lay persons, and can be readily interpreted irrespective of the shape of the normative distribution. The only disadvantage is the lack of uniformity in the units. In a normal distribution, differences in scores near the mean are exaggerated in the percentile transformation, whereas differences at the end of the distribution, which may be of practical importance, are artificially reduced.

Derived scores are an elaboration of the standard scores. Commonly used derived scores are T-scores, which are favoured by some psychometricians (e.g., Cronbach, 1984). The MMPI-2, for example, uses T-scores and these have a mean of 50 and a standard deviation of 10. On the MMPI-2 a T-score of 70 is used to identify significant psychopathology. With regard to the MMPI-2 this is now set to be equivalent to the 98th percentile rank (Pope et al. 1993).

A distinction must be made between a statistical abnormality and a diagnosis of mental disorder. As discussed above, a statistical abnormality indicates the frequency with which a specific test score occurs in a given normative population.

In contrast, the diagnosis of a psychiatric disorder is based on a clinical opinion of the presence of various signs and symptoms which can be classified as constituting mental disorder.

According to Valciukas (1995), forensic psychologists in the USA are increasingly being expected by legal advocates to use the DSM multiaxial classification system (DSM-IV) in their diagnostic evaluation of clients. This emphasis on mental state evaluation and diagnostic classification makes their evaluation similar to that of psychiatrists. There is no parallel development in the UK. Psychologists in the UK are not required or expected to place their findings within the DSM-IV or ICD-10 diagnostic classification systems. There are exceptions, of course. For example, a diagnosis of post-traumatic stress disorder often relies upon DSM criteria, as it did in the arbitration cases of the Zeebrugge disaster (see Chapter 8).

Mental age

Psychologists in England are sometimes asked to convert IQ scores to a mental age equivalent when giving their testimony, both in cases of children and adults. The legal advocates then use the mental age score as a frame of reference for interpreting the client's performance on the IQ score. In the present authors' experience, such practice is unwise for at least two reasons. First, modern intelligence tests for adults, like the WAIS-R, do not provide mental age equivalence scores. There is no ready and reliable way of calculating mental age and what is given to the court is a crude and subjective estimate. However, some children's tests, like the Stanford-Binet and the WISC-R, do have tables for calculating a mental age from the raw scores (Cronbach, 1984). Secondly, even when such calculation is possible to conduct accurately the mental age score can be easily misinterpreted (Wechsler, 1974; Cronbach, 1984).

The main problem is that when mental age is given on the basis of test scores often more than a definable level of performance on one test is implied. For example, describing an individual's performance on an intelligence test in terms of mental age may result in over-generalisation to other abilities. That is, a mental age score may be taken to imply performance in areas not assessed by the test, including social and emotional functioning. A good example of such misuse happened in the case discussed by Tunstall et al. (1982). In addition, general life experience cannot be ignored. A 50-year-old man, described as having a mental age of 10, has had very different life experiences from a 10-year-old child. It is meaningless to be describing such a person in terms of a mental age. All one could say is that his performance on a particular test is comparable to that found for the average child of 10. Such comparisons are commonly made, for example, in cases of literacy problems (reading, writing, spelling) and are quite legitimate for that specific purpose. From a court's point of view, a person described in terms of a mental age may be mistakenly perceived as somebody who should be treated like a 10-year-old boy. The present authors also know of cases where a reading age was confused with a mental age by court advocates. Therefore, expert witnesses should be careful in their use of such terms as mental age and reading age.

Reliability

The reliability of a test is measured by the test's consistency, either in terms of internal consistency of the test items or with a reference to the consistency of scores obtained by the same person when retested with the identical test or with an equivalent (alternative) form of the test. If a test was given to an individual on several different occasions then one would expect a good test to give consistent results over time, provided the person being tested has not undergone a fundamental change between testing sessions. The longer the test–retest interval the lower the reliability scores tend to be. That is, short-term temporal stability is typically greater than long-term stability. For example, the test– retest reliability for the MMPI, which is one of the most widely used personality/clinical measures, typically varies between 0.70 and 0.80 when people are retested within two weeks, but goes down to about 0.35 to 0.45 when the test is readministered after one or more years (Weiner, 1995). Weiner (1995) argues that such low long-term stability of a clinical test, measuring such symptoms as transitory anxiety and depression, does not invalidate the MMPI as a valuable clinical measure, but it poses a problem when a test is aiming to measure presumably stable and enduring personality traits, such as extraversion and antisocial attitudes or personality disorder.

There are several different methods for determining reliability, including Cronbach's Alpha for internal consistency, correlation coefficients for test–retest reliability, and Kappa for inter-scorer reliability. When measuring inter-scorer reliabilities, Kappa is a more stringent measure with categorical data than simple correlation coefficients (Bartko and Carpenter, 1976). The reliability coefficient obtained for a given test can range from 0 to 1.0. Typically for psychometric tests they range between 0.80 and 0.90 (Anastasi and Urbina, 1996; Klein, 1992).

The reliability coefficient makes it possible to compare the reliability of different tests and it gives an overall indication of the test's reliability. However, in order to interpret *individual scores*, the most appropriate way of evaluating reliability is by the test's *standard error of measurement*. This refers to the margin of error that can be expected in an individual score as a result of inherent unreliability of the test (i.e., deviation from the theoretical 'true' score). When individuals are tested on more than one occasion there is likely to be some variation in the scores obtained due to a variety of factors, including motivation, level of concentration, anxiety, fatigue, attitude towards the examiner and examiner's scoring errors. Once these factors have been averaged out by testing the individual on a number of occasions, his or her 'true' score on the test will emerge.

The standard error of measurement is computed from the reliability coefficient of a test and the test's standard deviation score. It is normally given in the published manual of psychometric tests. For example, the average standard error of measurement for Full Scale IQ on the WAIS-R (Wechsler, 1981) is 2.53. This means that there is 95 per cent chance that the individual's score lies within 5.06 points (twice the standard error of measurement) of the 'true' score.

Matarazzo (1990) argues for the importance of knowing the test's standard error of measurement when testifying in court:

> My experience in the courtroom, where more and more psychologists' conclusions are being vigorously challenged by attorneys, has led me to conclude that too many psychologists testifying for the plaintiff or defense, are unaware of the standard error of measurement of the scores (and the accompanying confidence intervals) produced by our batteries of tests.
>
> (p. 1,005)

Validity

The validity of a test is determined by the extent to which it measures what it is designed to measure. Unless a test is reliable it cannot be valid, but a reliable test may not necessarily be valid for the purpose it was designed. For example, a test may give similar scores when persons are tested on different occasions, but it may not be useful in measuring the construct or behaviour for which the test is intended. The three main types of validity, are referred to as 'content', 'criterion-related', and 'construct' validity, respectively.

Content validity refers to the item content of the test and how well it represents the behavioural domain to be measured. This is often important in the case of educational tests, but is less relevant for establishing the effectiveness of aptitude and personality tests which require more empirical verification (Anastasi and Urbina, 1996). Grisso (1986b) argues that some tests that are useful for clinical and forensic applications have poor content validity, which places a greater burden on their meeting other standards for validity.

In forensic practice item-to-item analysis of a test's content is sometimes undertaken by legal advocates and judges in order to see whether or not the test 'looks valid' (Tunstall *et al.*, 1982). This refers to 'face validity', which is not to be confused with content validity. Face validity provides a superficial impression of what the test appears to measure, which can be very misleading to the court. When items appear superficially to be irrelevant, inappropriate, simplistic, or not sufficiently subtle they may undermine the court's confidence in the test. Sometimes lawyers and judges take individual test items out of context and ask the psychologist hypothetical questions about them, or they may make derogatory comments about the test in court. The best way of handling such questioning is to point out that the validity of the test is based on an evaluation of the test as a whole and that one item by itself is of no significance.

Criterion-related validity indicates the effectiveness of the test in predicting an examinee's behaviour in relevant situations. Test scores are validated against external criteria, which are of two types, referred to as *concurrent validity* and *predictive validity*. Concurrent validity refers to correlation of test scores with another measure of the same type of behaviour given in the same time period. It is most relevant for predicting current status, such as mental state or clinical diagnosis, rather than predicting future behaviour. In contrast, predictive validity is the ability of the test to predict a specified behaviour on an occasion removed from the test situation. This may include IQ scores predicting future academic success or personality measures predicting offending behaviour at a later date.

Construct validity refers to the relationship of the test scores to a relevant theoretical construct or trait. As an example, much of the early work on the Gudjonsson Suggestibility Scale (GSS; Gudjonsson, 1984b) was concerned with establishing the construct validity of the test as a valid measure of interrogative suggestibility. The research 'used deduction of hypotheses based on theoretical relations between the construct of suggestibility and other personality constructs, then used the GSS as an operational definition of suggestibility to test these hypotheses' (Grisso, 1986a, p. 146).

Selection and use of tests

There are a large number of psychological tests available for forensic applications. Heilbrun (1992) provides useful guidelines for the use of psychological testing in forensic assessment. Some of these are as follows:

1   The test should be documented and reviewed in the scientific literature and it needs to contain a manual describing the test's development, psychometric properties and procedure.

2   The reliability and validity of the test should be considered carefully. Heilbrun argues that tests with a reliability coefficient of less than 0.80 are not recommended for forensic use and would require a justification by the psychologist using the test. The lower the reliability the poorer the validity of the test due to excessive error variance.

In the experience of the present authors, some psychologists regularly use short forms of tests or reduce the number of subtests they use on the WAIS-R. Such a procedure tends to reduce the reliability of tests and should be avoided. Considering that a few IQ points may make a difference to the outcome of a case it is important that the assessment conducted is as thorough and comprehensive as possible. When short forms or a reduced number of subtests are used this and the reasons for it should be made clear in the report.

Lezak (1995) makes the valuable point that examiners should always use the manual of the WAIS-R when administering the test and not rely on their memorised version of the instructions and test items. When questions have been memorised they may gradually become distorted and the meaning of the questions is commonly inadvertently altered. Some psychologists are also in the habit of not properly timing the client's performance as required by the test manual, as well as failing to put the test pieces in the standard arrangement. This practice is not acceptable, because it does not conform to the standardisation of the test and may give misleading results.

3   The test must be relevant to the legal issue addressed, or the psychological construct underlying the legal issue. Relevance should be supported by published validation research, although on occasions justification for using a particular test may be made on theoretical grounds.

4   The standard administration recommended in the test's manual should be used, which requires a quiet and distraction-free testing environment. However, this is not always possible in forensic practice and clients some-times have to be tested in a noisy prison environment. Such variations on the standard administration of the test will have to be taken into considera-tion and should be stated when interpreting the test scores.

5   The scores from a particular test should not be applied towards a purpose for which the test was not developed (e.g., making inferences about suggestibility from the results of IQ test scores). The interpretation of the test scores should be guided by population and situation specificity. This means that the closer the individual 'fits' the population and situation of those described in the validation studies, the greater the confidence one can express in the applicability of the results. Many tests used in forensic prac-tice are standardised on non-forensic populations, which limits the generalisability of the results.

6   There is controversy in the literature about clinical versus statistical predictions (e.g., Meehl, 1954; Sawyer, 1966). Using a combination of clinical data and actuarial data is preferable in forensic work. It is note-worthy that clinical judgments of intellectual skills and suggestibility traits are often grossly wrong (Gudjonsson, 1992a).

There are several advantages with administering a battery of tests rather than one single test. Firstly, using tests that measure different aspects of psychological functioning gives a broader base from which inferences can be drawn. For example, administering all the subtests of the WAIS-R gives a better indication of the client's intellectual strengths and weaknesses than the individual score from Raven's Standard Progressive Matrices. Secondly, using tests that measure similar aspects of psychological functioning may corroborate the findings from the two tests, although tests measuring similar theoretical constructs and psycho-logical functions sometimes give divergent results. For example, the correlation between the Hare's Psychopathic Check List and the Psychoticism dimension of the Eysenck Personality Questionnaire (EPQ) is very modest (Hare, 1982). One reason for such divergence is that tests measuring similar functions may measure them in different ways (Weiner, 1995).

Interpretation of test scores

It is rare in a forensic evaluation that one can rely on the results from one single instrument. Typically, test data will need to be integrated and interpreted in relation to other sources of data. Grisso (1986b) argues that one of the most important precautions in the forensic evaluation is to base interpretations and opinions on more than a single test score or sign. It is always unwise to over-generalise from single test findings. The examiner must be fully aware of the limitations of test data. All psychological tests, to a varying degree, are susceptible to numerous sources of error, including socially desirable responding and possible malingering. Test scores will therefore need to be evaluated within the frame of reference of other sources of information in the case. These other sources of data may include background information on the client, current mental state of the client and his or her demeanour during the assessment, findings from other similar or parallel tests administered as a part of the evaluation (e.g., when test batteries are used in the evaluation), and all relevant legal papers (e.g., case summary, client's proof of evidence, counsel's advice, witness statements, client's statements to the police, list of indictments, list of previous convictions). When acting as expert witnesses, psychologists sometimes have to listen to the client giving evidence in court and this may also form a part of their overall evaluation when testifying.

Client's background history

There are a number of aspects of the client's background that may need to be assessed during a forensic evaluation. The scope and amount of detail that are required about the client's background will depend on the individual case. Sometimes a great deal of information is known about the client's background from police reports, statements obtained by the client's solicitor, school reports, social enquiry reports, and previous medical, psychiatric and psychological reports. Background information is also commonly obtained from interviewing the client. This may need to be corroborated with other sources of information, such as interviews with informants and through previous documentation and reports. Good background information will often assist with identifying and evaluating the client's psychological problems with regard to the pending case. The following are often relevant to the forensic evaluation.

1   *Family history*   This includes information about the client's family constellation, upbringing, and relevant psychological and psychiatric problems within the family.

2   *Educational history*   Information about the client's educational history is often invaluable. Difficulties at school, including educational and behavioural problems, may be relevant to the forensic evaluation. Sometimes IQ scores are inconsistent with the client's educational background which may raise questions about malingering or undiagnosed organic problems.

3   *Occupational history*   The nature and number of previous jobs held by the client may provide important information about his or her skills and occupational stability.

4   *Medical history*   Major medical problems should be noted as far they are relevant to the psychological evaluation. Some medical problems, such as a heart condition or severe pain, may influence the client's ability to cope in stressful situations, including a police interrogation and custodial confinement.

5   *Previous psychiatric history*   A previous psychiatric history is often relevant to the current psychological evaluation. It may provide insight into the client's current mental state and that which existed at the time of the material event (accident, offence, police interrogation).

6   *History of previous psychological involvement*   Any previous psychological assessment and treatment should be noted and explored in detail if they are relevant to the current evaluation. Previous test results are often informative and may indicate a deterioration in mental functioning, which needs to be investigated further.

7   *History of drug and alcohol use and abuse*   A history of alcohol or drug abuse is an important factor that may influence psychological test results and the client's mental state during the psychological evaluation. It may also have had a bearing on the client's mental state at the time of the alleged offence (*mens rea*), as well as at the time of the trial (fitness to stand trial).

8   *History of sexual abuse*   In some cases a detailed sexual developmental history is relevant to the current psychological evaluation. Not uncommonly, a history of sexual abuse is reported and this may form an important part of the case. In addition, a history of sexual abuse may need to be taken into account when interpreting some psychological tests in order not to produce misleading conclusions (Pope *et al.* 1993).

9   *Previous forensic history*   A history of previous offending may be relevant to the psychological evaluation in so far as it provides information about the client's behavioural problems and experience with the criminal justice system.

Mental state examination

An evaluation of the client's mental state normally forms a part of any psychological assessment conducted for civil or criminal proceedings. At its most basic level, it consists of observation of the client's demeanour, attitude and performance during the assessment. These behavioural observations may identify important 'signs' or 'indications' of possible difficulties or mental problems. It is also good clinical practice to ask the client questions about his or her current mood, sleep, appetite, preoccupations and worries, medication, and drink and drug habits. These may reveal information about clinical 'symptoms'. Both 'signs' and 'symptoms' will have a bearing on the interpretation of psychometric test results and any diagnosis made.

CO-OPERATION AND MOTIVATION

Any lack of co-operation with the assessment will need to be monitored and interpreted appropriately. Poor co-operation may involve the client not being forthcoming with answers to the questions asked by the examiner, answering questions inappropriately, and refusing to complete some or all of the tests administered. There could be a number of reasons for the lack of co-operation, including the client not feeling well on the day of the assessment, lack of rapport with the examiner, feelings of apathy, lack of motivation, lack of understanding of the purpose of the assessment or its importance, suspiciousness, paranoia, evasiveness, defensiveness or malingering.

Before psychometric tests are administered it is important to establish good rapport with the client. A lack of satisfactory rapport with the client can have disastrous consequences when it is misinterpreted, as it did in the case of Engin Raghip, one of the 'Tottenham Three' (see Chapter 9 for a brief description of the psychological and legal issues involved). The psychologist commissioned by the defence prior to Raghip's trial had found Raghip very suspicious of him during the assessment, which he had mistakenly interpreted as an indication of malingering (Gudjonsson, 1992a).

The importance of trust and proper explanation for the assessment by the examiner are demonstrated in the work of Grossarth-Matick et al. (1995). The authors used four different methods of administering a questionnaire that was designed to predict future cancer and coronary heart disease in healthy individuals. The combination of trust and explanation about the nature and purpose of the questionnaire most effectively predicted illness in later life, while the absence of both trust and explanation produced the worst results. The more intimate the assessment, which is often the case when conducting sexual assessments, the greater the need for trust. Similarly, the greater the complexity of the assessment, including complicated questionnaires, the greater the need for an appropriate explanation for the nature and content of the assessment. Of course, these general principles are difficult to apply in forensic settings because of the lack of confidentiality (i.e., the intimate findings may be revealed in open court for everybody to hear), the potential aversive consequences of self-disclosure (i.e., findings may be used against the client in court and have serious legal consequences), and the increased risk of malingering when clients are fully briefed about the nature and content of psychometric tests. In spite of these potential problems, the present authors agree with Theilgaard (1996) that most clients in forensic settings will co-operate with testing if the purposes of the tests are explained and good rapport is established. However, a particular problem may arise in the case of paranoid clients. They are often suspicious of tests, particularly when the test is subtle ('non-transparent'), and they may try to elicit details from the examiner about the nature and content of the test before they are prepared to co-operate. The danger here is that giving them detailed information about the test may invalidate the results obtained by their being able to fake the answers successfully.

MENTAL ALERTNESS

The client's mental alertness is important for a proper evaluation to take place. Some clients are lethargic and mentally unresponsive during the assessment. The reason for this needs to be determined as well as the likely effects on the psychometric tests administered. Occasionally, clients are under the influence of illicit drugs or alcohol during the assessment, which impairs their mental alertness. In addition, the effects of prescribed psychotropic medication on test scores are unknown.

ORIENTATION

The client's orientation is noted by his or her awareness in relation to person, place and time. The client may be asked to give his full name, age, date of birth, as well give other significant names and dates. They may be asked to name the place where the assessment is taking place, the current date and time. Lack of orientation may suggest mental confusion and possible organic problems.

ATTENTION AND CONCENTRATION

Attention refers to the extent to which the client focuses his or her mind on specific stimuli within the environment. During the assessment the client may not, for a variety of reasons, attend fully to the questions being asked by the examiner or to test items. Another related problem that is often noted in clinical practice is impaired concentration. This refers to the difficulties some clients have with maintaining sufficient focus on relevant stimuli over a period of time. In order to remember things, including simple test instructions, clients have to pay attention to it and concentrate on it. There are a number of possible reasons for lack of attention and concentration, which fall into three groups. First, they may be caused by such factors as tiredness, sleeplessness or lack of interest. Secondly, they may be caused by mental problems (such as anxiety), mental preoccupation (such as worry over the pending court case), hallucinations, delusions, physical pain and a noisy environment, which can all cause 'distractibility' (distractibility refers to the readiness with which internal or external stimuli disrupt the client's focus of attention). Thirdly, attentional and concentration problems may have direct organic causes (Lezak, 1995).

DEPRESSION AND ANXIETY

It is generally recognised in clinical practice that depression may influence the performance on intellectual and memory tests (i.e., cognitive functioning). This is typically attributed to depressed patients committing less effort to tasks than non-depressed people (Smith et al., 1993). However, the relationship between cognitive functioning and depression is not always apparent and findings from different studies are inconsistent (Hale et al., 1993). The performance subtests of the WAIS-R may be more affected than the verbal subtests, because they depend on mental speed and accuracy. However, in a recent study of depressed patients and non-depressed psychiatric controls no significant differences emerged between groups on either verbal or performance IQ scores or with regard to an estimate of premorbid intelligence (Hale et al., 1993). Similarly, Sigurdsson et al. (1994) found that severe depression did not significantly impair immediate or delayed verbal memory on the Gudjonsson Suggestibility Scales. Interestingly, confabulation scores were significantly lower during the patients' depressed phase, and after recovery equalled that of normal controls. One explanation put forward by Sigurdsson and his colleagues is that when people are depressed their mind is less imaginative and creative, which impairs their usual tendency to confabulate. This is consistent with depressed people committing less effort to the task, although it does not necessarily impair the amount of correct material they are able to produce or make them more suggestible. Of course, depression may not be a unitary disorder and the above findings do not rule out the possibility that some depressed individuals are prone to confabulation.

There is no doubt that severe anxiety can impair performance on cognitive tests (Cronbach, 1984; Lezak, 1995). Typically anxiety impairs concentration and mostly affects tests requiring sustained concentration, such as the digit span, digit symbol and arithmetic subtests of the WAIS-R. However, when people are tested in a stressful situation, as when they are detained as suspects at a police station, their performance on cognitive tests may not be significantly impaired. For example, Gudjonsson et al. (1995) found that the state and trait anxiety scores of suspects detained at police stations were not significantly correlated with their performance on tests of intelligence and memory. This is in spite of the finding that many of the suspects were experiencing severe anxiety (Gudjonsson et al., 1993; Gudjonsson et al., 1995).

From the above discussion it is evident that anxiety and depression do not invariably or necessarily impair performance on cognitive tests. Nevertheless, it is important for the forensic psychologist to be aware that both anxiety and depression can severely impair performance in an individual case. Each case must be considered on its own merit and general rules or research findings do not always apply.

LANGUAGE PROBLEMS

Sometimes clients who speak little or no English have to be assessed. This can create major problems and it limits the nature and extent of the assessment (Gudjonsson, 1995b). Interviewing clients through an interpreter is always a disadvantage and inevitably hinders effective communication. Under such circumstances malingering and lying are more difficult to detect. Administering psychological tests, such as personality questionnaires and cognitive tests, which are translated by an interpreter during the assessment, is a very dubious procedure. Ideally, such clients should be administered tests that have been formally translated and standardised for their culture. This hardly ever happens due to the practical problems involved. What typically happens is that the psychologist limits the assessment to non-verbal and culture-fair cognitive tests.

READING PROBLEMS

Norms for personality inventories and questionnaires are based on the person being able to read the statements or questions contained within the instrument. Most well-known American personality questionnaires, such as the MMPI-2, the Millon Clinical Multiaxial Inventory, and the Basic Personality Inventory, require reading levels of at least the fifth grade (Schinka and Borum, 1993), which is equivalent to a reading age of about nine years.

In forensic practice, some clients are illiterate and the items have to be read out to them. The effects of this practice on the actual scores obtained is unknown. As far as the MMPI-2 is concerned, a tape-recorded version of the instrument is available from the publishers of the test (Hathaway and McKinley, 1989). Tape-recorded administration of the test has been shown to give similar results to the written format (Dahlstrom et al. 1972). Computer-based administration is also available from the publishers. Computer presentations of psychological tests are on the increase and have many advantages, including automatic and reliable scoring, immediate printout of the test results, and the storing of a data base (Klein, 1992).

CULTURAL FACTORS

When assessing people from different cultural backgrounds it is important to take into account factors that may influence idiosyncratic responses which are culturally determined. The MMPI-2 has been revised with this particular problem in mind (Pope et al. 1993; Butcher, 1996). In addition, some tests are more culture fair than others (Klein, 1992). Considerable work has gone into the cross-cultural use of the MMPI-2.

There are a number of ways in which questionnaires and other self-report inventories can be affected by response bias. There are three main types of bias, which are known as 'acquiescence', 'other-deception' or 'impression management', and 'self-deception'.

Acquiescence refers to the tendency to agree with a statement or a question irrespective of content. A test of acquiescence that one of us (Gudjonsson) has used extensively in forensic practice is that developed by Winkler *et al.*, (1982), which consists of twelve logically opposite pairs of items. Acquiescence is significantly negatively correlated with intelligence and has a number of forensic applications (Gudjonsson, 1990a).

Related to the concept of acquiescence is the 'irrelevant responding', which refers to clients not becoming psychologically engaged during the psychological testing and clinical interview (Rogers, 1988). This may cause them to respond inconsistently to items, including answering logically opposite questions either in affirmative (acquiescence) or in the negative ('No-sayer').

The scores on personality inventories are also influenced by the tendency of some clients to present themselves to others in a socially desirable way (other-deception) and to deny painful emotional experiences (self-deception). These two types of deception are only modestly correlated (Sackeim and Gur, 1979). Other-deception is more context bound than self-deception, but both are important in establishing if clients are likely to be presenting themselves in an unduly favourable light and denying possible underlying psychopathology (Gudjonsson, 1990b). Other-deception and self-deception are best viewed as an attempt to 'fake good'. In contrast, attempts to 'fake bad' are normally associated with the term 'malingering'.

Malingering and 'faking bad'

The term malingering is typically used to describe 'conscious fabrication or gross exaggeration of physical and/or psychological symptoms' (Rogers, 1988). Related to this is 'faking bad' on psychological tests.

'Faking good' and 'faking bad' are both very important forms of potential unreliability during the forensic evaluation. The incentive for clients to fake on psychological tests is often compelling and must be considered as a possibility in every civil and criminal case. There is no room for complacency with regard to the possibility of faking. On occasions faking does take place and it may not always be detected. On the other hand, unfounded assumptions about faking can also be very damaging to clients, and on occasions can result in a miscarriage of justice when they are wrongly diagnosed as being deceptive. Pankratz (1988) makes the important point in this context that 'The clinician should be careful not to prejudge patients on the basis of initial presentation or past reputation' (p. 192).

Concerning faking, there are two types of error that can occur during the forensic evaluation. First, faking may not be identified by the practitioner when it occurs. Secondly, genuine performance may be misclassified as faking. The first type of error is known as 'false negative error' and the latter as a 'false positive error'. Both types of error are important when methods are devised for detecting faking on psychological tests (Gudjonsson and Shackleton, 1986).

There are a number of areas where clients may attempt to fake bad during the psychological assessment. Gudjonsson (1988) discusses three main areas, referred to as 'faking of cognitive deficits', 'faking of amnesia' and 'faking of psychological and psychiatric symptoms'.

FAKING OF COGNITIVE DEFICITS

Impaired scores on cognitive and neuropsychological tests may be due to low motivation to do well or indifference as well as deliberate attempts at faking. Poor motivation is more difficult to identify objectively than deliberate faking, but it can sometimes be revealed by the client's demeanour during testing (e.g., giving up very easily on items, giving many 'don't know answers'). It is always difficult in practice to evaluate the precise effects of low motivation on test scores.

It is not known how often people attempt to fake a cognitive deficit during the forensic evaluation assessment. Kaufman (1978) argues that it is very difficult for people to fake convincingly on intelligence tests, while McKinlay et al. (1983) claim that the incidence of faking bad on cognitive tests has been exaggerated. The present authors have come across cases where faking on intelligence tests was either subsequently admitted by the client or strongly suspected. There is no doubt that faking on intelligence and neuropsychological tests sometimes does occur. When this is suspected the psychologist can administer a number of tests that have been found to be effective in detecting faking (Gudjonsson and Shackleton, 1986; Pankratz, 1988; Greiffenstein et al., 1994; Lezak, 1995).

FAKING OF AMNESIA

Amnesia refers to the pathological inability to remember facts or events. It is commonly reported after the commission of a violent crime (Kopelman, 1987, 1995; Schacter, 1986; Taylor and Kopelman, 1984). Claims of amnesia also occur in cases of personal injury (Guthkelch, 1980). There is a common assumption among the judiciary that defendants claim amnesia in order to escape prosecution or punishment and that plaintiffs in civil cases do so for financial gains (Brandt, 1988). What is not known is the proportion of amnesia that is actually genuine.

Schacter (1986) argues that there are two different methods of differentiating between feigned and genuine amnesia. The first method consists of looking at the psychiatric history of the amnesic person, the current psychological profile and the premeditation of the crime. The second method involves looking at the nature of the amnesia and devising subtle ways of differentiating between feigned and genuine amnesia. Schacter provides some evidence from controlled laboratory studies that 'feeling-of-knowing' ratings (i.e., the subjective feeling that one could retrieve the 'lost' memory if given the right cues) can differentiate between genuine and feigned forgetting. It is not known if the same differentiation holds for amnesia as opposed to normal forgetting. None of Schacter's suggested methods have empirical support.

FAKING OF PSYCHOLOGICAL AND PSYCHIATRIC SYMPTOMS

There is a range of psychological and psychiatric symptoms that clients may attempt to fake during a forensic evaluation. These include mental illness (Resnick, 1988a) and post-traumatic stress disorder (Resnick, 1988b). Symptoms of anxiety, depression and specific phobias may also be faked on occasions. Gudjonsson and Sartory (1983) used an experimental psychophysiological technique for diagnosing blood-injury phobia in a case of suspected drunken driving. Such techniques appear to be rarely used in practice, but hold considerable promise. The MMPI-2 has a number of built-in scales for detecting possible malingering and response style (Pope *et al.* 1993; Berry, 1995). This often proves useful in forensic practice.

Rogers (1990) provides an 'adaptational model' for understanding malingering, which focuses on the conscious decision making involved and its self-serving purpose (tangible gains, such as increased compensation in civil cases and reduced sentence in criminal cases). On the basis of this model, Rogers *et al.* (1992) have developed a formal assessment procedure for clinicians in order to detect malingering in forensic practice, referred to as the 'Structured Interview of Reported Symptoms' (SIRS). The SIRS consists of eight primary scales which measure feigned presentations and five supplementary scales which measure response bias due to such factors as defensivenesss and inconsistency in reporting symptoms. Unfortunately, a diagnosis of malingering on the SIRS is significantly correlated with acquiescence and yield suggestibility as measured by the Gudjonsson Suggestibility Scale (Pollock, 1996), which suggests that it may wrongly classify suggestible and acquiescent people as malingerers. In view of his findings, Pollock urges clinicians to proceed with caution when they attempt to determine malingering of mental disorder from structured interview approach, such as those recommended by Rogers *et al.* (1992).

Tests of competencies

An area that is increasingly recognised as being important in forensic evaluations relates to adults' capacity to make decisions (Murphy and Clare, 1995). These are related to various 'legal competencies', including the 'competency to stand trial', 'criminal responsibility', 'parental competency', 'competency to care for self or property', 'testamentary competency', and 'competency to consent to treatment'. Grisso (1986a) discusses these in detail and reviews a number of relevant psychological tests. He argues that each type of competency refers to different capacities, individuals, and circumstances. According to Grisso, legal competency focuses on the 'individual's *functional abilities*, *behaviors*, or *capacities*' and these are 'related to, but distinct from, psychiatric diagnosis or conclusions about intellectual abilities and personality traits' (p. 15). Grisso provides an important conceptual model for assessments of competencies, which focuses on guiding the collection of reliable case data, the use of empirical research to interpret data, and the development of new research, whilst advising that psychologists should be cautious about inferring legal concepts from psychological data. The central features of Grisso's conceptual framework are:

1 The measurement of functional abilities;
2 The relevance of the functional abilities assessed to contexts of legal competency;
3 The type of 'causal inferences' that can be drawn about the relationship between the functional deficits and legal competency;
4 The degree to which the functional ability or deficit interacts with the demand characteristics of the situation;
5 That legal competency constructs are 'judgmental' (i.e., they require a specific evaluation) and 'dispositional' (i.e., the finding of incompetency authorises a particular legal response).

The control of psychological tests

There are two main reasons for controlling the use of psychological tests. First, to prevent detailed familiarity with the test, which would invalidate its future application. Test content has to be concealed from potential examinees to prevent the possibility of their deliberately faking on the test. As was discussed in Chapter 4, the nature and content of psychological tests are sometimes revealed in open court, which poses a serious threat to the validity of some psychological tests. The second reason for needing to control the use of psychological tests is to ensure that the test is used by a qualified examiner.

It is also important that psychologists use the published forms of tests rather than using photocopies which may breach copyright.

Conclusions

Psychological testing forms an important part of the forensic psychologist's armoury. Psychologists are in a unique position to apply reliable and valid tests to a range of human behaviours, which are relevant to the legal issues in criminal and civil proceedings. There are a number of areas that can be assessed, including cognitive functioning, neuropsychological status, personality, areas of clinical concern, anger and sexual problems, and various legal competencies. Test scores should not be used in isolation from other types of information, including a clinical interview and the studying of relevant background documents. Normally, psychological testing only forms a part of the forensic evaluation. Its importance depends on the nature of the case and the issues being addressed.

7

PSYCHOLINGUISTIC
TECHNIQUES

Introduction

Psycholinguistics is that branch of psychology which deals with verbal communication. It embraces linguistics – the study of language, formerly known as philology – as well as the scientific study of receptive and expressive verbal behaviour, known in Europe as *Ausdruckpsychologie*.

The term 'psycholinguistics' was formally adopted in 1953 (Goldman-Eisler, 1976) but studies of the psychology of language go back to Wundt and his contemporaries of a century ago. The interest in language gave way to behaviourism for many decades, but when resuscitated after the Second World War, it benefited from the new techniques and theories which had developed during its latency period, including the statistics of information theory, electromagnetic recording instruments and computers, which opened up a new and wider world of language analysis inconceivable a decade earlier.

Forensic psycholinguistics refers to the application of psycholinguistic techniques to the collection, examination and presentation of verbal evidence for judicial purposes, and in the 1990s, two international associations concerned with forensic applications of linguistics have come into being. The first, the International Association of Forensic Phonetics (IAFP) was founded in 1991 at St John's College, York, and is the registered body for this speciality. It has a Code of Practice formulated by its Professional Conduct Committee, and its Research Committee awards grants, and co-ordinates international awards, for research into forensic applications of this area of expertise. The second, but larger of the two organisations, is the International Association of Forensic Linguists, founded at Birmingham University's School of English in 1992. Through conferences, newsletters, etc. it provides a forum for the interchange of information and ideas about all forensic applications of linguistic analysis, and is currently preparing a register of expert witnesses in the forensic linguistic field. Within a year of its foundation the membership already exceeded 150, and the growth and activity of these two bodies underlines both the development of forensic linguistics and its present demand by the legal profession. This speciality now has its own journal entitled *Forensic Linguistics: the international journal of Speech, Language and the Law*, published by Routledge, London since 1994.

In view of the growing importance of psycholinguistics in forensic work, we have devoted an entire chapter to the main techniques at present in use by forensic psychologists.

Stylometry

'Stylometry', also known as 'statistical stylistics', developed rapidly in the 1960s, gaining considerable publicity in the analysis of statements in Evans' case, (Svartvik, 1967). By the following year Bailey (1968) was able to publish an annotated bibliography of statistical stylistics containing well over 600 entries.

Stylometry began in the nineteenth century, but it was not until the 1930s that mathematicians and statisticians developed real interest in the field. Other disciplines have subsequently developed an interest in stylometry, which now encompasses psychologists, biologists, linguists, literary critics, biologists and forensic scientists. With computer technology and sophisticated statistical methods, the scope for carrying out detailed and complicated analyses has been completely transformed. It is no longer necessary to rely on the simple arithmetic calculations, although many problems in forensic psycholinguistics can be solved using a pocket calculator.

Stylometry is the most frequent and simple form of psycholinguistic analysis for forensic purposes used in the UK. It relies on objective facts, such as the rate of occurrence of some elementary feature of the English language. This measure can be used for both inter-document or intra-document analysis, differing figures derived in this way being tested for statistical significance by standard techniques, such as Fisher's Exact Probability method or Chi-square test.

In practice, the use of frequency counts by which verbal habits are most easily demonstrated, can be inaugurated after a preliminary perusal of the document in issue. Psychologists will find Crystal (1987) invaluable in the provision of letter and word frequency tables, and other linguistic data. In his book, the section entitled 'The Statistical Structure of Language' is especially recommended. The fact that the immigrant languages which the forensic linguist will encounter in the UK today, like the English language itself, follow Zipf's Law, means that such languages can be analysed statistically without knowing the meaning, although in some scripts, such as Arabic, it will prove difficult to separate letters and words without some familiarity. Zipf's Law states that the frequency(f) of a word in a given text and the rank order(r) of that word in frequency in the language are inverse functions of a constant(c), that is, $fr = c$. The constant approximates 30,000 in all written languages so far analysed.

Visual inspection alone will reveal the more obvious differences, which may be the repetition of certain words in one sample, and their complete absence in the other. Sometimes word tallies are identical, but their juxtaposition show significant differences; e.g., the word 'and' may be followed by the definite article in one sample, and by the indefinite article in another.

In both texts, if long enough, exceptions in one sample to consistent patterns of word groupings in another will emerge. This enables four-square contingency tables to be constructed, so that non-parametric analysis can be derived and this can be tested for significance.

Generally speaking stylometric analyses fall into one of three categories, namely:

1 Frequency and nature of errors of vocabulary, orthography, syntax or grammar.
2 Frequency of factors related to writing style, including average word length, average sentence length, and number of syllables, prefixes or suffixes per hundred words. These factors are usually combined together in some established formula to yield a readability index, some versions of which are described below.
3 Ratios of parts of speech, such as verb/adjective and verb/noun, and especially the Type Token Ratio, which compares in the form of a decimal fraction, the number of different words used with the total word count. Some clinicians will be familiar with the TTR, which has been used in clinical assessments for many years, being particularly sensitive to the effects of anxiety – a point which needs special attention when comparing two documents written under different circumstances. As a general rule, anxiety decreases the use of adverbs and adjectives, while anger and its concomitants, such as frustration and aggression, tend to increase descriptive words, and hence there is a difference in word count.

Beyond the comparative simplicities of stylometry lie an extensive range of other linguistic techniques. Some idea of the scope of this speciality is given in a useful and comprehensive introduction to the subject by Levi (1994), who describes a selection of forensic linguistic activities including the following:

a Voice identification and voiceprints, used in speaker identification and speaker profiling; 'voice line-ups' used in the investigation of false emergency calls, obscene phone calls, blackmail demands, etc.; phonetic similarity in trademark law; and validity of speaker recognition by witnesses.
b Linguistic morphology, such as dialectological analysis of old tribal treaties now being questioned in land ownership disputes abroad, and trademark infringements.
c Syntax analysis, to evaluate the comprehensibility of documents, and to detect anomalies which negate offences of non-compliance, sometimes encountered in social security tribunals.
d Semantics, which looks at the ambiguity of words and phrases, especially in 'small print' parts of documents, leading to types of behaviour which otherwise would not have occurred.
e Pragmatics, examining the context of communication and what is sometimes called para-communication, such as differences in completing questions on

forms depending upon what the respondent believes is required by the sender of the form, a problem frequently occurring when claimants for financial support are accused of falsifying answers. The psycholinguistic profiling of rapists is a recent use of pragmatics, and this branch of stylometry now has its own *Journal of Pragmatics*.

f   Conversational analysis, sometimes called sociolinguistics or discourse analysis, especially of taped conversations between suspects, between offender and victim, and between police interrogator and witness or suspect.

g   Text comprehensibility, involving some of the former types of analysis but also including vocabulary choice and document design.

h   Validity of transcribed confessions, which deals with the many complexities associated with the evaluation of confession evidence (see Gudjonsson, 1992a, for a detailed review).

Levi (1994) describes many legal cases which illustrate most of the applications listed above and has an up-to-date, extensive bibliography; her account provides a concise yet comprehensive introduction to the subject, reference to which is recommended. Levi and Walker (1990) also discuss language and the judicial process, Kaplan (1994) provides a brief overview of forensic linguistics, and Shuy (1993) gives a fascinating account of the use and abuse of language evidence in the courtroom.

Linguistic applications by computer

One of the first uses of cluster analysis in court is described by Nilbett and Boreham (1976), when it was used to dispute the authenticity of an alleged oral confession. The defendant claimed that the confession had been fabricated by the police, whereas the prosecution maintained that it contained a verbatim record of what the defendant had told the police. The stylistic experts had access to an undisputed police statement which had been made by the defendant during an interrogation concerning another case. The two sets of statements were sufficiently long to carry out meaningful statistical analyses on them. A computer programme was used to place the different words used, and their frequency, into natural clusters. The results showed that the two sets of documents fell into two distinct clusters, which suggested that the disputed and undisputed documents were unlikely to have originated from the same person. The evidence was presented to the jury who acquitted the defendant.

Some linguistic analyses, such as those used to determine the authorship of ancient texts, require computer applications which originally occupied much mainframe computer time, but in forensic applications the texts being analysed rarely extend beyond a few pages, and the personal computer has brought virtually every problem within solution by independent experts. The SSPS program is sufficient for the simpler stylistic analyses described earlier, but because of the diversity of problems which need a linguistic solution, there is no single computer program which would satisfy all demands. Some psychologists set up their own simple programs for the purpose, especially if they have a lap-top computer which enables them to analyse in situ documents which are not allowed to be removed from custody. Others usually have access to a computing department in their institution which can provide analytic services. Even among independent self-employed consultants, the computer-less psychologist is today a rara avis indeed. In the USA, psychologists have found one commercial programme of particular value in their psycholinguistic investigations for the court, and this is marketed as Prostyle. At the time of writing, this software is not marketed in the UK, but copies are already in use in this country, mainly by professional writers and teachers of English in higher education for whom it was originally programmed.

Prostyle provides an immediate analysis of any text entered, and provides a print-out of a variety of factors in numerical terms, which enable the statistical significance of any discrepancies in two texts (for example, a written confession and previous documents written by the accused) to be determined. Among the factors provided by Prostyle will be found the following:

1   Overall Legibility Index, which indicates how easy or difficult the text is to understand.
2   The FOG and the Flesch-Kincaid Readability Indices, which are discussed further below.
3   The Passive Voice Index, whose frequency of use in any one text is sensitive to individual differences, and which in this program is detected by an analysis of writing style.
4   The number of different words used, which when produced as a percentage of total words in the text, provides a measure of vocabulary usage.
5   The percentage of complex words; in linguistic analysis this concept is usually defined in terms of prefixes, suffixes, and number of syllables, but Prostyle uses only the latter count.
6   The average sentence length, which correlates positively with educational level.
7   The Reading Age represented by the text being analysed.
8   The style fault index, representing the number of faults in writing style discovered in the text. In this index, the faults have been defined by a consensus of literary experts, and each fault is counted separately. Prostyle also gives both on-screen and disk warnings as the text is entered and each style fault occurs, but when the program is used by professional writers who wish to use so-called style faults deliberately, such as the use of vulgar words to typify one character, a Style Filter can be activated which removes style fault indications in a range of levels, although these faults are still computed for the Style Fault Indices.

The faults computed consist of: abstract nouns, incorrect or clumsy grammar, common cliches, complex sentence constructions, misplacement of conjugates and prepositions, formal language, hidden verbs, jargon and vogue words, lazy and apologetic words, legal and archaic words, disturbances of passive voice, sexist assumptions, vulgar and obscene words, and weak English. Being North American in origin, the style faults do not match precisely the politically correct standards now being imposed in the UK, but the program tallies more than enough types of fault to provide a useful statistical analysis for forensic purposes, and the facts being counted are the faults themselves, and their meanings and sociopolitical implications are irrelevant to this task.

In addition to the numerical presentation of the Style Fault Index, the print-out also gives a five-level verbal rating of writing style from 'excellent' (scores less than 5) to 'unacceptable' (scores over 50), which itself may prove a useful discriminator.

This multi-factorial approach to linguistic analysis has the advantage that probability figures for the difference between means can be tested progressively and the analysis halted when an acceptable level of chance exclusion occurs. There is unlikely to be much, if any, correlation between the frequency of many of the style faults, archaic and vulgar words for instance, so that the product of the individual probabilities can be used as a crude guide of when enough data has been assembled. In criminal cases, psychologists will want to aim for high levels of statistical significance, but in civil cases, the criteria are substantially lower, as explained in Chapter 8.

Two of the readability indices embodied in the Prostyle program have been used independently by psychologists long before Prostyle became available. Used by many teachers to assess essays, and by some academic examiners when evaluating dissertations, the value of a readability index as a quick and easy way to compare the authorship of two documents was readily appreciated by forensic psychologists. At least five different readability indices have been published and are in use at the present time. Although all are intercorrelated, only two have been regarded as suitable for forensic linguistic analysis, namely the Flesch-Kincaid Index and the Gunning FOG Index.

The Flesch-Kincaid Index

The original Flesch Readability Index was published during the Second World War (Flesch, 1943, 1946, 1948) and was already in use by military psychologists charged with the task of designating the authors of captured enemy documents. One of us (Haward) was introduced to this index when examining enemy papers which were to be used as evidence in the forthcoming War Crimes Trials in Hamburg and Nuremburg, when authorship was important for attaching documentary evidence to a particular accused person. The index is calculated from the formula:

$$I = 0.39a + 11.80b - 15.59$$

where I = Flesch Readability Index, a = average sentence length in number of words, and b = average number of syllables per word.

Despite its acknowledged validity and reliability, the index never achieved its later popularity until Farr and Jenkins (1949) produced a graphical solution for the formula, in which the two factors were entered into a table of computed values for the index, the appropriate index being read off from the co-ordinates obtained from the particular text. Some forensic psychologists using linguistic analysis now carry a copy of the Farr-Jenkins table in their psychometric kit. The Flesch Index has been applied to a range of forensic problems concerned with the reading ease of documents, including the police caution (Gudjonsson, 1991, 1992a; Clare and Gudjonsson, 1992).

More recently, Kincaid developed a modification of the Flesch Index to provide a facile version for computer input which is now known as the Flesch-Kincaid Index. It has been embodied in a number of specially written computer programs, and is now of central importance in the Prostyle software. This readability index is certainly one of the most accurate, reliable and validly discriminating scales in forensic use today. The superior scientific status of the Flesch-Kincaid Index, compared with the FOG and other readability indices such as the Noon Clarity Index and the Dick Density Index – both crude variations of the Flesch scale – is shown by the formal adoption of the Flesch-Kincaid by the US government, where appropriate departments are subject to a standing rule that all documentation must demonstrate a satisfactory Flesch-Kincaid Index before being passed for publication. For authors of government documents, the value of the Prostyle program is that the value of the Flesch-Kincaid Index can be added to the script immediately word-processing is completed.

The Gunning FOG Index

The FOG Index, developed by Gunning (1945) became immediately better known than the Flesch scale and is in worldwide use. This is probably because the index can be translated immediately into (American) school grades, and is therefore popular among American teachers and educational psychologists as well as writers and journalists. Gunning uses virtually the same factors as those of Flesch, but the FOG Index is less discriminative and unsuitable for scientific use. The Flesch Index has therefore become the chosen analytic instrument of the psycholinguistic professional.

In the Prostyle program, the actual number of syllables, words and sentences in the text is computed to produce the various indices as well as being recorded as raw scores, as with the other factors. It will be noted that while the program provides a quick and facile technique for analysing texts, the factors themselves can be simply extracted by visual analysis. This can be a tedious and laborious task in the case of long and difficult texts, such as copyright infringements including cases of plagiarism, but for disputed statements written and signed during police interrogation – one of the more common documents tendered for psychological examination – the linguistic analysis can be accomplished without difficulty during a professional visit. This is particularly useful when a photocopy of the document is unavailable or prohibited. At the time of writing, some forensic psychologists performing linguistic analysis of the sort embodied in the Prostyle program still do so by hand rather than by computer.

Two other readability scales need be discussed only briefly, and then only to discourage their use for forensic purposes. The Noon Clarity Scale, devised by a business methods expert, is intended for office use only. It has insufficient sensitivity for use in forensic evaluations, and is little used outside the business community. The other readability measure is the Dick Density Index, produced by a teacher of journalism for use by writers. Using density as the antonym for clarity, Dick employs the two factors of Flesch but merely halves their sum, giving the Density Index poor differentiating power. Significantly, neither of these measures is included in the Prostyle computations, and they are unsuitable for professional use.

For very short pieces of text, it will be obvious that any one factor by itself is unlikely to be sufficient to show any significant difference when compared with a criterion text, and the value of the Prostyle program is that the sheer weight of its mathematical complexity ensures that overall differences will emerge when the author of the disputed text is different from that of the criterion text. At one time, a simple stylometric analysis of shorter texts found some difficulty in showing up differences between original texts of suspects and those allegedly doctored by the police. These days, the recruitment of police officers of higher educational quality than formerly, necessary in using the high technology now employed by the constabulary, has meant that in many cases their linguistic patterns are markedly different from those of their underworld clientele.

Corpus linguistics

One useful linguistic approach to forensic problems is known as corpus linguistics, a useful introduction to which is provided by Coulthard (1994). This provides not only a new kind of data for linguistic analysis, but a new way of carrying out linguistic analysis. Just as medical or insurance actuaries acquire base rates for the frequency of a given disease, or the lifespan of an individual of a given age, by reference to the population from which the individual was drawn, so in corpus linguistics the forensic psychologist matches some aspect of a text in dispute with a corpus of language from which the text is initially assumed to be a representative sample.

As in statistics generally, the size of the population governs the accuracy of prediction. The early corpora consisted of about a million words, but corpus linguists feel happier in their analyses if the corpus is more extensive. The Collins COBUILD project had accumulated 120 million words of written text by 1994 and has been growing rapidly ever since. It has been calculated by Sinclair (in Coulthard, 1994) that the average person uses approximately half a million words per week, so COBUILD represents about five years of talking and writing by one person.

In addition to a 'general population' corpus of words, special corpora are being built up by accumulating texts from some distinctive populations: the Forensic Linguistics Research Group at Birmingham, for example, has developed a corpus of forensic texts derived from suicide notes, threatening letters, transcriptions of unlawful telephone calls, court proceedings, police interview records, etc.

The corpus offers an entire range of linguistic factors with which any given text can be matched. Word frequency offers one of the simplest analyses, and counts can be made of the ten most frequent English words, which are 'the' (representing 6 per cent of the entire text) followed by 'of, to, and, a, in, that, it, is', and 'for', which together make up 20 per cent of the average text. The frequencies in the disputed texts can be matched against the corpus frequency, and the differences obtained in the two cases can then be tested statistically, or frequencies found in one text can be compared with those in a second text, and the difference subjected to statistical analysis. In the analysis of a single text, where the writer alleges some part has been falsified by some other person, the disputed part can be matched against the undisputed part: in such cases, the samples are necessarily small, so the most frequent ten words are particularly useful items to analyse.

Most texts and speech used in everyday life are drawn from a corpus of the most frequently used 2,500 words, so the occurrence of words outside this corpus has special significance. Coulthard (1994) cites a case in which a man of simple vocabulary alleged that his university-educated superior had rewritten his report. One of the words claimed to be inserted was 'enthusiast', which occurs only 2.5 times per million words, so an examination of relatively rare words provides high probabilities that they belonged to one person's vocabulary rather than another's.

Another informative frequency in corpus linguistics is collocations, meaning the co-occurrence of two or more specified words. Collocations can become highly personalised and are extremely consistent in usage. For example, a person who uses the collocation 'centred around' is never likely to use 'centred upon' instead. Similarly, while 'an engineer' is not uncommon as a noun, the derivative verb 'to engineer' is quite rare.

Other grammatical factors have useful frequency counts in corpora, such as present or past tenses, positive or negative clauses, passive or active verbs, omission of the definite article by either note taking or the use of plural nouns, and many other grammatical characteristics which enable the literary structure of a text to be compared with the corpus and hence with another text. Psychologists wishing to use corpus linguistics as one of their forensic techniques cannot do better than study Coulthard (1994) who not only explains a wide range of analyses for which there is no room here to detail, but gives an excellent collection of examples, all of which are pertinent to forensic work. His paper also explains how to present linguistic evidence in court by means of concordance lines, as well as giving details of how to gain access to COBUILD and the Birmingham Forensic Corpus.

The Cusum plot

The work of Morton (1978) has been important in raising the profile of stylometry. Morton was critical of using frequency counts of verbs, nouns and adjectives *per se*, and proposed that it is more meaningful to look at 'collocations', that is, the combinations and sequencing of words and their relative position in the script. Morton's argument is that collocations are a better reflection of habit (i.e., less consciously determined) than the choice of individual words. Morton considered simple and frequently used words as being of greatest value for stylistic analysis. Infrequently used words would be of very limited use unless one was analysing exceptionally lengthy documents. The basic assumption is that there is far greater variation in the use of collocations between different authors than found within documents written by the same author. The collocations analysed may be of varied type. An example of Morton's method of using collocations involves comparing the number of times the word 'and' is followed by 'the' with how often 'and' is not followed by 'the'. Contingency statistics (Chi-square tests) can be used to compare the frequencies of each combination for the disputed and 'control' documents respectively.

Totty et al. (1987) have made a serious study of Morton's methods and question their validity. The authors argue that a number of complicated issues need to be resolved before one can apply the techniques developed in the literary field to forensic problems. These include unknown base frequency characteristics of certain styles and the unknown effects of context and stress on the style of speech and writing. In addition, Totty et al. consider documents of less than 1,000 words to be unsuitable for reliable stylistic analysis, because of the problem with finding habits (i.e., consistent styles) that are sufficiently frequent to give valid results when tested statistically.

Morton and Michaelson (1990) have extended Morton's earlier work and provide a new technique for using cumulative sum charts as a way of reliably identifying authorship of documents. The technique, called the 'Cusum' method (Cumulative Sum Analysis), relies on sentence length distribution and word habit within each sentence, which are plotted on a graph and compared with known authentic manuscripts.

The Cusum method continues to be used in court proceedings as evidence, although many shortcomings of the method have been identified by researchers (Canter, 1992; Hardcastle, 1997). Both Canter and Hardcastle go so far as to suggest that the method is totally discredited and should not be used as providing reliable evidence of the authenticity of authorship of either written or spoken text.

Suicide note analysis

In many cases the person who commits suicide leaves behind a note, usually addressed to somebody close to them. A study of suicide notes has been made by Retterstol (1993), and shows how analysis of such notes can reveal motivations and other characteristics of the victim, which may be relevant to the proceedings in the coroner's court. He found that in the 148 suicides studied a note had been left in 22 per cent of the cases (by 15 per cent of the men and 65 per cent of the women).

Analysis of suicide notes can often distinguish between attempted suicide, where a genuine intention to die is present, and para-suicide, which is a feigned attempt usually interpreted as a cry for help or device for manipulating significant others, each of which calls for different decisions by the professionals involved.

Survivors of suicide pacts may both be prepared to take the blame for aiding, abetting or procuring, still a criminal offence under the Suicide Act 1961. In these circumstances, a note written before the attempt may provide evidence of which survivor was the instigator. A sole survivor of a pact is usually the prime suspect, but the converse also occurs. When a suicide note is absent, psycholinguistic analysis of other documents may be necessary, including recently written personal letters and the official case notes made by the professional concerned. In one case a psychologist was severely reprimanded in court for his failure to keep adequate records of his treatment. The absence of a suicide note and adequate records prevents even an informal semantic analysis of context, which may be crucial to the facts in issue.

In cases of suicidal behaviour the forensic psychologist has sometimes played, and will continue to play, a central role in the investigation by psycholinguistic analysis of cases of questionable suicide and attempted suicide. The main role in these cases is the determination of the intention of the deceased, the accused or of some other person critically involved in the event.

Analysing auditory material

So far in this section we have been concerned with written texts, but mention has already been made of voice identification as one of the problems to which forensic linguistics can be applied. Such problems occur mostly in the case of telephone calls or recordings of bugged conversations, but also occur in speech between the offender and his victim. In cases of robbery the communication is usually too brief to provide enough material for analysis or identification – when one of us (Haward) was robbed by a native of alarming proportions in Belize, the offender uttered only one word: 'Wallet!'

Where transcripts of recorded communication exist, the psychologist can deal with this as written text in the ways already described, but the auditory record is still open to analysis by various means, and this is the province of forensic phonetics. There are a number of computer-aided signal analyses available, although these are beyond the scope of this account. German experts probably lead the world in what is referred to as forensic speaker identification, and have already applied their techniques successfully in several thousand cases. The offences concerned include fifty-nine cases of homicide, as well as blackmail instructions, bomb hoax calls, kidnapping, terrorist threats and communications during rape. The German techniques have been admirably explained by Kuenzel (1994), who believes that there is a steadily increasing tendency for speech to be a concomitant of crime.

Voice identification is not the only use of auditory material used in forensic analysis. In one case, a prison officer reported that he overheard a prisoner confessing to his visitor that he had committed a certain crime. The prisoner was awaiting his appeal hearing, and the officer's statement, if believed, would obviously nullify any chance of his appeal succeeding. He denied making the confession, and gave a plausible alternative account of what he had said, but the question was which of the two accounts the appellate judges would believe was the true one. The prisoner realised that more credence was likely to be accorded to the prison officer, not only because of his status and the fact that he was supposedly on the side of law and order, but also because ostensibly the officer had nothing to gain by making the statement. In regard to the latter point, the prisoner pointed out that he himself had everything to lose by unnecessarily making a confession in a public place with prison officers present.

One of us (Haward) was approached and asked if there was any psychological evidence which would support the argument that the prison officer could have misheard the conversation. The experience of mishearing is well known, occurring either with impaired hearing, or when the signal:noise ratio is small. Without access to the officer's auditory efficiency, an experiment was set up to test the alternative explanation. A sample of adults listened to a tape-recording and wrote down what they heard. The stimulus consisted of the conversational hum recorded in a prison visiting room, on which had been superimposed, in sotto voce at the usual level of conversation between prisoners and their visitors, the statement he had allegedly made and which he claimed the officer had misheard. As expected, none of the experimental sample correctly reproduced the statement, neither had any of the responses a reference to crime. A report was submitted explaining that the probability of a conversation being misheard in the precise circumstances of a prison visiting session was significantly high, and detailing the evidence upon which this opinion was based. The prisoner lost his appeal on other grounds, but was satisfied that justice had been done on this point at least.

A possibly unique use of linguistic analysis occurred in another case, in which a man in a Trinidad court was convicted of murder and sentenced to death, some former colonies still retaining capital punishment. While on death row his only visitor was a nun, who reported on his strange behaviour. A group of abolitionists in London, anxious to save the man from the death penalty, believed from these reports that he might be insane, which by tradition, would enable the death sentence to be commuted to life imprisonment. An appeal was sent to the Privy Council, being the appellate court for former British colonies which were members of the Commonwealth, but it was rejected on grounds of insufficient medical evidence of insanity, the prisoner refusing to see a doctor.

The group decided to appeal to the Queen for clemency, and therefore prevailed upon the nun to secrete a tape recorder in her wimple, when visiting the prisoner. Eventually some forty cassettes were flown back to London where one of us (Haward) was afforded only a few days before the execution date to analyse the tapes for evidence of insanity. This form of linguistic analysis relied upon familiarity with psychotic speech, with which to compare the extensive samples, a task aided by Haward's early clinical experience on chronic psychotic wards prior to the introduction of antipsychotic medication. Transcripts of significant speech which resembled gross psychotic ideation were made, and on the day before the hanging was due, a motor-cycle courier stood by ready to take a formal appeal to the Queen. The affidavit was actually being signed when a radio message was received stating that the authorities had learned of the appeal, and brought forward the execution, which had just taken place.

The introduction of cockpit voice recorders has brought another source of linguistic evidence to the fore. Of growing importance in courts of inquiry following accidents to airliners is the analysis of crew speech before their death obtained from CVRs recovered from the wreckage. Hirson and Howard (1994) describe the use of spectrographic analysis in such cases, but acoustic phonetics can play a prominent part, especially when two languages are involved. The latter is more often the case than not, since English is the universal language for air traffic communications, but the majority of pilots using the world's airways will possess a different mother tongue, to which they may relapse in times of crisis. Psychologists of the Defence Research Agency are usually called upon to provide expert forensic input to these formal inquiries, but because insurance claims totalling millions of pounds are frequently involved, opinions are often sought from independent forensic psychologists. Whilst Ministry of Defence psychologists give evidence in their own right, CVR evidence can also be utilised as part of a psycholinguistic investigation which may be required by one or more of the many lawyers acting on behalf of representatives of the victims. These often take the legal form of class actions, when claims made on behalf of all the many victims are joined together in one mass claim, thus avoiding hundreds of repetitions of evidence, saving considerable court time and costs, with each individual claim supporting the others.

In one particular airline accident, one of us (Haward) was asked to provide a psycholinguistic analysis of evidence involving the captain of the aircraft. One of the contentious issues was whether his action which caused the crash was an inevitable consequence of his heart failure, or whether he had contributed to the latter by his behaviour before the cardiac crisis arose. Involving multimedia evidence for linguistic analysis, the forensic material was in three parts: first were affidavits made by airline staff present in the flight briefing room, which described the angry behaviour of the pilot prior to take off; second was the under-sheet from the cockpit notepad, bearing a readable note in unusually heavy indentation (evidence would be given that the note was written in bad temper and with such force that it broke the pencil); and third was a transcript from the cockpit voice recorder. Each called for a different psycholinguistic approach. In the first analysis, that of the pre-flight briefing, it was the *content* of what was said that was significant; in the second it was the *expressive behaviour* or *Ausdruckpsychologie*, notably the force of indentation on the notepad; lastly, in the analysis of the CVR it was the *emotional* nature of the utterances made to the other crew members on the flight deck. A fourth type of analysis could also have been made, that of spectrographic analysis of the voice tape: this was beyond the co-author's resources at the time, but was employed by another forensic scientist working for a different organisation.

The multimedia samples and their psychological analysis were significant as evidence in this case in showing the pilot's mental state prior to his accident. The implications of official inquiries into accidents for forensic psychologists are explained further in Chapter 9.

Davis *et al.* (1997) have recently developed a typology for analysing the use of language by rapists during the commission of the rape. This has the potential for building up a linguistic profile of individual rapists, which may well in future assist with their being identified and captured by the police.

The ESDA techniques

Mention has already been made of some of the many kinds of forensic texts which have come the way of the psychologist for examination – letters, suicide notes, disputed confessions, police interview notes, etc. The list was further extended in 1978 by the invention of ESDA – the Electro-Static Detection Apparatus. This provides a clear reproduction of any written document by operating on the seemingly blank under-sheet of paper in the writing pad. Of course, the contents of a missing document sometimes can be read from an under-sheet if the writer has pressed hard enough with his pen on the top-sheet, but such occasions are fortuitous and the results incomplete. ESDA makes a clear copy, every time, without any undue pressure being made. Its special value is that even if the under-sheet is removed as a precaution by the person writing or falsifying the top sheet, ESDA continues to reproduce the original from several pages down.

ESDA became world famous in 1986, when the West Midlands Serious Crime Squad came under suspicion of forging confessions in a number of notorious cases, and the linguistic analysis of ESDA-generated documents led to the release of a surprising number of long-term prisoners on the grounds of miscarriage of justice, and the final disbandment of the elite crime squad. The forensic linguist whose evidence shattered the public view of police integrity was Davis (1994), and his account of his role in the enquiries leading up to the successful appellate proceedings gives a practical insight into this method of linguistic analysis.

Graphical analysis

The techniques so far described in forensic linguistics have been concerned chiefly with documentation content and voice characteristics. Writing is also a form of expressive behaviour; basic knowledge of the latter is expected in all first degree courses, and competence in its analysis should be within the skills of the professional psychologist. Graphology itself, and the problems of the validity of graphological interpretations are too well known to require repeating here, but the scientific application of mensuration to writing samples can offer useful data of relevance to some forensic problems. Usually this will consist of measuring the dimensions of the letters and words, interword spaces and line spaces, angles of slope of characters, and any other aspects of the writing which lend themselves to measurement. Armed only with protractor and millimetre rule – more accurately navigation compass points – the psychologist can quickly elicit sufficient data to demonstrate differences between two samples of handwriting. These may be from different writers, or the same writer in different circumstances, e.g., under the influence of drugs, hypnosis or some emotional condition, thus providing some evidence on which to construe the state of mind at the time of writing. Indeed, a signature that deviates markedly from the person's normal signature, such as in size and steadiness, has been used in court cases as evidence of the defendant's disturbed mental state during the interrogation and confinement.

An example of an *Ausdruckpsychologie* problem in psycholinguistics is described by Haward (1997). This involved the analysis of changes in writing characteristics in a suicide note allegedly written under compulsion, and in two different lighting conditions, proof of which would confirm the presence of a second party. Measures of differences in slope and size of letters, words and spaces in the two lighting conditions were matched with those obtained from an experimental sample copying a typescript version of the text. Statistically signif-icant differences were found between lighting conditions and between samples, demonstrating the effects of the overdose of drug upon expressive behaviour, but the measured changes produced by the two lighting conditions failed to distin-guish the two samples. This supported the victim's case and criminal proceedings followed.

It will be appreciated that forensic linguistics offers unique techniques which offer a wide range of simple forms of analysis appropriate for use by any well-trained forensic psychologist, although in some instances they call for a high degree of knowledge and expertise in psycholinguistics. The ever-growing demands for linguistic analyses are such that failure to develop and use such skills calls into question the competence of any psychologist asked to address these kinds of problem.

Statement Reality Analysis

Techniques based on the principles of Statement Reality Analysis are widely used in continental Europe, especially in Germany, where it has been used in over 40,000 cases. This linguistic approach, originally developed by Undeutsch (1982, 1989), attempts to establish the truth or falsity of a statement by psychological enquiry. In Germany it has become routine in cases of alleged child abuse. The forensic psychologist in that country has a statutory and therefore automatic role in all juvenile cases; the German Supreme Court, as early as 1954, formally acknowledged that in assessing the truthfulness of a juvenile witness the expert psychologist has other and better resources than does the court.

Statement Reality Analysis takes as its starting point the finding that statements based on recall are qualitatively different to those deliberately fabricated. Genuine recall is more spontaneous and subjectively richer. The reality of a statement is judged on a number of set 'reality criteria', which fall under two main headings (Undeutsch, 1982):

1   Fundamental criteria   These consist of the clarity, vividness and wealth of detail of the statement; its originality, in respect of details not otherwise mentioned, its reference to details not normally within the experience of a child of this age, details of the offence itself, which are more specific than peripheral experiences, the reporting of expected and appropriate feelings, and the spontaneous correction or addition to detail.
2   Secondary criteria   These are all concerned with the consistency of the reported facts. Is the statement internally consistent? Do they equate with known scientific or psychological phenomena? Are they consistent with facts known about the child being interrogated? Do they match other facts known about the case? Is the statement consistent with the situation in which it was made?

There is obviously a strong subjective element in this technique, and it must be remembered that evidence of this kind is being accepted by continental courts which not only adopt the *inquisitorial* style of judicial inquiry, but are free from the restrictive rules of admissibility which exist in the adversarial system employed in the British Commonwealth and USA. That said, Statement Reality Analysis can be a powerful tool which, in experienced hands, directs attention to the acceptable facts of the case while avoiding misdirected enquiries.

Formal Structure Analysis

Sweden has been a recognised centre of linguistic expertise ever since Svartvik (1967) was brought over to the UK as a forensic linguist in the Evans case. In this context, Trankell (1972, 1982) developed a psycholinguistic approach he called Formal Structure Analysis. Like Undeutsch, his concern was principally to validate the statements of child victims and offenders in the juvenile courts, and while differing in details, the two approaches have much in common, although the Scandinavian technique, as one would expect, puts more emphasis on the linguistic analysis rather than on the consistency between the statement and reality. The technique is not dissimilar to the one described above, because it was largely based on Undeutsch's framework. It has been extensively used in Sweden.

Criteria-Based Content Analysis (CBCA)

Steller and Koehnken (1990) refined the system of Undeutsch and his followers by integrating the content criteria from different systems. This produced nineteen criteria, which fall into five separate categories, as follows:

1   General characteristics, which comprises three criteria:

    a   Logical structure
    b   Unstructured production
    c   Quantity of details

2   Specific contents, which comprises four criteria:

    a   Contextual embedding
    b   Descriptions of interactions
    c   Reproduction of conversation
    d   Unexpected complications during the incident

3   Peculiarities of content, which comprises six criteria:

    a   Unusual details
    b   Superfluous details
    c   Accurately reported details misunderstood
    d   Related external associations
    e   Accounts of subjective mental state
    f   Attribution of perpetrator's mental state

4   Motivation-related contents, which comprises five criteria:

    a   Spontaneous corrections
    b   Admitting lack of memory
    c   Raising doubts about one's own testimony
    d   Self-deprecation
    e   Pardoning the perpetrator

5   Offence-specific elements, which consists of only one criterion:

    a   Details characteristic of the offence

The CBCA refers to the analysis of the quality of the content of the accuser's statement by using the above nineteen criteria. The outcome is then interpreted in the context of other relevant information in the case, such as biographical, test and case data. This procedure is labelled 'Statement Validity Assessment' (SVA) and provides an assessment of the likelihood that the child has actually experienced the event described in his or her statement. According to Steller and Boychuk (1992, p. 49), the SVA includes:

a 'Careful review of the relevant case information'
b 'Preserved semistructured interview of the child'
c 'Criteria-based content analysis of the transcribed interview'
d 'Validity checks of additional case information'
e 'A systematic summarization of content analysis and validity checks'

The SVA and CBCA consist of a systematic approach to the forensic evaluation concerning the veracity of the child's accusation. They are not to be confused with a psychometric test. The CBCA criteria appear to have sufficient inter-judge and test–retest reliabilities to be used as a psychometric procedure, although adequate validity still needs to be demonstrated (Horowitz et al. 1997). The SVA method is particularly controversial in the USA and awaits validation (Steller and Boychuk, 1992).

It will be readily apparent that Statement Reality Analysis, Formal Statement Analysis and Criterion-Based Content Analysis are techniques which are similar in practice and have a common linguistic basis. Their exponents believe them to be valid because: (a) they work, in the sense that they induce a clear belief in all concerned that they validly reflect reality (i.e., they have 'face validity'); (b) they are readily accepted by the German courts by virtue of common-sense explanations relying upon analytic rigour rather than upon some esoteric theory incomprehensible to the judiciary; and (c) they lead to conviction, if the expert's conclusion points in that direction, on a foundation of expert evidence which has not yet been capable of refutation.

All this breeds a considerable degree of confidence in the practitioners who amass cumulative experience by the regular and frequent use of these techniques. In its turn, this experience provides an ever-increasing corpus of linguistic data which further serves to increase the validity of individual norms, and allows anomalies, peculiarities and deviations from general experience to be more validly delineated. As professional integration in European forensic activity develops, this group of linguistic techniques is likely to play an increasing part in UK forensic psychology.

Some UK forensic psychologists have chosen to extract what they believe are the more meritorious components of these three approaches and applied them to their professional advantage in their own forensic investigations regarding both adults and children. Educational psychologists have been undoubtedly active in contributing to juvenile forensic issues, but the contributions of some members of this speciality have come under some justifiable criticism, and in many cases show a lack of the substantial preparation of evidence which forensic psychologists elsewhere in Europe undertake.

These techniques demand a high level of psychological insight and considerable experience of child behaviour. It is well suited to the training and orientation of the European psychologist, but falls between the approaches of either the rigidly scientific psychometrists and those of more subjective and psychodynamic orientation. It is hoped that with increasing EU integration, the greater interchange of skills and techniques will provide advantages for all forensic psychologists throughout Europe. Raymond and Bornstein (1991) have discussed some of the expected problems in training, designation and practice of the increasing number of experts in the European Union, and British psychologists should be preparing themselves for a wider practice in continental Europe.

Conclusions

Forensic linguistics is a rapidly developing speciality which is now well established but a long way from reaching its full potential. More generally known as stylometry, sometimes as stylistics, it was first used to analyse texts to determine literary authorship, but its usage has expanded to determining other psychological features, including reading/writing ease and mental state. Many different kinds of analysis are used and these are explained in some detail above. Psychologists in Germany and Scandinavia first used forensic linguistics to validate evidential statements made by minors, and gained a recognised place in the legal system of their respective countries, particularly in Germany. Variations in analytic techniques have been developed in different countries, each bearing a different label, such as Statement Reality Analysis, Formal Structure Analysis and Criterion-Based Content Analysis. In the UK the use of forensic linguistics tends to be non-specific, selecting various elements appropriate to the forensic problem. Details of a computer program for linguistic analysis are also given. The analysis of suicide notes is described as one example of graphical text analysis, which while not strictly linguistic, is included within the corpus of expressive behaviour under which linguistics is subsumed. The development of voice analysis, particularly in aircraft investigations, which may have either civil or criminal implications, is also described.

8

CIVIL CASES

Introduction

Forensic psychologists may find themselves having to present written or oral evidence in a variety of legal settings. As far as courts are concerned, these involve three different jurisdictions, referred to as 'Courts of Civil Jurisdiction', 'Courts of Special Jurisdiction', and 'Courts of Criminal Jurisdiction' (Haward, 1981). The civil courts are discussed in detail in this Chapter, as well as some of the Courts of Special Jurisdiction. The Courts of Special Jurisdiction deal with matters which are not manifestly either public or private. These 'administrative' courts include the Coroner's Courts and Mental Health Review Tribunals, and Courts Martial.

Civil cases figure prominently in the forensic psychologist's caseload. They are mainly concerned with cases in which compensation is sought for injury or psychological trauma arising from the negligence of others. Most neuropsychologists involved in court work find their entire forensic caseload within the civil law. Problems of brain damage following a road traffic accident are commonly referred to psychologists because of the cognitive or behavioural deficits which may follow. Chronic physical pain arising out of negligence may result in litigation when it can be argued that it is interfering significantly with the complainant's regular activities and quality of life, and post-traumatic stress disorder is a relatively new concept which has brought clinicians into the witness box.

In addition to cases involving compensation, psychologists are expected to deal with a wide range of other problems which are brought to the civil courts, such as cases involving family disputes and child custody, mental capacity to make a will or look after one's financial affairs, sudden death, immoral behaviour of clergymen, and the special problems arising at work, in commerce, and in ships at sea.

Civil law

In order to adapt to the rich diversity of problems brought before the courts, since the twelfth century civil law has developed a specialised corpus of law for each set of problems which have some common basis and for which specific remedies have been created. Civil law in its entirety thus embraces the laws of tort, contract, trusts, probate, as well as maritime, mercantile and family laws. In earlier times these were mostly dealt with in their own separate courts; today those specialised courts are now divisions or sub-divisions of the High Court, with family law, because of ubiquitous litigation, using County and Family Proceedings Courts as well. In addition, the Ecclesiastical Courts – the oldest existing courts in the land – and the Coroner's Courts also have non-criminal jurisdiction. In the last half century there has also been a proliferation of sub-judicial courts and tribunals which administer administrative law and modern legislation concerning relations between citizen and government.

Figure 8.1 gives a brief outline of the criminal justice system in England and Wales as it relates to the civil and special jurisdiction courts. It provides the framework for the remaining discussion in this chapter. All courts are ultimately answerable to the European court.

Civil and criminal law: similarities and differences

Most forensic psychologists deal with both civil and criminal cases, and need to be aware of significant differences between tendering expert evidence in civil and criminal courts respectively. Civil actions, that is, those taken by one party who has been personally offended by another, predate criminal prosecutions by untold centuries; they stem directly from the *Lex Talionis* – 'an eye for an eye' – which marked individual and family feuds before civilisation itself became established. During the first millenium AD no distinction was made between criminal and civil offences. It was not until the Norman kings took over formal control of English law in AD 1066 that the separation of civil and criminal cases began to be recognised.

These two branches of English law had, and still have, certain things in common. Although both predate common law, each became formalised and unified in common law. Both civil and criminal proceedings follow the adversary system, in which one side is said to 'win' and the other 'loses'. Both eschew any search for 'the whole truth', excluding from court any facts which may be relevant to the case but which are not directly related to the pleadings as presented in court. Both follow Rules of Evidence by which facts which would be admissible under an inquisitorial system can be excluded on a number of different grounds.

Both rely upon various legal presumptions, some of which are irrebuttable, whatever the scientific evidence to the contrary. Both cases are argued by lawyers before a judicial officer. In both cases, the legal maxim is that 'the burden of proof lies on he who asserts', that is, the party bringing the case. In criminal cases this will usually be the Crown Prosecution Service, although any citizen possessing prima facie evidence of a crime may prosecute. In civil cases the

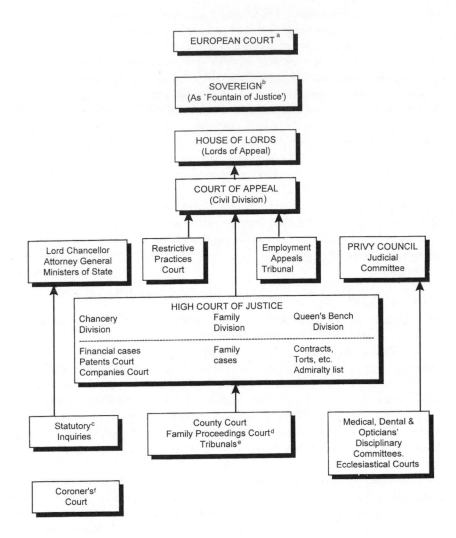

Figure 8.1 The Civil Courts in England and Wales

Notes:

[a] Appellants normally exhaust lower appellate courts first, but can supplicate to take their appeal direct when the contentious issue is not appropriate to existing legislation.

[b] The sovereign retains power to grant pardons but now only does so in consultation with the Secretary of State for Home Affairs.

[c] Official inquiries have various appellate channels, and some have no rights of appeal.

[d] These are held in the Magistrates' Court.

[e] Most tribunals have an appellate channel to the High Court, but a few, like the General Medical Council, refer appeals elsewhere.

[f] The Coroner's Court has no appellate channel.

asserter will be the aggrieved party, called the pursuer in Scotland, and the plaintiff elsewhere in the UK.

The differences are less fundamental, but are generally of more direct practical importance to the forensic psychologist. Civil and criminal cases are heard in different courts. Another difference is that the Magistrates' Court is the court of first instance for criminal prosecutions, whereas many civil actions are first heard in the High Court, the lower courts dealing with reclamation of debts below a certain sum, and the more simple or urgent family disputes. A third difference is that the evidence admissible in each is regulated by different statutes, such as the Police and Criminal Evidence Act 1984 and the Civil Evidence Act 1972.

Another difference is that of trial by jury. First established by the Assize of Clarendon in AD 1166, the jury system is an established principle which rests on the belief that justice is best served when accused persons are tried by their peers. In contrast, the actions heard in civil courts often involve such difficult legal arguments, or extremely complex scientific, medical or financial concepts, that most civil cases are heard in the absence of a jury. An exception is made in the case of libel, where the essential question is one of damaged reputation, this being a social issue which a jury is believed competent to address.

There are differences with regard to the sanctions imposed. Criminal law is public law, developed to protect the crown and the public at large; its sanctions are therefore directed against the offender to discourage repetition of the offence and if necessary keep the offender from doing so by detention in prison or security hospital. Punishment was the central feature of criminal law, which had no interest in the victim as such and the idea of compensating the victim of a criminal offence is of very recent origin. In contradistinction, civil law is private law, based on the policy of redressing a wrong imposed by one particular party upon another. The emphasis is on remedying in some way the aggravation or injury caused by the offence, rather than punishing the offender. An exception to this lies in those offences, such as defamation, where proof of malice may lead to punitive damages, or where the plaintiff is right in law but deemed to be morally blameworthy, in which case damages of one penny (the smallest coin of the realm) may be awarded with all costs payable, producing the equivalent of a very severe fine. The judge in a civil court may order specific performance on the part of the defendants, making them comply with a contract or agreement, or restore the plaintiff's situation to the status quo ante. The judge may also issue an Injunction to stop the defendant from continuing to commit the offence, but in most cases damages in the form of a specified sum of money is seen as the most realistic way of compensating the victim of a civil offence.

Important differences lie in the level of proof required in civil and criminal cases. In criminal trials, the burden of proof normally remains with the prosecutor, and the accused person is under no compulsion to defend himself in any way. In common law, the accused need not utter a word, the onus being on the prosecutor to prove his case beyond all reasonable doubt. However, by the Criminal Justice and Public Order Act 1994, the age-old right to silence was modified and adverse inferences can be drawn by the court if a suspect chooses to remain silent when questioned by the police or refuses to testify in court (see Chapter 9).

An exception to the burden of proof lying with the prosecution occurs in those cases where the accused pleads absence of *mens rea* (guilty mind) by reason of some mental condition, such as insanity or 'diminished responsibility'. In such a case, the burden of proving the absence or impairment of *mens rea* lies on the defendant on the balance of probability. In civil actions, however, the burden of proof moves alternately from one party to the other as each relevant piece of evidence tendered is countered and rebutted by evidence from the opposing side. In complicated cases this may produce an alternating battle of wits, with further evidence and counter evidence required by each side. Psychologists involved in such cases may find themselves testifying initially on one issue, e.g., the existence of brain damage, and then changing their role from clinician to experimentalist or actuary to produce evidence on some other issue, such as contributory negligence, or loss of expected earning power.

In some cases, for example Scane's (1959), described by Haward (1981), the psychologist may be required to adopt each of the four roles discussed in Chapter 6 in succession, and in civil actions this is not an uncommon occurrence.

It will be obvious that civil cases can create professional demands different from those of criminal cases, where the requirements of the case are usually known from the start. Also, civil cases often extend over a much longer period of time: one case took twelve years of litigation and four changes of solicitors before compensation was obtained. A corollary of this is that permission to leave court after testifying, often implicit in criminal proceedings, may require to be requested explicitly in a civil court. In such cases, the psychologist may be asked to remain within the precincts of the court if there is the possibility of being recalled later that day, or to 'hold in readiness' for a possible recall on some subsequent date. Often the psychologist, after testifying on one particular issue, will be asked to attend a counsel's conference held after the next adjournment, in order to discuss what contribution can be made to the next issue which has arisen.

In contrast to criminal trials, where no out-of-court settlement takes place, 97 per cent of High Court actions are settled out of court; of the 3 per cent which come to trial, only a few are real contests of liability (Barker *et al.* 1993, p. 178). Because most claims are covered by insurance, such as house, motorcar, public or professional liability, etc., insurers find it less expensive to settle out of court as soon as prospects of a quick settlement disappear. In some cases, the facts produced by the psychologist from experimental work or literature research are of such cogency and so overwhelming that the parties are prepared to negotiate a settlement immediately. While in criminal trials it is open to the judge to instruct the jury to bring in a 'not guilty' verdict when the prosecution case has collapsed, or some informal plea-bargaining can take place to limit the expected sentence when a 'guilty' verdict is probable, criminal cases themselves cannot be settled out of court once proceedings have commenced.

Probability in civil actions

Differences between civil and criminal actions differ not only in the *burden* of proof, but in the *weight* of evidence required to furnish proof. In theory, under English criminal law, proof of innocence is not required (though lack of it, for example, by failing to provide an alibi, may substantially weaken the defence when other circumstantial evidence exists). Proof of guilt, on the other hand, must be *beyond reasonable doubt*. The simplicity of this phrase belies its complex psychological character. The authors have been involved in a number of cases in which quantitative psychometric data have been presented to the court, which in scientific terms of statistical probability have amply supported proof of some issue before the court. The decision of the jurors is, of course, reached on the basis of probabilities often below their level of awareness, and the subconscious probability which becomes acceptable as fact will vary from one juror to another, and the combined probabilities as perceived by two different juries may differ significantly in offences which appear to be identical. The many simulated jury studies reported in the psychological literature and conducted using students as 'jurors', have failed to take into account the fact that most students, by virtue of their statistical training, may have a different concept of probability than the average juror.

The judiciary's view of statistical evidence

In criminal courts, the judiciary have shown themselves unwilling to accept any quantitative measure to separate reasonable from unreasonable doubt, since this is a matter, not for the expert, but for the court to decide. The problem in criminal law of an ever-shifting level of probability, beyond which guilt is assumed, is not present in civil law. The rule here is that the parties to an action whose evidence tips the balance of probabilities in their favour wins the suit. Perhaps because of this essential difference in 'weight of evidence' or 'burden of proof', quantitative data is more acceptable in civil courts. Another factor is that many of the cases hinge on technicalities arising from industrial accidents, where, for example, the issue may concern differences in safety wire measured in microns; divisional judges selected to try such cases are highly numerate and well versed in dealing with quantitative evidence.

When the psychologist is submitting a variety of data, based upon findings which have no intercorrelation, then the overall probability will be the product of all the individual probabilities, which usually builds up quickly to a scientifically acceptable level of significance. (Where intercorrelations exist and are known, these are entered into the equation, of course.) However, the standard levels of significance adopted in statistics are themselves quite arbitrary and clearly unrelated to the level of evidence accepted in the civil court. Some psychologists may feel that their integrity as scientists is compromised by tendering any evidence which falls short of the conventional levels. Others believe that the interests of justice over-ride any arbitrary rule devised by statisticians, and are prepared to tender any psychometric or research evidence relevant to the case, irrespective of its probability value, adding any necessary qualifying statements, including, of course, the degree to which chance may have produced the same result.

To conceal from the court 'statistically non-significant' evidence favouring one party (even worse, to present it as a negative finding) when the other party may be presenting evidence of even lower statistical significance, gives the latter an unfair advantage and is patently unjust. On entering the witness box, the expert witness swears to tell the whole truth, and the legal rule regarding the balance of probabilities demands that all relevant evidence should be tendered. Some psychologists deliberately avoid the use of the 'level of significance' and merely talk of the chance effects, leaving the counsel and judge to interpret these in the final addresses and summing-up. This is a fundamental problem in scientific evidence which has not yet been adequately addressed within our profession. The use of confidence levels goes some way towards reducing this problem, but employing any statistical terms in the examination opens the door to misleading enquiries in cross-examination, and only the most well-prepared psychologist can evade the resulting quagmire of confusion and misapprehension which a good advocate can use to entrap the expert witness and belittle the evidence to the jury.

Branches of civil law

Mention has been made that unlike the criminal courts, which have equivalent jurisdiction (though not equivalent sentencing power), the High Court of Justice has various divisions which have a specialised function, and in some of which the judiciary are highly competent, well experienced, and expert in that particular branch of civil law. The legal presumption is that 'everyone knows the law', and ignorance of the law can be embarrassing for so-called experts if they display their ignorance of some essential feature of the law relevant to their case. When appearing in one of the divisional or sub-divisional courts of the High Court, it is preferable to have some idea of the particular branch of civil law administered in that court. Some examples of forensic work involving these various branches of civil law follow.

Law of contract

Problems encountered in contract law rarely concern the psychologist as an expert witness (although they have done as a professional practitioner – see Chapter 4) as they are concerned mainly with financial transactions and conditions of service. These are dealt with in the County Courts for small sums and in the High Court for larger sums or where the conditions of the contract are complex. At present, the High Court deals with about 150,000 claims each year whereas the County Courts process some 1.5 million cases. The need for psychological evidence mainly arises when breach of contract by non-payment relates to psychological treatment or the defendant's mental state is in issue.

Law of tort

Tort, from the Norman French meaning 'a wrong', is the interference of one party's rights by another, for which the law can provide a remedy. Compensation is the principal remedy, but the High Court, where cases of tort are heard, can also use remedies from the law of equity, such as orders for specific performance (for example, forcing the defendant to dismantle a new building which infringes the plaintiff's right to reasonable light), or the injunction, which prevents the defendant from continuing a particular interference, such as harassment. Compensation cases represent the majority of those for whom expert psychological evidence is required, usually where cognitive impairment or emotional trauma has been suffered, or earning potential has been adversely affected as a result of some action for which the defendant is being held responsible. Most cases of this kind require clinical training, but occupational psychologists have an important role to play in cases involving work-related accidents, and in assessing working capacity and earning potential. In its time, the National Institute of Industrial Psychology was an important source of such expertise, and furnished a useful earnings-rate index. Given the present cognitive efficiency of the plaintiff, it was possible to predict from this scale (Table 8.1) the plaintiff's approximate earning power, once the current base wage was known.

While the courts have always been sympathetic to the plaintiff's case when *medical* evidence of physical injury is offered, within the law of tort it has been more difficult to convince the court, especially when medical evidence is lacking or psychiatric evidence that psychological trauma can be as debilitating as a physical injury is opposed by the defence. A major legal development has occurred recently which has had an enormous impact on both criminal law and the law of tort, and it relates to the establishment of the diagnosis of post-traumatic stress disorder (Stone, 1993).

Post-traumatic stress disorder (PTSD)

The identification of PTSD symptoms can form the basis for defining psychological injury in civil (compensation) cases as well as negating culpability or mitigating sentences in criminal cases (Colman and MacKay, 1995).

In the UK an important early case was the arbitration in February 1989 between passengers on the ferry which capsized off Zeebrugge in March 1987 and the P & O European Ferries (Dover) Limited and the Peninsular and Oriental Steam Navigation Company. One of us (Gudjonsson) testified at the arbitration hearing on behalf of three of the claimants. The ten 'test cases' that were subject to arbitration set the standards whereby other claimants' compensation could be

Table 8.1 Mean rates of income

Barr-Fryer Value	Occupational group	NIIP Index
a	b	c
20	Professional	5.0
19	Managerial	4.5
17	Semi-professional	3.0
16	Clerical / sales	2.7
14	Skilled	2.5
11	Semi-skilled	2.1
8	Unskilled	1.5
5	Domestic service	1.2
4	Fishing industry	1.0

Notes:
[a] Fryer (1922). See also Lorge and Blau (1942).
[b] Standard occupational groupings.
[c] NIIP multiplier of basic national earnings. This is the British adaptation by NIIP from tables by Gray (1946). The IQ values, now being out of date, have been omitted.

evaluated. The respondents admitted liability for the claimants' injuries, loss and damages, which were referred to arbitration primarily to consider damages for 'nervous shock' and the applicability of the diagnosis of PTSD to each claimant, according to the DSM-III-R criteria. The arbitration also evaluated the importance of pathological grief where claimants had lost one or more relatives in the disaster. The arbitration was important because for the first time in Great Britain PTSD became recognised as a legitimate condition for compensation. Secondly, the judgment emphasised that disaster victims may be left 'vulnerable' to the risk of further psychiatric illness and that this must be taken into consideration when awarding compensation.

Family law

This is a relatively new branch of civil law, a consolidation of divorce law developed in the twelfth century as part of canon (ecclesiastic) law, with more recent legislation introduced to deal with modern family problems and the protection of children. Until the Reformation, so-called divorce, permitted on grounds of adultery, cruelty or unnatural practices, was actually equivalent to judicial separation, since remarriage was not permitted. In earlier times, the wife and her property became possessions of the husband on marriage, and the latter had full rights over his wife and children who had no recourse to the law. English literature of the 18th and 19th centuries provides a vivid and accurate picture of the misfortunes suffered by such human chattels devoid of all legal rights. Since the Reformation divorce was available only by a private act of parliament, and was thus limited to landed gentry with sufficient influence in parliamentary affairs. It was not until the Victorian Matrimonial Causes Act 1857 that true divorce with right to remarry became available to the public who could afford it; the grounds remained the same as they were in the twelfth century, and remained so until the Divorce Reform Act 1969. Until then, many psychologists, including one of us (Haward), spent much time in the divorce courts giving evidence on mental cruelty and/or unnatural practices, mostly (but not exclusively) for the wife as plaintiff. The Married Woman's Property Act 1882 went some way to providing some measure of independence to the wife who brought substantial property into the marriage, but this development had no implications for forensic psychology unless the husband claimed mental incompetence on the part of his wife and sought to take over power of attorney.

The civil law's concern with children came late in legal history, parental rights to do what they would with their children being held paramount. Children appear in late-nineteenth-century court records only in relation to custody problems following divorce, and these were usually settled according to long-standing rigid rules such as the Tender Years Doctrine which stipulated that a child of tender years should automatically go to the mother. In the 1920s legislation protecting the interests of children appeared, such as the Adoption of Children Act 1926 and the Infant Life (Preservation) Act 1929, but the greatest developments came after the Second World War, when social concerns expressed in the Beveridge Report, 1942, laid the foundations for the postwar Welfare State. The Education Act 1944 had already anticipated some concerns about children's welfare by the creation of the Education *Welfare* Officer, replacing the School Board Attendance Officer, but the most far-reaching legislation for the protection of children was embodied in the Children Act 1948 which opened the door for a range of forensic contributions from educational and clinical psychologists.

Family law is administered in the Family Division of the High Court, in County Courts, and in the Family Proceedings Courts chaired by specially trained magistrates. Parker (1987) estimated that some 200,000 reports containing psychological evidence are annually put before Family Courts. Of special concern is the poor quality of school reports produced in court, which have been heavily criticised by the National Association for the Care and Resettlement of Offenders (NACRO, 1984) for relying on hearsay and unsubstantiated remarks, and the use of emotive language. Examples described by

Ball (1981) amount to little more than character assassination under cover of a psychological opinion, and Nash (1982) putting a solicitor's point of view, describes educational psychologists' reports which repeat the conclusions of social workers, who in turn have repeated the conclusions of teachers.

All courts administering family law have equal jurisdiction; parties to a private dispute not involving the local authority can choose whichever level of court they wish, but all care proceedings, which are brought by either the local authority or NSPCC, start in the Family Proceedings (Magistrates') Court, where the justices' clerk allocates the case to the most appropriate court. Cases which have some urgency because the child is believed to be at risk go to the local Family Proceedings Court where the magistrates can empower the immediate removal of the child or of the parent posing a threat to the child's safety. The Children Act 1989 governs most of the current proceedings, Section 1 laying down the fundamental policy that the welfare of the child must be paramount (Bridge et al., 1990). The child's welfare is not easy to assess, as Taylor (1979) explains: the psychologist is caught between two parents or one parent and the social services, and has the problem of applying data from two-parent traditional homes to a single-parent family. Cases can become quite complicated when some psychological feature is the central issue; when one parent sought denial of custody to a homosexual father, the psychologist concerned was required to give extensive evidence on the nature and aetiology of homosexuality, and its paternal effects upon child development (Taylor, 1979).

In looking at each case, the court uses a checklist, which could also be used by any psychologist tendering evidence to the court. The checklist enumerates all the facts relevant to the case which the court is required to consider before reaching a decision and making the necessary order(s) designed to rectify or ameliorate the situation.

CHILD PROTECTION CHECKLIST (SEE BRIDGE ET AL., 1990, FOR DETAILS)

Information required by the Family Proceedings Court:

1   The ascertainable wishes and feelings of the child concerned, considered in the light of the child's age and understanding.
2   The child's physical, emotional and educational needs.
3   The likely effect on the child of any considered change in the family circumstances.
4   The relevant personal characteristics of the child, such as age, sex, upbringing, culture, etc.
5   The harm suffered or risk of suffering in the foreseeable future.
6   The capability of the parents, guardian or others in loco parentis of meeting the child's present needs.

The information required by the court emphasises the need to assess the family as a whole, and the Home Inventory has been found useful in assessing the families of children under investigation (Bradley *et al.*, 1992), but specialised assessment methods, such as the Child Abuse Potential Inventory (Milner, 1986) may also be required.

The Children Act empowers the justices to make a wide range of orders to deal with most situations which arise, full details of which are given by Carr (1992). In addition, family law makes use of other legislation, such as the Adoption Act 1976 for adoption orders, the Education Act 1944 for education supervision orders, the Domestic Proceedings and Magistrates Courts Act 1978 for children's maintenance orders, and so on.

The administration of family law has been developed and consolidated in the Family Law Act 1996 which absorbs, modifies or repeals sections of nearly fifty preceding acts. At the time of writing not all of the schedules of this Act have come into force, but since it will have a significant effect upon expert evidence, psychologists working in family law cases should make themselves aware of its provisions, the best current source being La Follete and Purdie (1996).

Scotland uses a different system. Cases which in England would come under one of the family law courts are heard by the Sheriff, who deals with the whole gamut of Scottish law, including property, divorce, juvenile crime, sudden death and child custody. Children in need of compulsory care are referred to a Children's Hearing by three lay persons drawn from a special Children's Panel set up by the local authority.

Maritime law

Maritime law – the law of the sea – is now generally referred to as admiralty law because it was originally administered in the Court of Admiralty, now the Admiralty Division of the High Court. Maritime law has strong elements of international law embodied in it, developing as it did from the maritime trade between many different countries. So far, problems arising at sea which have been brought to the forensic psychologist have been extremely rare. Occasionally, when a person at sea disappears, the case divides itself into two parts, one concerned with whether a crime has been committed, the other concerned with presumption of death and subsequent proceedings for the probate of the missing person's estate. For both issues a psychological autopsy may be appropriate, whereby the psychologist is asked to piece together the available evidence to show the probable state of mind of the person concerned prior to his disappearance. This may give compelling weight to a finding of suicide being more likely than accident or murder, and so make a decisive impact upon the consequences. Certification of death would be a matter for the coroner. Probate, if disputed, would then go to the High Court, while a question of murder would be taken up by the appropriate authority and end in the criminal court. Accidental death would raise questions within the Admiralty's jurisdiction regarding safety at sea, central to this court's present responsibilities.

The psychological autopsy is well established in the USA and has been shown to have a statistically significant impact on the determination of death, especially in equivocal cases (Jobes *et al.*, 1986). It is much less common in the UK, where in the past it has been more concerned with sudden deaths in mental hospitals. The validity of diagnoses obtained through psychological autopsies has been confirmed by Brent *et al.* (1993). In maritime inquiries the psychologist's careful examination of possible motivating factors, based upon the nature of the person evaluated by a consensus of evidence from others, and upon the probable precipitating factors in the environment at that particular time, undoubtedly yield a more realistic and comprehensive picture from which a professional opinion can be derived. The assessment of the presence of depression, based on information given by other passengers or shipmates and by enquiries based on one of the many depression scales available, is particularly useful when suicide is suspected. In a fairly recent USA admiralty case of 'wrongful death' (Calderon v. Spencer and Hughes case, 1990) the psychologist's evidence was the key issue and determined the nature of the charges subsequently made.

Another area of maritime law which has involved the forensic psychologist is that concerned with accidents to vessels rather than to people; claims for compensation would go to the High Court (Queen's Bench Division) rather than to the Admiralty Division. In the past decade, a series of disasters at sea, notably among vehicular ferries, have introduced the question of post-traumatic stress disorder, discussed earlier. Such accidents have brought the behaviour of ship's masters and their crew into question, and so for one particular episode at sea psychologists could find themselves involved not only in the initial shipowner's inquiry, but also in the divisional court dealing with admiralty affairs concerned with crew conduct relating to safety at sea and the safety of the vessel itself, the High Court where class actions for compensation take place, the Crown Court if the evidence points to criminal negligence on the part of crew members, the Coroner's Court if loss of life has occurred, and an Industrial Tribunal if crew members appeal against sanctions imposed upon them by the shipowner.

In one preliminary enquiry, one of us (Haward) carried out experiments in a hired vessel and was able to show that an apparent misjudgment by the captain was due to a perceptual parallax error induced by a newly installed portside lighting system. Such evidence in mitigation is often of great importance in changing the adjudicator's view of presumed incompetence to one of unavoidable error, and so saving the master his ticket and future career. The diminution of sea traffic since 1945 has meant that involvement of psychologists in maritime enquiries is reducing in frequency, although each year still sees a number of accidents at sea within territorial waters. Churchill and Love (1988) provide an up-to-date account of maritime law.

Mercantile law

The Commercial List of the High Court, which now embodies the old Courts Merchant, is increasingly concerned with what are now called consumer affairs. Forensic psychologists providing evidence for this court are usually university-based faculty members specialising in some appropriate branch of social or cognitive psychology. Many of the reported cases featuring expert psychological testimony concern perceptual problems: it will be remembered from Chapter 2 that Munsterberg pioneered the way in mercantile law by solving the problem of the Flemish weavers with reference to Helmholtz's work on colour vision. In 1921, the Coca Cola Company sued the Cheo Cola Company in the first of a long series of *passing off* lawsuits which have continued to this day. A psychologist provided evidence in the original hearing which demonstrated that some purchasers misperceived the cheaper product for 'the real thing' and his study set the pattern for this kind of forensic problem. Sixty years later, one us (Haward) was repeating this approach in respect of two similar packagings of baked beans, and at the time of writing the makers of two different chocolate wafers are in litigation over confusion in packaging.

The growing emphasis on creating experimental evidence for specific forensic problems raises two further points to be emphasised. The first is that when the forensic psychologist produces experimental data that significantly affects the issue, the case usually ends, like the majority of civil actions, with an out-of-court settlement, and goes unrecorded in the law reports. This makes it all the more important for details of such work to find permanent availability in the professional literature. Fortunately, the number of publications of forensic interest is increasing, but there is also a wide range of specialist journals where such studies could be, and have been, appropriately reported.

The *Milwaukee Journal*, for example, published a consumer analysis from 1922 to 1931, which was sufficiently detailed to provide formulae for establishing the price of various commodities, and so making exposure of unfairly high profits a valid and easy process. Like much social data, many of the findings are tied by time and place, but other data remain valid, such as the dates when brand names became generally established in the public mind. Although most of this early work emanates from the USA, much of it is still reasonably valid for UK populations, for many of the products on sale in the UK originated from manufacturers in the USA. Very often, a pilot experiment, or small sampling procedure, provides sufficient contemporary data to enable the earlier data to be validated or updated.

The other point to be made is that in searching psychological literature one must be prepared to go back considerably more years than is customary. Mention has been made of the Oswald trial and the reference made there to Munsterberg's study of aural discrimination conducted more than half a century earlier. There is a wealth of good experimental data to be found in that more leisurely age of the interwar years, particularly in the 1930s, and the work of Bartlett (1932) on memory recall, conducted during this period, has been frequently quoted in the witness box. Psychology journals of the 1920s were particularly rich in consumer research data. Reliance on a computer search may be adequate if sound data of direct relevance to the problem is thrown up, but making inferences from data derived for a different purpose or from a dissimilar sample to the parties in question when better data already exists in the archives is not only poor applied psychology, but offends the 'Best Evidence Rule'. If the psychologist acting for the other party has taken the trouble to dredge the literature to some depth, and has obtained facts of direct relevance to the problem, the probability of a successful judgment in favour of his own party will be considerably enhanced. More importantly, the slipshod expert could then be sued for professional negligence by the party whose case he has then lost by his own shortcomings. The law always demands the very best an expert can offer, and in an increasingly litigious society the second best often suffers the penalty it deserves.

Law of equity

Equity was developed in medieval times by the Lord Chancellor, to improve the inequities of a rigid judicial system. Unless there was a specific writ which matched the plaintiff's case, the Court of Common Pleas was powerless to intervene. Appeals to the King, as 'The Fountain of Justice', were passed to the Lord Chancellor, who then provided equitable solutions. For many years the law of equity was administered only in the Court of Chancery, but today it is valid in all courts, and many of the remedies in cases of tort, such as injunctions and orders for specific performance come from this source. In Chapter 4 we saw the law of equity at work in developing equitable obligations as the basis for new torts such as breach of confidence, as well as new defences in duty of care. One of the Royal Prerogatives established by Henry II in AD 1154 was the safeguarding and management of the lands and estates of 'idiots' until their death and 'lunatics' until their recovery – an exceptionally early record of this differential prognosis. This task was delegated to the Lord Chancellor, in the Court of Chancery, and later a Court of Protection was established which acted as trustee to property under a Master in Lunacy. The Court of Chancery also administered the estates of minors and those unfit to manage their inherited estate by reason of low intelligence. Nearly nine centuries later it is still difficult for those 'in chancery' to regain control of their own property, but the advent of the forensic psychologist has improved significantly their chances of success.

Court of Protection

Since the Mental Health Act 1959 the Court of Protection has been administered by the Supreme Court of Judicature under Section 8 of that Act. Until the abolition of the Victorian asylums in recent years, Hospital Management

Committees put into the Court of Protection the substantial affairs of those 'certified' mental patients (apart from those known legally as 'pauper lunatics' supported by local taxes) where no relative was known who could be granted power of attorney. Some 25,000 mental patients have their affairs in the Court of Protection (Barker *et al.*, 1993, p. 197). Scotland has no Court of Protection or court of equivalent function, but the Sheriff can appoint an official known as a *curator bonus* to handle all the affairs of any person proved to be *incapax*.

Clinical psychologists played an active role in assessing competency for the Court of Protection or Curator Bonus as part of their clinical duties, but are sometimes retained to assist discharged patients to regain custody of their own funds. When patients recognise their own incapacity and agree on some designated person to be awarded power of attorney on their behalf, the matter can be undertaken by their solicitor in a simple procedure, laid down by the Powers of Attorney Act 1971 and Enduring Powers of Attorney Act 1985. An alternative process is the use of an Appointee, referred to as 'The Poor Man's Court of Protection' and appointed under Regulation 26 of the Social Services (Claims and Payments) Regulations 1981. The Appointee is authorised to collect all moneys payable to the Social Services beneficiary. It is only when the allegedly incompetent person fails to recognise the need for, or to agree to, the transfer of financial power, and is of sufficient financial standing to justify a judicial process, that the powers of the Court of Protection are invoked. Usually it is relatives or others with vested financial interests who initiate the proceedings as soon as they become concerned that the patient's behaviour could be detrimental to their 'expectations', since it is the heirs and successors to the estate who might have their rights jeopardised. Normally such disputes would go to the High Court, but where there is a prima facie case for the compulsory appointment of an independent trustee, the Court of Protection becomes involved.

Mental incompetency

Assessing mental competency is one of the major activities for some psychologists, and extends beyond the Court of Protection. It is the only problem which to date has brought the psychologist into the courts which administer the law of trusts. Competency problems of this sort fall into one of three categories:

1   Levels of incompetency which remain relatively constant, generally due to poor intellectual endowment, but sometimes occurring in states of relatively non-progressive cognitive impairment due to brain damage, or a chronic stage of psychosis. This type of case generally comes to court only where the estate is of some substance.
2   Levels of incompetency which can be predicted to decline with time and whose restoration is beyond the ability of contemporary medicine. These cases involve mental deterioration, which can arise from senile and presenile dementia.

3   Transitory levels of incompetency which may fluctuate or improve with
     time, often associated with psychotic episodes, but which may involve toxic
     conditions produced by industrial chemicals.

The first two categories have fairly clear-cut requirements. It is the third category
which causes some special difficulty; it is not feasible for the court to consider
changes in the short term, for the time lag in hearing cases may be much longer
than the interval of lucidity. In psychiatric patients both spontaneous remission
as well as unpredicted relapses are known to occur, and the policy has been to
continue the legal status quo in those cases which pursue a cyclic or recurrent
course of mental disability. However well the patient may have recovered from a
mental disorder, it would be an act of unjustifiable temerity for a psychologist to
swear on oath that this state of mind will continue into the foreseeable future.
Where industrial toxins have been indicted and the patient is no longer in
contact with them, the situation is, of course, different.

While the psychologist may be expected to provide the traditional clinical
assessment to support the medical evidence of mental disability or otherwise,
patients who are struggling to free themselves from the Court of Protection need
in addition evidence which is essentially practical. What the court requires here
is clear and unambiguous evidence that the appellant is actually capable of
handling his or her own affairs. Obviously, some formal assessment must be
made, for the patient concerned may have some disorder in which mental deterioration could be expected and whose present condition belies his premorbid
occupational status or educational level. Older medical records labelled
'dementia praecox' imply this decline, while younger patients in a brief but
deceptive remission often have case notes referring to one of the progressive
cerebral diseases, so the antecedents of the case deserve careful study, and
psychometric data obtained in earlier days can be repeated and prove valuable in
plotting any possible deterioration.

The court, however, will not be impressed by anything as simple as an IQ score.
The courts have seen enough defendants of below average intelligence who nevertheless run thriving businesses as well as academically bright bankrupts completely
lacking in business acumen. What the court really requires is evidence which
demonstrates in a practical way that appellants understand the nature and value of
their property and income. The court will be interested also in the ability of the
patient to handle day-to-day financial transactions, such as checking the change
after buying a paper, or crossing a cheque when drawing one.

The Court of Protection acts as a kind of public trustee: it accepts legal
responsibility for every item of the estate; when it surrenders control back into
the hands of the patient, it becomes accountable for any later loss in value due to
unreasonable disposal of funds or property by the patient who owns the estate.
The court is therefore unwilling to relinquish its responsibility until absolutely
convinced that the owner is *compos mentis* and capable of administering the
property and finances in a prudent manner.

Forensic psychology has clarified the relevant evidence enormously. The psychologist can not only provide an acceptably accurate assessment of relevant cognitive efficiency, as described by Grisso (1986a), but can describe in quantitative terms and with first-hand personal experience the patient's practical ability in everyday shopping and in handling documents. There has been an increasing demand for forensic psychological advice since the change from in-patient care, where the spending patterns of the psychiatric patient could be closely monitored and influenced by nursing supervision, to community care in which the patient is free to waste personal assets and is vulnerable to the influence of fellow patients sharing supervised accommodation. An even greater risk comes from predatory individuals offering fraudulent advice for their own financial advantage whose success against even mentally competent citizens appears weekly in the crime columns of local papers.

Assessing competence to handle own affairs

The assessment is generally carried out in three phases. First, a diagnostic assessment is necessary to ascertain the cause of the alleged incompetency. This enables the psychologist to predict whether the condition is likely to improve, continue as it is, or decline in the foreseeable future. In the second phase, cognitive testing will enable the patient's intellectual functioning to be evaluated. This should be both in terms of overall level, where reference to the earning power at various IQ levels shown in Table 8.1 will prove helpful, but especially in terms of quality and consistency, as shown by WAIS sub-test scatter, for example.

The third phase, from the legal point of view, is the most important. This consists of a practical evaluation of financial competence. One helpful way of starting this part of the assessment uses one of the formal checklists published for this purpose or by following the guidance provided by such authors as Grisso (1986a), Culver and Gert (1990) and Freedman et al. (1991). Mental competence in civil law is essentially concerned with financial acumen and with knowledge and understanding of possessions. In contrast, competence in criminal law is concerned with accused persons' ability to distinguish right from wrong and to form an unlawful intent, as well as a clear knowledge of their actions at the time of the offence, and the ability to explain the circumstances to their legal advisors and to understand their advice. Another way of looking at this difference is to consider that in criminal law competence is mainly of retrospective importance (with the exception of fitness to plead and stand trial issues), whereas in civil law it is of prospective importance.

Bespoke assessment

Following the use of one or more of the published guidelines, a made-to-measure test of *valuation* can be administered, based on items familiar to the patient, and if possible including some of his own possessions, provided their value can be independently determined. If the patient owns a house or a car, their market value can be readily obtained. Antiques, objets d'art, and pictures should be excluded, for only collectors and connoisseurs can estimate current values within a reasonable bandwidth. Discrepancies are quantifiable, and can be given standard deviation scores by reference to norms easily obtained by local small-group sampling. It is customary to find significant differences between those who, despite over- or under-pricing, are nevertheless not altogether unrealistic in their valuation, and those whose valuations bear little regard to reality. In the latter case it is not uncommon to find simple items like a hammer or cheese grater valued at a higher sum than an armchair or a bicycle. It is instructive to list the items in ordinal order of the patient's valuation and correlate these with the mean valuations of the normative group. The resulting rank-order correlation co-efficient can then be tested for significance, adding quantitatively to the basis for an opinion which can be proffered to the court with a satisfying degree of confidence.

By this time, the psychologist has data on how well the patient comprehends his or her personal and social situation, the composition of family and their possible financial dependency, the extent of personal possessions and a reasonable idea of their value, the source and amount of existing and anticipated income, and a workable framework for knowing how much to pay for common domestic and personal goods likely to be purchased in future. At this stage the psychologist should be able to make a provisional judgment on whether or not the patient is safe to be given complete and unsupervised control of his or her affairs. A useful criterion is to ask oneself whether one would trust the patient with a shopping list and one's own money, and expect to receive goods shrewdly bought and of satisfactory quality.

The accuracy of one's judgment is confirmed from the next stage of the assessment. Patients discussing their financial matters in the consulting room is one thing, handling finances in practice is another. Accordingly, courts have signified their appreciation of the critical evidence provided by the forensic psychologist which demonstrates this latter ability. In dealing with this type of case, one of us (Haward) regularly went shopping with the patients concerned, either to a general store or hospital shop at a slack period, arranging for the patient to tender currency which required the receipt of change in coinage, and paying for each commodity separately. Prior briefing with the retailer enables the change to be given in two parts with a short delay between them. Despite prior warning to patients to check change conscientiously, it is common to find them accepting the first part of the change and turning away to look at other goods on their shopping list, and the percentage loss by this behaviour can be calculated and provides a very practical and meaningful figure when their financial competence is being assessed. There are many variations for this technique, and an hour's practical shopping provides data which are valid and more closely relevant to the issue at hand than the same time devoted to standard psychometric testing in the consulting room.

The final report will thus contain quantitative information on both testamentary capacity and the client's financial acumen in everyday affairs, together with the psychologist's opinion on how this compares with those of the ordinary citizen. The psychologist's qualitative appraisal is particularly important, because while the numerical data show the discrepancy between the patient's financial competence and the ideal, the court will also want to know how the former compares with the patients' assumed premorbid competence, judged by that of their peers. Many people pocket their change without checking it, and it would be unrealistic to require the patient in chancery to meet a significantly higher standard than normal.

Law of probate

Probate was originally administered under canon law but was transferred to its own Court of Probate in 1857. In 1971 probate disputes were transferred to the High Court, contentious cases going to the Chancery Division and non-contentious cases going to the Family Division. As with mental competence discussed above, psychologists are occasionally involved in providing evidence for probate, usually in respect of patients they have already seen for assessment. Disputes occur among relatives concerning the disposal of the deceased's estate, however modest, and the validity of the will is frequently questioned. The law recognises only two reasons for interfering with the dispositions of a will, namely 'undue influence' by persons close to the deceased, and 'mental incompetence', both of which may concern the psychologist. Situations where a nurse or carer benefits unduly from a patient's will are not uncommon, and clinical psychologists have been asked to interview staff and patients and report their findings on this issue. Companions or housekeepers with the sole responsibility for looking after an elderly and infirm individual sometimes receive the entire estate, including the house, causing the natural heirs and successors, often noticeably absent from the scene until then, to oppose probate. In such cases, the beneficiary may well have earned the bequest, but the circumstances demand investigation. Perr (1981) discusses the problem of undue influence, which by law must be not automatically presumed, but which must be considered in cases of long-term care or dependency upon the beneficiary (Howe's case, 1909).

However, mental capacity is the central issue in most cases of contested wills, and is regarded somewhat differently from the legal, as opposed to the medical, point of view (Grainger, 1991). The Beaney's case (1978) established the current legal view, and Edmunds (1993) discusses the psychiatric viewpoint. It was sadly ironic that one of our leading forensic pathologists, who has contributed so much to both legal and medical aspects of competency should himself have been the subject of such a dispute, due to a malignant brain tumour (Simpson v. Simpson, 1992). This case was important in establishing the principle that the level of competency required should be proportional to the percentage of assets being transferred.

139

In the early postwar days, most new admissions to hospital received a psychological assessment, and psychologists were expected to undertake a regular ward round. Deterioration Scales, such as the Shipley-Hartford (Shipley, 1940) were routinely used in the psychogeriatric wards, so that a continuous record of this aspect of mental competence was available. This made it possible to make a reasonable retrospective assessment of testamentary capacity. The profession's move away from routine psychometric assessment has removed this useful source of quantified data, and the psychologist now has to make his retrospective assessment by other means, usually by a controlled interview with nurses or carers, using appropriate items from the mental state examination to elicit subjective statements from those in daily contact with the deceased. Evaluating mental impairment in the elderly is made difficult because while mental test scores separate the mentally confused from the normal aged, they do not differentiate the confused from the demented (Hodgkinson, 1973).

The situation is much easier when the question of testamentary capacity arises at the time of making the will. Redmond (1987) and Spar and Garb (1992) provide a psychiatric approach to the assessment which provides a useful background to the psychologist's more quantitative approach. The legal requirements to establish testamentary capacity are that testators:

1 Know and understand that their own will is being prepared at that time.
2 Know the nature and extent of their estate in terms or real and personal property, goods and chattels.
3 Know who are their natural heirs and successors. (Even if they are to be excluded, the testator should know who might *reasonably* expect to inherit a bequest, in the order of a) family, b) close friends, c) business associates, d) servants, other carers.)
4 Understand the *effects* of their dispositions. (They should also appreciate the consequences, at least within the family, of members being excluded.)

Coroner's Court

The office of coroner was instituted in 1194 by Richard I to collect extraneous revenue from wrecks, royal fish, treasure trove and fines from the Saxons of all Hundreds where a Norman died unexpectedly. Wrecks are now dealt with in the Admiralty Division of the High Court, royal fish are no longer claimed by the crown, and only treasure trove and sudden death remain within the province of the coroner (the name means crown officer). There is no coroner in Scottish law, enquiries into sudden death being undertaken by the Sheriff. In English law the jurisdiction and procedure are laid down by the Coroners Acts 1887 and 1954. The coroner may convene an inquest into any death, but is obliged to do so in cases of violent death by murder, manslaughter, infanticide, death in prison, transportation accidents or notifiable diseases or from an unknown cause. Some inquests may be held without a jury, but a jury of seven persons is required in cases of suspected homicide, infanticide or road traffic accidents. The coroner can no longer indict a named person for a criminal offence, but states the cause of death. When the evidence is insufficient to establish the cause of death, for example when the circumstances make it impossible to distinguish between accident or suicide, the verdict is left 'open'.

The inquest is essentially a fact-finding rather than a blame-apportioning procedure, and is intended to be inquisitorial. In recent years, relatives of the deceased often seek to make someone responsible for the death of the victim in order to secure compensation, and use legal representatives to appear in the Coroner's Court on their behalf: this has the effect of creating an adversarial conflict which appears to be taking over the former non-adversarial enquiry.

Some clinicians will already have had some experience of the Coroner's Court, when patients under their care have died suddenly, and the question of death by suicide or misadventure is raised. According to Barker *et al.* (1993), suicide is the most likely source of contention in the Coroner's Court, despite the succession of High Court judgments which make it clear that only the most unequivocal evidence should support a verdict of suicide, which has a negative social connotation and may nullify any life insurance claim by executors to the victim's estate. Goldstein (1987) questions whether psychiatrists do not exceed the limits of their scientific expertise in determining suicide but there is no doubt that the evidence of the psychologist in supporting medical opinion has often proved helpful.

Suicide is one of the major causes of death, there being approximately ninety per week in the UK and nearly 600 per week in the USA. The incidence of suicide in the UK has almost rivalled that of road traffic deaths for the past thirty years (Hays, 1964; Registrar-General's Mortality Statistics, 1994) and is six times greater than the homicide rate. Since over 800 deaths per annum have an undetermined cause, and many suicides are believed to receive an accidental death verdict, the true incidence of suicide is believed to be significantly greater than the official figures suggest. Christian ethics regard suicide as a sin and under canon law the body was refused Christian burial. As social attitudes changed, the former strictures of canon law relating to suicide disappeared and gave way to the common law crime of suicide. Since an attempt to commit a crime is also a crime in its own right, attempted suicide also became a crime, but in the context of the postwar Welfare State, the criminal proceedings against persons whose attempted suicide had failed were seen as an obstacle to their subsequent treatment, and the crimes of both suicide itself and attempts to commit it were abolished by the Suicide Act 1961. Nevertheless, case precedents make it explicit that society does not approve of suicide, and to discourage suicide Section 2 of the Suicide Act makes it an offence to assist another person to commit suicide by aiding, abetting, counselling or procuring the suicide or its attempt by another. In England and Wales there were thirty-one convictions in the decade 1982–1991. The questions of whether allowing terminally ill patients to refuse treatment, or Jehovah's Witnesses to refuse life-saving blood-transfusions, or failing to force-feed prisoners who go on hunger strike (all arguments with a psychological component), are forms of encouraging suicide have been raised in a number of cases in the criminal courts. Institutional suicide still occurs in the prison service at some sixty per annum (Crighton and Towl, 1997) creating a problem with which the prison psychologists are concerned (Towl, 1996).

Suicide pacts

Since it is still a criminal offence to encourage another person to commit suicide, suicide pacts involving two persons may lead to prosecution of the one who may survive the joint attempt. A survey (Cohen, 1961) found that the national incidence of suicide pacts is approximately one per cent of all suicides, but a more recent study in South Hampshire found an incidence of 2.5 per cent (Brown et al. 1995), although the two populations are not strictly comparable. When both parties survive a suicide pact, due to incompetency in method or some fortuitous intervention, both generally take the blame for initiating the event, making it difficult to determine which was the offender. In these circumstances a note written in anticipation of a successful suicide may help to identify the offender. A sole survivor is often the prime suspect, but the converse is known. Notes in such cases are less common than in single suicides, and the value of the psychological autopsy is then manifest. Multiple suicides, which have occasionally occurred under some form of religious influence, form a psychological study of their own, as do those who immolate themselves for political purpose.

Para-suicide

Para-suicide is a pseudo-attempt in which there is no intention to end life, and is usually construed as a cry for help, or as manipulative behaviour in a difficult relationship. It needs to be distinguished from a genuine, if abortive, intention. The pseudo-suicide may claim the attempt was genuine, but any suicide note left behind usually betrays the true intention of the writer. In one study, 65 per cent of female maximum security hospital patients who had suffered self-harm, later admitted that their intention had been to kill themselves (Liebling et al. 1997). A general psychological assessment is necessary if the individual is to be offered appropriate help, but differentiation between true and para-suicidal intent is not easy, especially as most para-suicidees show both severe depression and suicidal ideation (Beck and Steer, 1987, 1991).

Hawton and Catalan (1982) published a useful *Six-point Post-suicidal Attempt Assessment*, the abridged features of which are:

1 explanation (reason, goals, precipitating event);
2 degree of real suicidal intent;

3   present suicidal risk;
4   existing problems (both acute and chronic);
5   psychiatric status, relevance and diagnosis;
6   appropriate help available and its acceptability.

These authors also provide a list of suicidal risk factors (item 3 above) consisting of:

a   problems with alcohol;
b   anti-social personality;
c   previous psychiatric inpatient residence;
d   previously a psychiatric outpatient;
e   previously made a suicidal/para-suicidal attempt;
f   living alone.

Para-suicide, as well as some auto-erotic practices, can sometimes go wrong and lead to accidental death which has all the hallmarks of a true suicide. In para-suicide, any note left behind for effect becomes important evidence in teasing out the true intention. This is more than of academic importance, because a coroner's verdict of suicide is likely to invalidate any life insurance taken out by the victim, and the surviving family members may suffer substantial financial loss as a result. Other consequences are less tangible but may affect the family more immediately, such as feelings of shame or guilt, or loss of esteem in the neighbourhood. Conversely many genuine suicidal attempts fail for various reasons, and the attempter is likely to deny a true intention out of shame.

Canon law

Canon law is administered in the Ecclesiastic Courts, which were unknown in Britain until after AD 1066 when William I separated secular and ecclesiastic jurisdiction. The church courts had wide powers including the burning of witches and heretics, and the imprisonment of parishioners for moral offences. Until the Justices of the Peace Act 1361 under Edward I, law and order among the common people was mainly and effectively in the hands of the parish priest, but the church courts had declined in influence by the turn of the seventeenth century and in the nineteenth century many historic ecclesiastic courts, such as those of the Prince-Bishops, were abolished, and their jurisdiction transferred to secular courts. Disputes over wills went to the Court of Probate, and matrimonial disputes to the Divorce Court. Some other ecclesiastic offences, such as defamation, became civil offences and were transferred to the High Court, while certain other offences, such as brawling in the churchyard, became crimes and the province of the magistracy.

Nevertheless, this still left canon law to deal with a wide range of offences of both clergy and laity, which remained virtually unchanged until reformed by the

Ecclesiastical Jurisdiction Measure 1963. This Act swept away a host of canonical offences, some of which had existed from Anglo-Saxon times, and canon law today is only a minute remnant of an all-pervasive legislation that originally penetrated every aspect of social and family life.

The Established Church of England now has only four permanent ecclesiastical courts. These are the Diocesan Court, the appellate courts of the two Archbishops, the Court of Ecclesiastical Causes Reserved (which deals with offences relating to church ceremonial, doctrine or ritual), and the Queen in Council, who, as the 'Fountain of All Justice' is, in theory at least, the ultimate appellate authority for all British courts. Psychologists, when providing evidence in ecclesiastical cases, have so far as is known, been restricted to the Diocesan Courts, sometimes referred to as the Consistory Court. This court is conducted similarly to High Court proceedings, and follows the rules of the Civil Evidence Act. The Chancellor hearing the case has similar powers to a High Court judge, and can sub-poena witnesses, enforce the production of documents, impose sanctions for contempt of court, and make orders for costs. The expenses for expert and lay witnesses are also taxed in the same manner as in the High Court, but by tradition, the court receives evidence primarily in the form of affidavits. Psychologists may be asked to tender their report in this form. More commonly, they are asked to provide a report at the preliminary inquiry, held by the bishop. Except in serious cases where criminal proceedings are also involved, the bishop will take appropriate action without invoking formal court proceedings.

By far the most frequent cause of complaint referred to the psychologist is sexual behaviour of varying degrees of seriousness, either involving parishioners or members of the choir, the juvenile participants of which are particularly vulnerable to exploitation in a religious setting. Some of these cases receive media attention and prosecution may follow, but many minor cases do not come within the criminal law, although still proscribed by canon law, and can thus be handled directly and more discreetly by the church. It is important to understand that canon law concerns *moral offences*, not civil or criminal ones, although there exists some overlap with both.

If a psychological opinion is thought to be helpful, psychologists who are regular church attenders and on the parochial register, will probably be the first choice, since their familiarity with both the normal behavioural requirements of conducting services and the settings in which they occur can be taken for granted. In other cases, the psychologist may come to the notice of the church authorities by virtue of his professional relationship with clergy possessing psychological problems. Erring clerics who realise that their chosen career is at stake, may call in a solicitor to help them, and some referrals reach the psychologist in this way. With the establishment of residential centres to help erring clergy, in which staff psychologists play a prominent role, both in the UK and North America, there is a growing tendency by senior clergy to by-pass formal proceedings and direct suitable miscreants to these centres for treatment and penance. Camargo (1997), for example. illustrates the magnitude of the problem in his retrospective analysis of 1,322 male clergy referred to one centre in Canada.

Courts convened under the Benefices Act 1898, the Pastoral Measures Act 1968, the Ecclesiastical Jurisdiction Measure 1963, and the Court of Faculties, are unlikely to need a contribution from forensic psychology.

It will be apparent that ecclesiastical offences which concern the psychologist form only a small part of canon law, although in terms of frequency of occurrence they are perhaps the most significant. Such offences as conduct unbecoming to a clerk in Holy Orders, neglect of pastoral duty, dishonesty, disorderly behaviour (usually arising from participation in public protests), immoral behaviour (including participation in divorce proceedings as co-respondent), adultery, receipt of affiliation or matrimonial orders, desertion and wilful neglect of wife or child appear to be increasing, although most cases are dealt with informally and do not go on record. In contrast, some of the older offences, such as *simony* (the trafficking in spiritual benefits for money) seem to have disappeared.

Administrative law

Administrative law is created by statute and governs the organisation, administration and powers of central and local government, the civil service, and those co-opted to serve its purposes. The modern administrative state is essentially a twentieth-century product, especially of the postwar Welfare State, although late Victorian times saw the introduction of such treasury-funded officials as the state schoolteacher, the postman, the factory inspector and the tax collector. Under the aegis of administrative law, two forms of proceedings have been introduced to protect citizens against the abuse of power by the government and its delegated bodies, and to provide a simpler, speedier, cheaper and more accessible justice for them. The two proceedings are the administrative tribunal and the statutory inquiry, respectively.

Administrative tribunals

Each tribunal is created and empowered by an Act of Parliament dealing with the subject to which the tribunal refers. Thus the Mental Health Review Tribunals were created by the Mental Health Act 1959, Section 3; the Industrial Tribunals by the Employment Protection (Consolidation) Act 1978, Section 128; the National Health Service Tribunals by the National Health Service Act 1977, Section 46, and so on. There are approximately 2,100 administrative tribunals at present, from the Agricultural Land Tribunal to the Wireless Telegraphy Tribunal. Many of these tribunals are extremely active: those dealing with supplementary benefits from the social services handle over 45,000 appeals per annum, and valuation courts run a close second with over 40,000 appeals each year. The tribunals are politically independent, and usually consist of a legal chairman aided by two experienced lay persons with opposing interests, and the applicant has right of appeal to the High Court. For many tribunals a psychological input would be irrelevant, and space allows mention of only a few in which psychologists have been involved with some frequency.

Mental Health Review Tribunals (MHRTs)

The MHRTs were established to protect patients from abuse of medical powers, and have been mainly concerned with compulsory hospital admission, which was introduced to obtain an opportunity for observation, treatment and the physical protection of the patient and others. Gostin *et al.* (1984) give a detailed account of the tribunal procedure, which is administered by a lawyer as chairman, a medical practitioner and a lay person. The dissolution of the county mental hospitals with their closed wards has significantly depleted the facilities for compulsory admission, and whereas clinical psychologists were regularly assessing patients on appeal at a rate of 1,000 each year nationwide, today the psychological input appears to be largely confined to psychologists working in special hospitals and in regional secure units. In the USA, where hospitalisation has been generally more restrictive for those unable to afford private facilities, release is normally obtained, where appropriate, by a writ of *habeas corpus* in a judicial proceeding rather than a tribunal.

The value of psychological input in appeals against compulsory detention is that it approaches the problem from abnormal psychology, that is, as a deviation from normal behaviour, rather than from the disease model adopted by hospital authorities and psychiatrists. One other advantage that the psychologist's nomothetic model has over the psychiatric disease model, is that the focus of the judgment then centres upon the actual evidence upon which the risk to the patient or to society is based. Diagnosis then becomes of secondary importance in predicting such issues as dangerousness or self-harm, which may be validated more by the history of previous similar behaviour than by the diagnostic label attached to the patient.

Disciplinary tribunals

The General Medical Council (GMC), established under the Medical Act 1858, was one of the earliest of professional disciplinary tribunals, being independent of the British Medical Association and answerable only to the Privy Council, its appellate court. It can put medical practitioners 'on trial', and suspend or cancel their licence to practise and hence abolish a career in their chosen profession. Other disciplinary committees include the Bar Council controlling the professional conduct of barristers, the General Dental Council, the General Nursing Council, the Central Midwives Board, as well as the disciplinary committees of other chartered professions such as accountants, surveyors and opticians.

The British Psychological Society created its own ethical committee under Professor F.V. Smith in the early 1950s, which has developed into a disciplinary committee to take an active role in controlling the conduct of its members. It has an investigatory committee to evaluate the allegations of professional misconduct made against members (127 in 1966, many of these against non-members, but up 24.5 per cent on 1995 figures). After screening by an investigatory panel and dealing with minor breaches of society guidelines, only a few cases each year are serious enough to be referred to the Disciplinary Board itself and receive either suspension for up to two years or expulsion from the society.

Most trade unions have their own disciplinary committee, but have lost much of their earlier significance. Many health authorities have disciplinary committees to deal with their own staff, and psychologists are usually involved when psychological factors, including stress at work or home is cited as a causal explanation or in mitigation. Many disciplinary committees provide for appeal to the High Court, and it is at the appellate stage that forensic psychologists will be more formally involved.

General Medical Council

Because of the special nature of medicine, appeals from its disciplinary committee go direct to the Judicial Committee of the Privy Council, which also deals with appeals from courts in the British colonies, and psychological evidence has also been given before this committee. Most misconduct by medical practitioners is of a type for which the services of a psychiatrist rather than a psychologist is preferred, if only to keep the proceedings within the same profession, but in cases of acute alcoholism or drug addiction, especially in general practice where the partners want the afflicted physician removed, the clinical psychologist is generally called in to provide quantitative data of the alleged professional incompetence. Cognitive testing, especially using neuropsychological assessment, sometimes betrays the residual impairment brought about by the substance abuse, but frequently the test data obtained from a subject when cold sober or drug-free bears little relation to those obtained when drunk or in a drug-induced state, a condition in which the psychologist rarely has the opportunity of making a psychometric assessment. The resulting report is open to misuse by the appellant's legal representative unless this caveat is made explicit in the report itself.

In recent years, government economies have discouraged tribunals from calling expert evidence unless regarded as essential to an equitable decision. As a result, psychologists who do appear to give evidence in quasi-judicial courts, are more frequently there as employees of the organisation concerned, speaking either for a staff member on the one hand, or the employing authority on the other. Examples of the latter would be a clinical psychologist representing a health trust, an educational psychologist a local education committee, an occupational psychologist a factory management, or psychologist-councillor the district council.

Industrial tribunals

A major appellate function of Industrial Tribunals is the hearing of appeals against unfair dismissal. While there are many causes of dismissal, many follow allegations of theft or fraud. Where such offences involve significant amounts, or are accompanied by evidence of conspiracy to steal or defraud, or form part of a regular ongoing pattern, the commission of the offence is generally provable, and the justification for instant dismissal substantiated, although for various reasons a formal charge is not always laid against the accused to secure prosecution. Sometimes dismissal occurs for latent reasons, using theft as the excuse, and really being a strict interpretation of what are generally considered to be perquisites or 'perks' such as using office stationery for personal use. Psychologists can usually demonstrate by observation and enquiry that such conduct is within the norm for a particular company, and that to dismiss one offender without dismissing the other offenders is inequitable, and this ploy has proved successful. In other cases, some member of staff becomes suspect without sound evidence of guilt, but may be asked to resign as an alternative to prosecution.

Statutory inquiries

The second quasi-judicial procedure under administrative law is the statutory inquiry. There are two forms, prospective inquiries, which are usually planning inquiries, and retrospective inquiries, which are usually accident inquiries. The statutory inquiry, like the administrative tribunal, is basically a product of the Welfare State during the past half century.

Tribunal and inquiry are both empowered by statute and regulated by administrative law, Both have a primary fact-finding function, and both receive evidence whose admissibility is discretionary, although when the chairman is a qualified lawyer, the admissibility generally conforms to the Civil Evidence Act.

The differences are more important. The tribunal is independent, and completely free from political interference: the inquiry goes before a minister who has power to ignore it, suppress it, or postpone its publication until a more politically propitious moment. The tribunal reaches a decision and acts upon it immediately, and has power to enforce it: the inquiry can only make recommendations to the minister concerned, but has no power to force its adoption, even in part. The tribunal sits with politically independent members: the inquiry with nominated civil servants. The tribunal has consistent rules of procedure: the inquiries vary considerably between themselves. All tribunals have the right of appeal: some inquiries have no right of appeal. In the USA, statutory inquiries are created under the Administrative Procedures Act 1946 and are based on a significantly different policy from the UK inquiry; in the USA statutory inquiry,

'He who hears, decides'. This decision-making policy of the American inquiry therefore makes it more equivalent to the UK tribunal than to the UK inquiry. It differs, too, in its more formal and consistent procedure.

Prospective statutory inquiries

The very first prospective statutory inquiry is said to be the national survey ordered by William I in the eleventh century for which the Domesday Book was the final report, and there have been a number of historical examples since then. Modern statutory inquiries are used to seek public reaction and guidance before carrying out some major change, such as constructing a new road system or large-scale building, or the introduction of legislation which would have a major impact upon a particular workforce, such as the fishing industry. In this type of inquiry, the social and experimental psychologist is in demand, and treasury-funded grants are made available for special psychosociological studies to assess the impact of the proposed change upon the communities likely to be affected by it. Such activities are generally carried out by university staff, often supported by postgraduate research students. However, independent psychologists are often in demand in more local issues, as in the appeal against a property developer who wanted to build a funeral parlour in a retirement village.

Probably the equivalent of a statutory inquiry which employed the greatest number of psychologists was the US Presidential Commission on Obscenity and Pornography, requested by Congress and created pursuant to Public Law 90–100, Section 5(b) in 1967, in anticipation of changes in the law regarding the control and possible censorship of sexual material and activities. Psychological research spread over two years was funded at a cost said to be 'millions of dollars' (Barnes,1970) and involved the staff of innumerable psychology departments nationwide. The resulting report ran to 700 pages, much of it in twenty-point font, and supported by ten volumes of scientific research reports.

Retrospective statutory inquiries

The inquiries described above were created in anticipation of legislative activity. In contrast, retrospective inquiries are held into events which arouse public concern and create demands for government action to prevent their reoccurrence. In some cases there is a need to attach responsibility on to some causal agent, whether company or individual. Statutory inquiries looking retrospectively at past events are of two kinds; the most common are those concerned with major transportation accidents and other disasters, such as that at Aberfan; the other kind looks into certain activities of the legislature or executive which have aroused public concern and media attention of such magnitude that verbal reassurances are no longer sufficient to placate the electorate. The Tribunal of Inquiry (Evidence) Act 1921 was legislated to allay public disquiet of this kind, and provided the powers of the High Court for this purpose. Statutory inquiries of this type have included government leaks likely to endanger the security of the realm, gifts to members of parliament, armament supplies to Iraq, and police brutality, and at the time of writing there is a call for an inquiry into the Gulf War syndrome.

Homicide inquiries

In 1994 the Department of Health made it mandatory in England and Wales for a public inquiry to be set up after a homicide committed by a mentally disordered person who had recently received psychiatric or social care (Department of Health, 1994a). Prior to that date there were some homicide inquiries, but they were not mandatory and only occurred in selected cases. The purpose of the inquiry is to establish what lessons can be learned from the homicide (i.e., to identify relevant deficiencies) and to make recommendations about improved service care in order to prevent a similar incident happening in future. A homicide inquiry therefore does not take over the function of the coroner, who attempts to establish the *cause* of death as opposed to the lessons that can be learned from the incident.

The effectiveness of homicide inquiries in reducing the likelihood of future homicides by psychiatric patients is much in dispute (Peay, 1996). One major problem is that there is no follow-up to the recommendations made by the inquiry team, they are very expensive for the health authority concerned, and appear to provide the incentive to find a scapegoat to blame for the tragedy.

Homicide inquiries can be conducted either in public or private, but in either case the findings are made public in some form, usually in a published report. Recent reviews have been conducted into the findings of homicide inquires on behalf of the Zito Trust (Sheppard, 1995, 1996). These reviews, titled *Learning the Lessons*, made a number of recommendations from inquiries into services after patients' deaths and other violent incidents involving mentally disordered patients. The reviews have recently been criticised by Petch and Bradley (1997), who have provided their own recommendations for practitioners and researchers. One recommendation is the need for meaningful research into the relationship between service provisions and patient violence.

Another related development in the early 1990s was the establishment of supervision registers in England and Wales for psychiatric patients who were being treated in the community (Department of Health, 1994b). The aim of the register was for the patient's consultant psychiatrist to identify and register three main 'risk groups', that is, where there was a significant risk of suicide, risk to others, or risk of severe self-neglect. In spite of considerable opposition from some mental health professionals the government has gone ahead with implementing the supervision register (Cohen *et al.* 1996; Baker, 1997).

Members of the Royal College of Psychiatrists feel sufficiently strongly about supervision registers and homicide inquiries to recommend 'Abandoning ineffective policies such as supervision registers and mandatory enquiries' (Royal College of Psychiatrists, 1997, p. 1).

Accident inquiries

The transportation accident inquiries differ considerably according to the type of transport involved. Shipping accidents are formal sittings under the Wreck Commissioner as judge, and have the rights to call witnesses, to cross-examine them, and to appeal to the High Court. In contrast, railway accident inquiries have no rules of procedure, no rights to a legal representative or to cross-examine witnesses, and no right of appeal. Although the Secretary of State is empowered to order a formal inquiry before a County Court judge, this has only happened on two occasions – the Tay Bridge disaster in 1879 and the Hixon Level Crossing disaster in 1968.

Airliner accidents have yet a different procedure, coming under the control of the Attorney General. The Commissioner is always an experienced senior barrister, and is supported by two highly qualified assessors from the aviation industry, all being appointed by the Lord Chancellor.

As with the planning inquiries, psychologists are frequently involved in accident inquiries. The King's Cross fire disaster led to major research for the inquiry at Surrey University's psychology department, and one of the present writers (Haward) has conducted research in a number of aircraft accidents, both into attitudes towards fire risk, as well as using the psychological postmortem technique to elucidate the pre-accident behaviour of the deceased pilot.

Conclusions

Civil actions occupy much of the forensic psychologist's time, and for some psychologists prove to be the most satisfying. They pose to some psychologists a much wider range of interesting questions than criminal cases, avoid the more sordid aspects of the criminal world, and proceed on a much longer time scale that enables preparatory work and court appearances to be more conveniently fitted in with routine commitments. While laboratory and field experimentation is sometimes a necessary feature of both criminal and civil problems, in the former there is usually insufficient time to undertake the more elaborate experiments that can produce important data used as evidence in civil actions.

Psychologists undertaking forensic work privately should note that solicitors are not usually prepared to pay for expenses incurred in experimental work, other than modest sums financed at petty cash level, such as questionnaire printing and distribution. For more ambitious projects a detailed proposal resembling a research grant application has normally been required, together with a fairly convincing argument that the experiment will yield information supporting their client's case.

However, one of us (Haward) has found that much useful forensic research can be completed on a shoestring budget financed out of time-based fees, using extra-mural psychology students and other volunteer participants, and finding local companies particularly generous in providing facilities free of charge. In past cases, these have included a supermarket outside opening hours, a factory workshop, a manual working seam in a coal mine, a general stores and a pier with docking facilities. The most expensive resource to date has been the leasing of an aircraft for an airborne experiment, but even this expense could have been avoided had today's wealth of simulators then been available.

Psychologists will not need reminding that developing valid and reliable psychometric instruments and psychological experimentation are the only two functions unique to their profession, and the bedrock upon which all their other activities should be based. With this in mind, salaried psychologists undertaking forensic work have successfully argued the case for devoting a reasonable proportion of their official time and facilities to this work, on the grounds that such an experience is a valuable enhancement of their professional skills, which require constant practice not always provided in their routine activities. Where fees are involved, some financial arrangement with the employing authority can be made, which may include some provision for paying a proportion of the overheads where facilities, such as laboratory, test material, office space, and secretarial assistance, are involved.

More often perhaps, psychologists prefer to work in their own off-duty time and entirely independent of their institution. Leave days are sometimes taken when attendance at court is protracted, but since staff, such as magistrates, district councillors, school governors, etc., are traditionally allowed authorised absence without penalty for purposes deemed to be of public benefit, there is usually no objection to absences at court, when not too excessive. Forensic psychology is now opening up in the UK as a full-time career (although this raises difficult professional and jurisprudential issues) and many of the present problems concerning fees, allocation of time, and research expenses and facilities will be resolved for those undertaking salaried forensic work. Meanwhile, the development of private incorporated companies of forensic psychology associates is bringing a new perspective into the situation, and the question of research costs and facilities in this setting has yet to be addressed.

Civil law differs from criminal law in many respects. It is administered in different courts, many having different procedures. The evidence is regulated by different statutes, with different levels of proof and admissibility. The requirement for juries is different, and out-of-court settlements are the general rule in civil hearings but never in criminal trials (plea-bargaining may take place out of court in some jurisdictions, but the termination of all criminal trials is in the hands of the judge). Criminal courts are hierarchical with ascending appellate functions, while civil hearings have different rights and sources for appeal.

The law of tort covers much of forensic psychology's contribution, which deals with compensation cases. Clinical psychologists provide most of the expertise, but there is also an important role for occupational psychologists to discuss working practices, earning power, etc., and from this speciality has come the IQ-Earnings Table which is sometimes used in recommending compensation levels.

Family law provides the problems which concern child, clinical and educational psychologists alike. Divorce has ceased to be a psychological issue, but child custody is a growing problem, and allegations of child abuse, both physical and sexual, have created a great deal of demand for psychology services.

Maritime law concerns sea-going problems in which forensic psychology has played an infrequent but significant part. Mercantile law deals with consumer affairs and retail trade problems, in which psychological experimentation has played a rare but useful role since the century began.

The law of equity provides the courts and the remedies for protecting the estates of minors, psychiatric and dementing patients, and those of low intelligence. It also provides remedies for tortious acts which would not otherwise be available under the law of tort itself. The Court of Protection is concerned with mental competence, the assessment of which is explained, and probate, which is dealt with in various courts depending upon the contentious nature of the will in question, has engaged the services of psychologists when testamentary capacity is in question.

The Coroner's Court brings to the psychologist problems of suicide, for which the technique of psychological autopsy is admirably suited. Attempted suicide and para-suicide are psychologically different if behaviourally identical, and carry different levels of risk. Psychological differentiation between the two is an important contribution of the psychologist, and following changes in some hospital admission rules, routine screening may become a new role for the psychologist. Checklists for this purpose are discussed, and these, together with the psychological autopsy, and the psycholinguistic analysis of suicide notes, have enabled the psychologist to make decisive contributions to coroner's enquiries.

Canon law is church law, and today applies only to the clergy of the established church. Psychologists have been involved in providing evidence on the psychological status of erring clerics, and are becoming employed for assessment and treatment in special centres, not unlike forensic psychiatry units in the UK, being set up in Europe and North America for transgressing clergymen.

Administrative law provides great diversity of forensic problems and procedures. It creates by statute both administrative tribunals and statutory inquiries. There are too many of each to be discussed individually. The Mental Health Review Tribunals were the first to employ the services of psychologists, but disciplinary and industrial tribunals of varying sorts now appear to use psychological help more frequently, although incidence figures are difficult to obtain. Statutory inquiries are both prospective, as in planning inquiries, and retrospective, as in inquiries into disasters and homicides. Each form of transport has differing procedures and legal rights. Statutory inquiries are usually overseen by ministers of state or lawyers of high judicial office, such as the Lord Chancellor or Attorney

General, and treasury funding is often available for large-scale psychological research, normally carried out by faculty staff in selected universities. Civil law, with its diversity of interesting problems and procedures and the opportunity for good experimental work by individuals or groups with relevant specialised interests, make it attractive to forensic psychologists. It is more demanding of sound knowledge of psychological theory relevant to the subject matter, professional skills in experimentation, and in the presentation and interpretation of facts and opinion, than in criminal law, where the problems are more limited and experience can be built up more quickly.

9

CRIMINAL CASES

Introduction

Forensic psychologists may find themselves having to present written or oral evidence in a variety of legal settings. As far as courts are concerned, these involve three different jurisdictions, referred to as 'Courts of Civil Jurisdiction', 'Courts of Special Jurisdiction' and 'Courts of Criminal Jurisdiction' (Haward, 1981). The civil courts are discussed in detail in Chapter 8. The Courts of Criminal Jurisdiction are the primary focus in this chapter and will be discussed in some detail.

The Courts of Special Jurisdiction deal with matters which are not manifestly either public or private. These 'administrative' courts include the Coroner's Courts and Mental Health Review Tribunals (see Chapter 9), and Courts Martial. Courts Martial deal with personnel of the armed forces under army, navy or air force law (McPherson, 1990; Lande and Armitage, 1997).

This chapter addresses primarily criminal law in England and Wales. There are historical differences in the ways in which the legal system has developed within the individual countries of the United Kingdom (Barclay, 1995). England and Wales, which are treated together, differ in some salient ways from both Scotland and Northern Ireland. The legal system in Northern Ireland is very similar to that which operates in England and Wales, whereas the Scottish system is very different. The Isle of Man and the Channel Islands also have their own legal systems, which are similar to those in England and Wales.

The legal provisions in other countries, including Scotland, Northern Ireland and the USA, are discussed where appropriate. The textbooks edited by Bluglass and Bowden, *Principles and Practice of Forensic Psychiatry*, and Gunn and Taylor (1993), *Forensic Psychiatry* (1990), provide an excellent background to the relevant legislations in different countries and jurisdictions, which are relevant to forensic psychiatry and psychology. There is an important difference between psychological and psychiatric assessment in that the latter more commonly focuses on the presence or absence of mental disorder, which makes psychiatric reports more dependent on provisions of the Mental Health Act. Those readers who are interested in the Mental Health Act provisions which are available in criminal cases should consult the above mentioned textbooks, as well as the recent book by Montgomery (1997). Stephenson (1992) and Kapardis (1997) provide excellent accounts of the interface between psychology and criminal justice.

It is important to remember that major changes in legislation with regard to the criminal justice system frequently occur and it is difficult for practitioners to keep up with all the changes. The most important changes, as far as criminal case work is concerned, are the Police and Criminal Evidence Act 1984 (Home Office, 1985) and its current Codes of Practice (Home Office, 1995a), the Criminal Justice and Public Disorder Act 1994 (Home Office, 1995b) and the Criminal Procedure and Investigations Act 1996 (Leng and Taylor, 1996).

Courts of criminal jurisdiction

Cases heard in the criminal courts are those considered to be a matter of public interest. They are generally brought against defendants by the Crown Prosecution Service in England and the Procurator Fiscal in Scotland, under the Lord Advocate, who are acting on behalf of the state. Sometimes members of the public may take out private prosecution in criminal cases (Barker *et al.* 1993).

Figure 9.1 gives a brief graphic illustration of the legal system in England and Wales as far as criminal cases are concerned (there is a separate figure in Chapter 8 concerning civil cases and the administrative courts). As far as the criminal courts are concerned, the lowest court is the Magistrates' Court, which consists of two criminal subdivisions, the 'adult court'and the 'youth court' (a family court and a 'coroner's court' are also housed within the Magistrates' Court, but these fall under a civil and special jurisdiction, respectively – see Chapter 8).

Appeals against conviction or sentence in the Magistrates' Court are heard in the Crown Court, where a judge sits with two lay magistrates to hear the grounds for appeal. Further appeals are heard in the Court of Appeal, which is divided into Civil and Criminal Divisions. Final appeals, which are generally on points of law and of general public importance, are heard in the House of Lords.

In Scotland the Lord Advocate presides over 'Sheriff Courts' and 'District Courts', which are the lower courts, as well as over a 'High Court of Justiciary' (criminal) and 'Court of Session' (civil). There is no appeal to the House of Lords in criminal cases, but there is in civil cases.

All courts in Britain are ultimately subordinate to the European Court, whose decisions are binding on member states.

In England and Wales there are 12 Law Lords, 35 Lord Justices of Appeal, 96 High Court Judges, 557 Circuit Judges, 332 District Judges, 913 Recorders, 348 Assistant Recorders, 87,081 solicitors, 8,935 self-employed barristers, 30,374 unpaid lay magistrates, 89 full-time stipendiary magistrates, and 89 acting stipendiary magistrates (*The Mail on Sunday Review*, 25 May 1997).

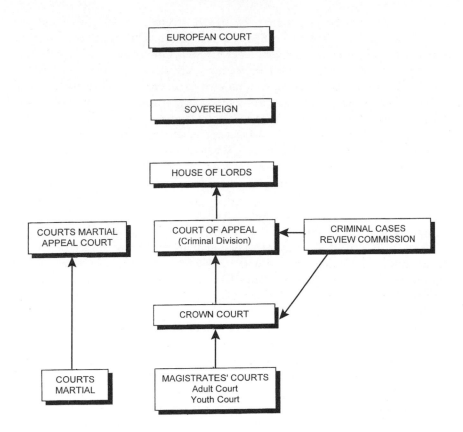

Figure 9.1 The Criminal Courts in England and Wales

Criminal offences in England and Wales are divided into three classes, which are referred to as 'summary', 'indictable' and 'either-way' offences. The specific offences which apply to each of the three groups vary over time and there is a general trend to increase the powers of the Magistrates' Court in order to reduce defendants' right to a jury trial (Lloyd-Bostock, 1996).

Summary offences are the less serious type of offences (e.g., traffic violations) and can only be tried in the Magistrates' Court by either justices of the peace (lay magistrates) or stipendiary magistrates. Lay magistrates are unpaid and work part time. They are not required to have any legal qualifications and are appointed by the Lord Chancellor. They normally sit on the bench in a group of three and this is particularly important in disputed trials, where two magistrates might disagree. Stipendiary magistrates are full-time, salaried magistrates and sit alone. They are qualified and experienced lawyers (i.e., either solicitors or barristers) and tend to preside over the longer and more difficult cases. Some Magistrates' Courts do not have any stipendiary magistrates and all cases are presided over by lay magistrates.

Indictable offences (i.e., those tried on indictment), on the other hand, are tried by jury in the Crown Court in contested cases. They represent the most serious offences, such as murder or rape. Either-way offences, which include theft, burglary and indecent assault, are those which can be tried either within the jurisdiction of the Magistrates' Court or the Crown Court. The mode of trial is decided by the magistrates, but the defendant has the choice to be tried in the Crown Court, even if the magistrates accept jurisdiction. If the magistrates accept jurisdiction then the defendant, if convicted, may nevertheless be sent to the Crown Court for sentencing. This happens when the magistrates consider that they have insufficient powers to sentence the offender after having heard all the evidence. Magistrates can only sentence offenders to a maximum of six months' imprisonment for one offence or for twelve months when two six months' sentences are running consecutively.

The Magistrates' Courts try the great majority of all criminal cases (about 97 per cent), as well as dealing with bail applications and committal to the Crown Court in the more serious cases or where a defendant has opted for a jury trial in an either-way offence. The Magistrates' Courts also process some civil cases, such as domestic disputes and child care proceedings. The Family Law Act 1996 (Bond *et al.*, 1997), has important implications for the Magistrates' Court concerning issues of child protection and domestic violence, although divorce law remains the domain of the county court.

Clinical psychologists sometimes give evidence in the Magistrates' Court, particularly in the youth and family courts (Lane, 1987; Parker, 1987). Family disputes fall under civil jurisdiction and are heard in the family court. Youth cases which fall within the criminal jurisdiction are heard in the youth court by specially trained magistrates, and deal with young persons aged between 10 and 17 inclusive (almost all fall in the age group 14–18 years). The procedure is similar to that found in the adult court, although there are differences (Barclay, 1995). In the youth court the proceedings are conducted in private (i.e., it is not open to the public like the adult court), although the proceedings may be reported in the press but generally without identifying the young person. The case must be committed or transferred to the Crown Court if the young person is charged with murder or manslaughter.

Youth courts were abolished in Scotland in 1971 and all such cases are heard by welfare tribunals (known as children's hearing), which are staffed by lay persons (Morris and Gelsthorpe, 1993). It is evident from Chapter 3 that psychologists in Scotland are actively involved in providing expert evidence in these children's hearing cases.

In England and Wales, jurors are used in all cases in the Crown Court where the accused pleads not guilty and this represents about 2 per cent of all criminal trials (Lloyd-Bostock, 1996). In England over 100,000 defendants are dealt with annually by the Crown Courts and of those about two-thirds plead guilty to all counts. In England juries have twelve members whereas in Scotland there are fifteen. Unanimous verdicts in England, Wales and Northern Ireland were abolished in 1967 due to police fears of jurors being bribed or intimidated by criminals (Lloyd-Bostock, 1996). Jurors can bring in a majority verdict of 10–2. In Scotland there is also a majority verdict, but it represents a majority of 8 out of 15. In contrast to England, in Scotland there are three possible verdicts in criminal trials: 'guilty', 'not guilty' or 'not proven'. A majority verdict refers to 'guilty' versus either 'not guilty' or 'not proven'.

An important development in Northern Ireland was the introduction in 1973 of the so-called 'Diplock Courts', which allows certain categories of serious crime to be tried without a jury (Jackson and Doran, 1992).

Criminal Cases Review Commission

The Criminal Cases Review Commission (CCRC) is an independent body set up under the Criminal Appeal Act 1995. It commenced work on 1 April 1997. It has responsibility for investigating suspected miscarriages of criminal justice in England, Wales and Northern Ireland, which had previously been the responsibility of the Home Office. The CCRC has fourteen members, who are supported by case workers and administrative staff. It receives representations from persons who feel they have been wrongly convicted or sentenced. The Commission will normally only consider cases which have already gone through the ordinary appeal system. In order for a case to have a chance of success there has to be an argument or evidence presented which has not already been raised during the trial or any appeal.

If a case is successful then the commission will refer the case to the Crown Court, if the original trial took place in a Magistrates' Court, or to the Court of Appeal concerning cases which were heard in the Crown Court. The CCRC can also refer cases to the Home Secretary where it believes that a Royal Pardon should be considered.

The Court of Appeal may on occasions ask the CCRC to investigate or settle an issue before it decides a case. In addition, the Home Secretary may ask the CCRC for advice when considering advising Her Majesty the Queen to issue a Royal Pardon.

Stages in criminal proceedings

Criminal proceedings in the Magistrates' Court and Crown Court involve three distinct stages, which are referred to as *pretrial*, *trial* and *sentencing*. Each stage consists of distinct legal issues and the contribution that psychologists can make at each stage varies considerably. It is essential that psychologists, who are preparing court reports, are familiar with the relevant legal concepts and issues relevant at each stage of the proceedings.

Pretrial issues

There are two main pretrial issues in criminal cases: whether or not the defendant is to be prosecuted and, if so, the defendant's fitness to plead and stand trial may be raised before commencement of the trial (Briscoe *et al.*, 1993). Fitness in this context relates to the defendant's current mental state and not that which existed at the time of the offence. It is determined by a jury. Where the defendant is suffering from medical, psychiatric or psychological problems the Crown Prosecution Service may not consider it to be in the public interest to proceed with the case and the charges may be dropped or left on file. Similarly, where the state of mind or the credibility of a main prosecution witness is in doubt the case may not proceed. For example, the police and the Crown Prosecution Service seem reluctant to proceed with cases of complainants whose allegations are based on so-called 'recovered memories' (Gudjonsson, 1997b; see later discussion in this chapter).

Fitness to plead, known in the USA as 'competency to stand trial', is principally related to whether or not a defendant has sufficient cognitive abilities to make a proper defence. This happens when the defendant's physical or mental state at the time of the trial is thought to interfere with the due process of the law (i.e., the defendant would not have a fair trial if the case proceeds). If found unfit to plead and stand trial there are a number of important consequences which follow, including that the trial will be postponed, commonly for an indefinite period, and in the meantime the defendant is detained compulsorily in hospital. In view of this legal and clinical significance, fitness to plead and stand trial issues are typically only raised in serious cases (Chiswick, 1990; Harding, 1993; Grubin, 1996).

Harding (1993) provides an excellent comparative review of the fitness to plead in criminal trials across a number of countries, including Austria, Denmark, Switzerland, Australia, Canada and the USA. He shows how the concept of fitness to plead and stand trial is confined to countries that rely on the adversarial system of justice. This includes England, Scotland, Australia, the USA and Canada. In contrast, countries that are inquisitorial in nature, such as Denmark, Austria and Switzerland, do not have legislation dealing with fitness to plead or stand trial. All accused persons must appear before an examining magistrate and if there are concerns about the accused's mental state during the proceedings a psychiatric report will be requested in order to assist the court in their decision-making process. In countries where issues of fitness to plead and stand trial issues form a part of the legal proceedings, the precise criteria used to determine unfitness may vary considerably.

Grubin (1996) discusses the development of the concept of fitness to plead from medieval England to current usage. The concept was recognised as early as the fourteenth century (Walker, 1968) and by the nineteenth century the criteria by which defendants were found unfit became determined by case law. The cases dealt with at that time were mostly concerned with the fitness of defendants who were deaf and dumb and unable to communicate. The two leading cases are those of Dyson (1831) and Pitchard (1836). Both were deaf-mutes who were insane and detained under the Criminal Lunatics Act 1800 (Grubin, 1996). The case of Easther Dyson was the first where criteria for fitness were clearly formulated. Dyson was indicted for the murder of her illegitimate child. A plea of not guilty was recorded against her, but she proved unable to understand her right to challenge jurors. Pitchard was indicted for bestiality and the jury considered him unable to stand trial. The Pitchard case refined and developed further the criteria for determining fitness to plead and stand trial. The central feature related to sufficient intellectual understanding to comprehend the charge, the plea, the challenging of jurors and court proceedings. One further criterion has been added during the past decade, which relates to defendants' ability to instruct their legal advocates (Mitchell and Richardson, 1985).

Briscoe et al. (1993) list the current criteria for determining fitness to plead and stand trial as follows:

a   being able to plead with understanding to the indictment;
b   being able to comprehend the details of evidence;
c   being able to follow court proceedings;
d   knowing that a juror can be challenged;
e   being able to instruct legal advisers.

The legal process concerned with those found unfit to plead, which originally followed the provisions of the Criminal Lunatics Act 1800, has been modified twice in England and Wales, first by the Criminal Procedure (Insanity) Act 1964, and more recently by the Criminal Procedure (Insanity and Unfitness to Plead) Act 1991. Those found unfit and detained under the Criminal Procedure (Insanity) Act 1964 should have been admitted to hospital under conditions which are equivalent to a hospital order under the Mental Health Act 1983 (Section 37) with Home Office restriction on discharge without time limit (Section 41). The Criminal Procedure (Insanity and Unfitness to Plead) Act 1991 made two important reforms (Briscoe et al., 1993). Firstly, that where defendants are found unfit to plead there has to be a trial concerning the facts of the case in order to determine the likelihood that the defendant committed the offence. If the evidence against the defendant is found to be weak then the charges are dropped and he or she is discharged. Secondly, the new Act introduced a range of new sentencing options for those persons found unfit to plead, including an absolute discharge and a hospital order without restrictions.

It is important to recognise that although mental disorder is relevant to the determination of fitness to plead, mental disorder does not per se make a person unfit to plead and stand trial. It is a question of how the mental disorder affects the defendant's current functional abilities within the context of relevant legal criteria for determining fitness. Similarly, amnesia, or pathological loss of memory, does not by itself make the defendant unfit to plead and stand trial (Shapiro, 1990; Grubin, 1996).

Grubin (1996) provides important data on 295 cases, involving 285 defendants, who had been found unfit to plead in England and Wales between 1976 and 1988. (The reason for the larger number of cases relates to some defendants being found unfit to plead on more than one occasion.)

The number of cases during each of the thirteen years ranged between twelve and forty-one. There has been a clear decline in the number of cases found unfit to plead each year, a trend which appears to have begun after the First World War (Grubin, 1996). In Grubin's study the majority of the cases involved defendants who were charged with violent offences, such as assaults (31 per cent) and homicide (9 per cent). However, offences of theft were also common (27 per cent) as well as arson (11 per cent) and sexual offences (11 per cent). Schizophrenia was the most common diagnosis (57 per cent), followed by mental handicap (21 per cent). Only five per cent of this unfit-to-plead population had been transferred to hospital prior to their being found unfit by the court. As far as outcome is concerned, over half (58 per cent) of the defendants were sent to a local psychiatric hospital, 30 per cent were sent to one of the special hospitals, and 10 per cent to a medium security hospital. Nine defendants (3 per cent) were not admitted to hospital at all. Six regained fitness to plead while still in prison and three were discharged from prison before their hospital transfer lapsed (i.e., by law the transfer to hospital had to take place within two months). As far as the long-term outcome is concerned, as of the end of September 1989, 26 per cent of the defendants had returned for trial, 22 per cent had their restrictions lifted, and a further 22 per cent had been discharged, either conditionally or absolutely.

Grubin makes the point that over the thirteen-year research period, where just over twenty cases of unfitness were found annually, between 700 and 800 hospital orders were issued by the courts. This is in addition to many mentally disordered offenders who are annually dealt with by the courts giving them conditional discharges and probation orders. Many others would have been diverted from the criminal justice system prior to any court attendance (Robertson et al., 1996).

The research by Grubin makes it very clear that unfitness to plead in England and Wales has been declining over the past seventy years and currently very few, or approximately twenty defendants per year are found unfit to plead. Grubin recommends that fitness to plead should be turned to as a last resort, for example when the provisions of the Mental Health Act 1983 have been exhausted or when they do not apply.

Grubin (1996) highlights some differences between England and Scotland with regard to fitness to plead issues, which include greater legal authority in Scotland for determining unfitness and the fact that unfitness can be determined by both the High Court and the Sheriff Courts (the latter also deal with summary jurisdictions). This means that fitness to plead issues are more commonly raised in Scotland than they are in England.

The USA has the most extensive case law and judicial process in relation to 'competency to stand trial' and in all federal and state jurisdictions a defendant must be judged mentally competent to stand trial before the trial can proceed (Harding, 1993). This means the issue of fitness to plead and stand trial is much more frequently raised in criminal cases in the USA than in England and Scotland and it takes up much of the time of forensic psychiatrists and psychologists (Blau, 1984; Shapiro, 1990).

The criteria used to determine competency to stand trial in the USA differ somewhat from those in the UK, and even within the USA statutes vary slightly between different states and jurisdictions. However, the basic criteria are similar to those in the UK in that 'the defendant must have an understanding of the charges and an ability to assist in his or her own defense' (Shapiro, 1990, p. 2). Shapiro discusses the importance of the standards set in Duskey's case (1960), where a defendant is 'considered competent to stand trial if he or she possesses a functional understanding of the proceedings, a rational understanding of the proceedings, and is able to consult with counsel with a reasonable degree of rational understanding' (p. 2). Functional understanding, which is the one most commonly understood of the three criteria, means that the defendant is able to accurately state the charges against him or her. Shapiro provides some excellent case examples about how the three criteria are assessed in actual cases.

Although there is some dispute in the USA about the burden of proof in cases of competency, the level of proof is based on the 'preponderance of evidence', which means that in order to consider a defendant fit to stand trial, the clinician must be '*slightly more certain than not*' that the defendant meets the criteria for competency' (Shapiro, 1990, p. 15).

The main problem for forensic psychiatrists and psychologists, which applies equally to UK and American expert witnesses, is that the legal constructs of fitness criteria are not well defined and described in case law which means that the expert may find it difficult to evaluate the defendant's psychiatric and psychological vulnerabilities within the context of the legal criteria. As a result, the psychiatric evaluation is often going to be peripherally related to the legal criteria (Grisso, 1986a).

A number of special instruments, referred to as 'Competency Tests', have been developed by American psychologists in order to assess objectively the functional deficits that are relevant to the legal issues (Blau, 1984; Grisso, 1986a; Shapiro, 1990). Recent factor analytic studies into 'Competency Tests' have raised concern about the lack of stable factor structure across different subject samples (Bagby *et al.*, 1992). Bagby *et al.* recommend that what is needed is a further development of empirical measures that better match the legal construct of competency to stand trial.

In the UK, psychiatrists are traditionally more commonly commissioned than psychologists to assess fitness to plead and stand trial. However, in recent years psychologists in England are increasingly commissioned by defence lawyers to carry out a psychological assessment on such cases. The psychological assessment provides the court with an objective and standardised assessment of the defendant's functional deficits. This may involve an assessment of the defendant's intellectual and neuropsychological status, as well as an assessment of problems related to severe anxiety and depression. Severe depression may, in certain circumstances, make it impossible for defendants to assist in their defence. For example, in a major fraud trial at the Central Criminal Court, one of us (Gudjonsson) testified with regard to one defendant's fitness to plead and stand trial. He argued successfully that the defendant's cognitive abilities had deteriorated after his arrest as a result of severe clinical depression. In view of the defendant's functional problems and the complexity of the trial proceedings it was thought unlikely that he could concentrate and understand the court proceedings and properly assist with his defence. He was fit to plead, but not fit to stand trial. Two years later, after receiving medical treatment for his depression the defendant was fit to stand trial and was convicted of the offences and given a long prison sentence.

Trial issues

In English law, a criminal offence contains a number of different elements which fall into two main categories, which need to be proved by the crown beyond reasonable doubt (except in cases of 'strict liability', see below). These are known as *actus reus* and *mens rea* (Leng, 1990). The former comprises elements pertaining to the crime itself and requires the crown to prove: (a) that a criminal offence was committed; and (b) that the defendant committed it. The *actus reus* element not only includes the commission of the act; it may also deal with the consequences of the act (e.g., death in cases of murder) and the surrounding circumstances (e.g., in a case of rape that the woman did not consent to the sexual act).

The term *mens rea* is used to refer to the defendant's state of mind at the time of the alleged offence. Here the focus is on the question of guilty intent and knowledge of the wrongfulness of the act. The crown has to prove that the offence was committed either recklessly or intentionally. The concepts of responsibility and free will are important here. The criteria for establishing *mens rea* are related to the nature of the offence, because each offence is defined separately in law and there are no standard criteria for defining *mens rea* across different offences. Certain offences, such as many of those embodied in the Road Traffic Acts, do not require an element of *mens rea* for the defendant to be convicted (i.e., they are offences of 'strict liability' and the crown only has to prove *actus reus*). However, in such cases, when the defendant is convicted a mental condition relevant to *mens rea* can be used as mitigation at the sentencing stage.

Psychologists in England are often instructed to prepare court reports which are relevant to both *actus reus* and *mens rea* issues and their involvement in such cases is expanding. As far as denial of *actus reus* is concerned, the defence may offer alibi evidence to indicate that the defendant was not present during the commission of the offence. When the defendant has made self-incriminating admissions or a confession to the police then this may be disputed at trial either on the basis that the admissions are unreliable or obtained unfairly. Psychologists are becoming increasingly involved in this area of work, both in the UK (Gudjonsson, 1996a) and USA (Shapiro, 1990; Ofshe and Leo, 1997). There are a number of ways of analysing the credibility of such confessions which focus on police behaviour (i.e., interrogative and custodial factors) and psychological vulnerabilities (Gudjonsson, 1992a, 1997e; Ofshe and Leo, 1997). Psychologists have also provided experimental evidence supporting the defence contention that no *actus reus* could have taken place, e.g. Haward (1963).

The contribution of clinical psychologists to *mens rea* issues complements that of their psychiatrist colleagues. However, psychiatric evidence at trial typically focuses on mental disorder in relation to the defence of insanity, infanticide, diminished responsibility (in cases where the charge is murder), and non-insane automatism (Briscoe *et al.*, 1993). Sometimes psychologists have a role to play in these cases, but most typically their role is to complement that of the psychiatric evaluation. Below we will discuss three issues where psychologists are commonly asked to evaluate defendants concerning their *mens rea*. These are: (1) duress and coercion; (2) absentmindedness, and (3) diminished responsibility in cases of homicide.

Duress It is sometimes argued by the defence that the defendant was coerced into crime by another person. This may be raised at trial in relation to *mens rea* or at the sentencing stage in form of mitigation (Gudjonsson, 1996b). The standard for determining duress as a defence at the trial stage can be viewed legally from two perspectives (Leng, 1990). First, was the defendant's will over-borne by the threat? This essentially relates to the defendant's subjective experience (i.e., it contains a subjective element). Secondly, is the nature of the threat such that a reasonable person would have given in to it? The latter standard, which contains an objective element, is the one used since Graham's case (1982). Graham was involved in the killing of his wife by another man, called King. Graham's defence was that King's violent behaviour in the past had made him fearful of King and unable to resist his command, especially since Graham's ability to resist pressure had been weakened by drugs and drink. The Court of Appeal upheld Graham's conviction and stated that the relevant test is whether a 'sober person of reasonable firmness, sharing the characteristics of the defendant' would have responded to the threat in the same way as Graham did (Leng, 1990, p. 248). The judgment makes it clear that the voluntary consumption of alcohol or illicit drugs is not relevant to the defence of duress.

The defence of duress can only succeed if the defendant can show that he or she was placed in an *unavoidable dilemma*. This means that the defendant had only two choices, either he or she committed the offence or submitted to the threat. There is no unavoidable dilemma when the defendant has an opportunity to get away from the situation (i.e., when there is a realistic option or opportunity of escaping from the situation). The threat does not have to be carried out immediately after the refusal, although this is typically the case. What the jury has to consider are factors like the defendant's age, the surrounding circumstances, and the risk involved in avoiding the threat (Leng, 1990).

One of us (Gudjonsson) has assessed a number of defendants where one defendant alleges that he or she was coerced, threatened or led into participating in the crime (Gudjonsson, 1996b). Such cases involve identifying enduring psychological vulnerabilities, including undue tendency towards compliance, lack of assertiveness and susceptibility to intimidation. In view of the nature of these cases Gudjonsson (1989, 1997a) developed the Gudjonsson Compliance Scale to assist with the assessment of these cases.

Duress is a very difficult defence to win at the trial stage, unless the threat is very real, severe, immediate and the defendant is in some way psychologically vulnerable (e.g., abnormally compliant and fearful, very young or very old) and there was no opportunity of escaping from the threat. More commonly, the psychological findings are used at the sentencing stage to mitigate the severity of the sentence.

Crimes committed under duress can be viewed as criminal acts committed vicariously by one party inducing a second party to perform the act. In this sense, crimes allegedly carried out under hypnotic suggestion would fall into the same category as those committed under duress. At least twenty-one such cases are on record. The prosecuting authorities usually deny that hypnotic control, if in fact it existed, was sufficient to absolve the offender from responsibility for his acts, but courts have acknowledged acceptance of this possibility through verdicts of not guilty or by significant leniency in sentencing. Psychologists have not yet proved conclusively that criminal conduct can, or cannot, be induced by hypnosis.

Absentmindedness Absentmindedness or forgetfulness is often raised as a defence in cases of shoplifting, but in these cases the question of mental abnormality does not normally arise (Bluglass, 1990b). However, psychiatrists and psychologists are sometimes asked to conduct an evaluation of a defendant in such cases and they may have to testify in court for the defence as to their findings. A leading case is that of Ingram (1975), which involved the successful appeal against conviction for shoplifting on the basis that the appellant, who was a practising lawyer, had placed the taken items in his pocket in a moment of absentmindedness. The judgment in the *Ingram* case is important because the Court of Appeal affirmed that absentmindedness can be a defence to shoplifting.

Reason and Lucas (1984) argue that absentmindedness is common in cases of shoplifting and the condition is exacerbated during a period of stress. When people are experiencing stress they sometimes become preoccupied and distracted, which may on occasions result in their walking out of a shop after having forgotten to pay for items. What is important in these cases is to study all the factual evidence in the case as well as assessing the defendant. For example, in one case a man was observed and recorded on store video looking carefully around the shop immediately before placing items of goods into his coat pocket and then slowly walking out of the shop without paying. At trial he claimed to have no memory of having placed the items of goods into his pocket and unsuccessfully argued for absentmindedness as a defence.

Diminished responsibility The defence of diminished responsibility was introduced in England and Wales under Section 2 of the Homicide Act 1957. As in the case of provocation and suicide pacts, it involves cases where there may have been 'malice aforethought' (i.e., an intention to kill another person or inflict grievous bodily harm), but there are mitigating circumstances which reduce the charge of murder to manslaughter (Hamilton, 1990).

The death penalty was abolished in 1965 (the last two men to be executed in Britain were Peter Anthony Allen and Gwynne Owen Evans who were hanged on 13 August 1964; Honeycombe, 1984). The sentence for murder was replaced by mandatory life imprisonment. In cases of murder, the defence can sometimes successfully argue for manslaughter on the basis of diminished responsibility, which means that the trial judge has a number of sentencing options available, including a probation order with psychiatric conditions. The burden of proof is on the defence but the standard of proof is on the balance of probabilities. Section 2 (1) of the Homicide Act 1957 states:

> Where a person kills or is a party to the killing of another, he shall not be convicted of murder if he was suffering from such abnormality of mind (whether arising from a condition of arrested or retarded development of mind or any inherent causes or induced by disease or injury) as substantially impaired his mental responsibility for his acts and omissions in doing or being a party to the killing.

The authoritative interpretations of the terms 'abnormality of mind' and 'substantial impairment' date back to the case of Byrne (1960). These are discussed in detail by Hamilton (1990). Byrne's case involved an abnormality of mind arising out of personality disorder. Clinical depression accounts for a substantial proportion of cases where the defence successfully argues for diminished responsibility, followed by the diagnoses of psychosis and personality disorder (Mitchell, 1997).

It is evident from the results of the BPS survey, discussed in Chapter 3, that psychologists do commonly provide psychological evaluations in murder cases where the question of diminished responsibility is being addressed. Such assessments address the defendant's mental state at the time of the offence and may include, in addition to a mental state examination, testing of intellectual functions, neuropsychological assessment, and psychometric tests like the MMPI-2 and the Gough Socialisation Scale (Gough, 1960). On occasions the Gudjonsson Blame Attribution Inventory (Gudjonsson and Singh, 1989) may also be administered to assess the defendant's perceptions of the offence (see later in this chapter).

Sentencing issues

After a defendant has been found guilty of a criminal offence the judge has to impose an appropriate penalty. Various sentencing options are available. The sentence imposed will depend primarily on the nature and seriousness of the case, as well as the aggravating features, surrounding circumstances and mitigating factors. Financial penalties are generally imposed for the less serious offences, whereas a probation order, a community service order up to 240 hours, or a prison sentence are given for the more serious offences.

Psychologists are increasingly being asked to provide reports about factors which are relevant to mitigation and sentencing. This may involve offering an opinion about treatment options and prognosis. The recommendation may involve offering treatment to persons convicted of sexual offences (Clare, 1993; Lang, 1993; Allam et al., 1997), anger problems (Towl and Crighton, 1996), compulsive shoplifting (Gudjonsson, 1987), and car theft (Brown, 1985). Towl and Crighton (1996) provide a very useful guide to 'risk assessment' of suicide and violence, which they define as, 'a combination of an estimate of the probability of a target behaviour occurring with a consideration of the consequences of such occurrences' (p. 55).

Probation orders

Under the powers of the Criminal Courts Act 1973 a probation order can be made for a period between six months and three years. The offence must be considered 'serious enough' to warrant a probation order being imposed. The offender must be at least 16 years of age and he or she must consent to the requirements of the order. The purpose of imposing a probation order is to protect society from reoffending and to rehabilitate the offender (i.e., make him or her a more responsible citizen). One of the conditions of that order, for either the whole duration or a part of that order, may be that the offender undergoes psychiatric treatment, either as a resident or non-resident patient. According to the Powers of the Criminal Courts Act 1973, the treatment has to be provided by a 'duly qualified medical practitioner', which means that he or she has to be approved under Section 12 (2) of the Mental Health Act 1983. However, the Criminal Justice and Public Order Act 1994 makes provisions for the treatment attached to the probation order to be provided by a psychologist who is registered as a 'chartered psychologist' by the British Psychological Society. The current position is that while 'chartered psychologists' can carry out the relevant treatment, it still remains essential that a 'duly qualified medical practitioner' provides written or oral evidence for the need for that treatment before a court will make a probation order with a condition of psychological treatment (Wasik and Taylor, 1995). This change in the law with regard to the introduction of chartered psychologists to the treatment of mental problems of offenders placed on probation represents an important step for the psychology profession. It indicates the recognition by the probation service and the judiciary of the important contribution that psychologists have made in the treatment of offenders.

Admissibility of expert evidence

From the lawyers' point of view, the history of forensic psychology has been primarily concerned with the extent that psychological evidence has been admissible in court. For evidence to be allowed in legal proceedings it has to be both relevant and admissible. Relevance is determined by the probative value of the evidence, whereas admissibility refers to evidence which is legally receivable irrespective of whether or not it is logically probative (Curzon, 1986). This means that evidence may be highly relevant but it is inadmissible for legal reasons (e.g., because it was obtained unfairly or illegally, that it is based on 'hearsay' or 'opinion', or that it is within the knowledge and experience of the ordinary person). According to Ormerod (1996), in recent years English courts have become more strict about the interpretation of relevance with regard to both prosecution and defence evidence.

The question of admissibility can arise with regard to any evidence placed before the court. When lawyers seek to introduce expert psychological or psychiatric evidence, then the judge will decide on the admissibility of the evidence. Submissions and legal arguments are heard by the judge in the absence of the jury (known in England as a 'voir dire' or 'trial within a trial'). In the USA, voir dire refers to the examination of potential jurors by psychologists in order to discover any prejudices which could influence their deliberations (Darbyshire, 1992).

The basic criteria for the admissibility of expert testimony in England were stated by Lord Justice Lawton in Turner's case (1975) These are: 'An expert's opinion is admissible to furnish the court with scientific information which is likely to be outside the experience and knowledge of a judge or jury' (p. 83). The appellant was convicted of the murder of his girlfriend. He alleged that he had been provoked into violence when his girlfriend confessed to relationships with other men. At the trial the defence requested the court's permission to call a psychiatrist to testify on the issue of provocation. The appellant had not been mentally ill at the time of the homicide, but his mental state and personality were considered such that he would have coped poorly with provocation. The trial judge refused to allow the evidence. The Court of Appeal held that the ruling of the trial judge was right. The psychiatric evidence was considered to be inadmissible because in the absence of mental illness it fell within ordinary human experience.

According to the principle developed in the Turner case, it is not admissible for psychiatrists or psychologists to give evidence about how an ordinary person is likely to react to stressful situations. Neither can they give evidence about matters directly related to the likely truthfulness of witnesses or defendants. According to Fitzgerald (1987), MacKay and Colman (1991), and Colman and MacKay (1995) English law has quite a restrictive approach to the admissibility of evidence from psychologists and psychiatrists. This means that, in theory at least, psychologists are not allowed to give evidence on such matters as eyewitness testimony, unlike psychologists in America (Davies, 1983). This follows from the strength and influence of precedential law, for the admissibility of psychological evidence under English law was originally granted to psychologists appearing as *medical witnesses*, as explained earlier, where their evidence, like that of psychiatrists, has to deal with the presence of mental abnormality. When this involves mental illness, learning disabilities or other diagnosed mental disorder (e.g., personality disorder) the evidence is readily admissible. However, the way the English courts allow or disallow psychological and psychiatric evidence is commonly inconsistent (Gudjonsson, 1992a, 1992b; Colman and MacKay, 1995). Moreover, exceptions to the restricted admissibility of psychological evidence do occur (Gudjonsson, 1992b). Indeed, one of us (Haward) has not infrequently testified in court with evidence challenging the eyewitness testimony of police officers (e.g., Haward, 1963). It should be noted that in the USA, psychologists tendering eyewitness evidence present a corpus of existing research data and then argue from the general to the particular, drawing conclusions by deductive reasoning relevant to the eyewitness in question; contrariwise, in the UK the practice of one of us (Haward) has been to initiate specially designed research which reproduces accurately the conditions under which the eyewitness made the critical observation, and then argue that since the alleged observation cannot be reproduced by observers placed in an identical situation, the original observation is likely to embody some form of misperception. He always makes the point tactfully that this implies that the observer concerned was honest but mistaken; it enables this explanation to be accepted without loss of face, especially when the court is told why, in the circumstances, misperception not only occurred but, in the particular circumstances, was probably inevitable. The alternative explanation questioning the observer's veracity could not only be unfair but would be difficult to prove.

Other examples of psychological evidence in criminal proceedings unrelated to mental abnormality, described in Haward (1981), include data on perception of oblique vehicular speed and identity from clothing.

There have been some significant recent legal developments in the UK with regard to the admissibility of psychological evidence in cases of disputed confessions, which has resulted in a more receptive attitude of the courts towards such evidence. Of fundamental significance was the judgment of the Court of Appeal in Raghip's case (1991). The case concerned a major public disturbance in 1985 on the Broadwater Farm Estate, North London. A police officer, PC Blakelock, was descended upon by a crowd of between thirty and fifty people and murdered. Three defendants, Winston Silcott, Mark Braithwaite and Engin Raghip, were convicted of Blakelock's murder in 1986 and sentenced to life imprisonment. Braithwaite and Raghip had made signed confessions, which they subsequently retracted. Raghip had been assessed by a psychiatrist and a clinical psychologist prior to his trial, but because the findings were not favourable their reports were never used at the time of Raghip's trial. One of us (Gudjonsson) was asked to assess Raghip in 1988 and discovered that both the psychiatrist and the clinical psychologist had failed to identify Raghip's relevant psychological vulnerabilities. After having seen the fresh psychological report, both experts changed their opinions and the case went to the Court of Appeal where it was heard at the end of November 1991.

Three psychologists testified at Raghip's appeal. The psychological evidence consisted of demonstrating Raghip's Borderline IQ (Full Scale IQ of 74) and his abnormal personality traits (i.e., high suggestibility and compliance), which were considered to undermine the reliability of his confession to the police. The judges fully accepted the psychological findings and Raghip's conviction was quashed. He had spent six years in prison for PC Blakelock's murder.

The specific importance of the ruling in Raghip's case for psychology is as follows:

1   The judges were 'not attracted to the concept that the judicial approach to submissions under Section 76(2)(b) of the Police and Criminal Evidence Act, 1984 (PACE) should be governed by which side of an arbitrary line, whether 69/70 or elsewhere, the IQ falls'. It means that in future cases trial judges should not rely on arbitrary IQ points when deciding on the admissibility of psychological evidence. Therefore, successful submissions under PACE might involve borderline IQ scores, as in the case of Raghip.
2   The judges recognised the potential importance of psychological evidence in cases of disputed confession and differentiated it from expert evidence that addressed defendants' *mens rea* (i.e., guilty intent). According to the judges, expert evidence on the reliability of any confession needs to be considered in accordance with the question, 'Is the mental condition of the defendant such that the jury would be assisted by expert help in assessing it?'
3   The judges considered that potential vulnerabilities to erroneous testimony, such as high suggestibility and intellectual deficits, could not be satisfactorily detected by observations of the defendant's performance in the witness box. The jury would be greatly assisted by a psychological assessment which has specifically tested for relevant vulnerabilities.

Following the judgment in the case of Raghip many legal arguments have subsequently taken place by defence advocates using the facts in that case about test scores and applying them to another case. In Raghip's case an IQ score of 74 was used to define mental handicap in accordance with Section 77 of the Police and Criminal Evidence Act 1984 (Home Office, 1985). In Kenny's case (1994), the Court of Appeal decided that it was wrong to take the IQ scores from one case (e.g., Raghip) and apply them slavishly to another. Each case has to be decided on its own merit and no rigid rules can be applied.

Another important achievement for forensic psychology is the judgment in case of Kane (1997), which was heard in the Court of Appeal in Northern Ireland. Patrick Kane was sentenced to life imprisonment. On 20 June 1997, the judges made their ruling and quashed Kane's 1990 conviction for aiding and abetting the IRA's murders of two British soldiers in 1988 (Randall, 1997). At the time of his trial in February 1990 Kane was assessed by one of us (Gudjonsson) at the request of the defence. The findings revealed an exceptionally anxiety prone and compliant individual of borderline intellectual ability (Full Scale IQ score of 78), who would have been considerably disadvantaged during the police interrogations into the two murders. His anxiety proneness was such that combined with his high compliance and modest intellect, he was more likely than the average person to have only considered the perceived immediate consequences of his self-incriminating admissions to the police (i.e., the interrogation terminating, being released from custody), rather than the long-term consequences (i.e., being convicted of a serious criminal offence and receiving a life sentence). The psychological report was not used at the trial, because the legal team did not think the findings would be admitted in evidence due to the fact that Kane was not found to be mentally ill or suffering from learning disability in accordance with Section 77 of the Police and Criminal Evidence Act. After his conviction Kane's case featured in a BBC television 'Rough Justice' programme. Following that programme the Secretary for Northern Ireland, Lord Mayhew, referred the case back to the Court of Appeal on the grounds that the psychological report constituted important new evidence. The Court of Appeal ruled that the evidence of Gudjonsson on the appellant's mental and psychological state was relevant and admissible and his testimony was received before the three appeal judges on 28 May 1997. In his ruling Lord Justice McCollum said the Appeal Court was persuaded by the evidence of Gudjonsson and the conviction was considered unsafe and quashed. Kane was immediately released from custody, after having spent nine years in prison.

A major legal development has occurred in relation to the diagnosis of post-traumatic stress disorder (PTSD), which has had an enormous impact on both civil and criminal law (Stone, 1993). The identification of PTSD symptoms can form the basis for defining psychological injury in civil (compensation) cases as well as negating culpability or mitigating sentences in criminal cases (Colman and MacKay, 1995).

As far as the standards for the admissibility of expert testimony are concerned, there have also been important legal developments in the USA. In the landmark case of *Daubert* (1993) the United States Supreme Court decided that the *Frye* test from 1923 has been superseded by the Federal Rules of Evidence. Carson (1993) and Colman and MacKay (1995) provide a review of the Daubert Decision and its legal implications. The relevant Federal Rules of Evidence are as follows:

> Rule 402. All relevant evidence is admissible, except as otherwise provided by the Constitution of the United States, by Act of Congress, by these rules, or by other rules prescribed by the Supreme Court pursuant to statutory authority. Evidence which is not relevant is not admissible.
> Rule 401. 'Relevant evidence' means evidence having any tendency to make the existence of any fact that is of consequence to the determination of the action more probable or less probable than it would be without the evidence.
> Rule 702. If scientific, technical, or other specialised knowledge will assist the trier of fact to understand the evidence or to determine a fact in issue, a witness qualified as an expert by knowledge, skill, experience, training, or education, may testify thereto in the form of an opinion or otherwise.

The Federal Rules of Evidence are clearly more liberal with regard to the admissibility of expert evidence than the Frye test, which stipulated that the expert evidence had to be 'generally accepted' within the scientific community to be admissible. The 'general acceptance' rule does not feature in the Federal Rules of Evidence, but the judgment makes it clear that any expert evidence must be reliable as well as relevant (Colman and MacKay, 1995).

Profiling as expert evidence

Offender profiling, which refers to the use of information from crime scenes, and sometimes also witnesses' accounts, to infer characteristics about the likely offender, has in recent years gained increased publicity in the UK. Two of the main profilers, David Canter and Paul Britton, have written accounts of their own work (Canter, 1994; Britton, 1997). American profilers have also written books of their profiling experience (Ressler and Schachtman, 1992; Douglas and Olshaker, 1996; Holmes and Holmes, 1996).

When profiling a case there is no opportunity for directly assessing the individual suspect, in contrast standard psychological assessments often rely on direct observations of the client and the results of standardised tests. Profiling represents an indirect way of conducting assessments, which typically involves intuition, psychodynamic ideas and a limited repertoire of behaviour from which to extrapolate (Gudjonsson and Copson, 1997).

Offender profiling is best viewed as an investigative tool in police investigations. However, expert evidence with regard to offender profiling has in recent years been brought before the courts both in the USA and the UK. Such evidence is usually introduced by the prosecution, but it can also in certain circumstances be introduced by the defence, for example where there are co-accused defendants (Ormerod, 1996).

Ormerod discusses in detail the evidential implications of offender profiling and makes some interesting comparisons between the English and American courts. There are a number of difficulties with the admissibility of offender profiling in criminal trials in the UK and the USA, which have to do with issues of relevance and reliability. As far as relevance is concerned, offender profiles only give a general indication of the *type* of person who is likely to have committed the offence rather than indicating any one individual, who happens to fit the profile. That is, the expert witness is not able to say on the basis of an offender profile that it is more probable than not that this defendant committed the offence. When introduced at trial by the prosecution there is a risk that such evidence can be more prejudicial to defendants than probative.

Another problem with offender profiling relates to uncertainty over the reliability and validity of the techniques used. There are no empirical findings to support the reliability and validity of offender profiling in solving crimes and some profilers are apparently more successful than others. Indeed, profiling very rarely assists the police in solving the case or opening up new lines of enquiry (Copson, 1995). Offender profiling relies on expert's opinion, which is not necessarily based on a sound theoretical or empirical foundation, rather than factual evidence.

In spite of the legal difficulties over admissibility, there are at least two known cases of psychological evidence involving profiling having been adduced at trial (Gudjonsson and Copson, 1997). In addition, in the Torney case (1996) in Northern Ireland, a psychologist and a psychiatrist gave evidence during a jury trial for the crown on matters which related to offender profiling. The case involved a police officer who was charged with murdering his wife, son and daughter. The defendant blamed the murders on his 13-year-old son, whom he claimed had 'gone berserk' and shot to death his mother and sister, after which he had committed suicide. One of us (Gudjonsson) had studied all the relevant case material, including the crime scene photographs and video, and testified that the murders of the daughter and mother were not consistent with an act that had resulted from loss of temper of a person who has gone 'berserk'. The murders appeared to have been carefully and efficiently executed by a person who was familiar with the use of firearms and had the confidence to use them. Indeed, the murders looked more like planned executions than a sudden outburst of violence. This made it more probable than not that the defendant rather than the son had committed the murders. The defendant was convicted of the murders.

The case of Colin Stagg

When the expert profile opinion is admissible then the court will have to decide upon the appropriate weight to give such evidence. The leading judgment in the UK is that of The Honourable Mr Justice Ognall in the Stagg case (1994). Colin Stagg was charged with the murder of Rachel Nickell on Wimbledon Common on 15 July 1992. In September 1992 Mr Stagg was arrested on suspicion of having committed the murder. He was detained in custody for three days, during which time he was extensively interrogated. He gave full accounts of his movements and persistently denied the murder. His home was searched and nothing incriminating was found. He was then released from custody. In January 1993 the police commenced a 'covert operation', which was carefully planned and operated in co-operation with a clinical psychologist, Mr Paul Britton, where a female police officer, code-named Lizzie James, befriended Mr Stagg. There is no doubt that Miss James' brief was to elicit a confession from Mr Stagg to the murder of Rachel Nickell by employing psychological ploys and manipulations, or if this was unsuccessful, to elicit responses and sexual fantasies from Mr Stagg which were consistent with the profile Mr Britton had produced of Miss Nickell's murderer (i.e., the murderer was diagnosed as a psychopath who possessed deviant sexual fantasies).

The covert operation lasted seven months, during which time Mr Stagg repeatedly denied the murder, but he eventually produced deviant sexual fantasies which could be construed as being incriminating, provided one accepted Mr Britton's profile of the murderer. Indeed, following the covert operation Mr Britton went as far as to suggest that Mr Stagg's 'behaviour was indistinguishable from that expected from the murderer of Rachel Nickell'. This was a very strong conclusion indeed.

The crown argued that there was a precise overlap between Mr Britton's profiled killer and Mr Stagg. They maintained that Mr Stagg's responses to Lizzie James were progressive, spontaneous, voluntary and reliable. The crown wanted the profile to be used as proof of identity of the murderer and argued for Mr Britton, the profiler, to be accepted in court as an expert witness.

The defence argued that Mr Britton's opinion was inadmissible in proof of identity. Firstly, Mr Britton's opinion did not amount to expert opinion as traditionally recognised by the court. Secondly, at its best the opinion did not go any further than to demonstrate a propensity to commit the crime alleged, which in law does not amount to admissible evidence.

Prior to the trial the defence had commissioned two reports from one of us (Gudjonsson) who comprehensively assessed Mr Stagg while he was on remand, as well as analysing in detail all the relevant material in the case. One report focused on the psychological assessment of Mr Stagg, while the second report focused on the covert operation and addressed the following questions:

1 Are the fantasies produced by Mr Stagg in his letters and conversations with Miss Lizzie James likely to be the product of a process of influence instigated by Lizzie James?

2 If so, is it safe to rely upon these fantasies as resembling Mr Stagg's genuine fantasies?

The detailed psychological assessment of Mr Stagg revealed no evidence to indicate that he was a 'sexually deviant psychopath', a description Mr Britton had attributed to Miss Nickell's murderer. The second report concluded that:

> There is no doubt that Miss James subjected Mr Stagg to psychological manipulation in order to elicit responses from him that fitted Mr Britton's profile of Miss Nickell's murderer. His 'fantasies' involving domination, humiliation and aggression were clearly a product of a subtle process of influence and should not be relied upon as representing Mr Stagg's genuine sexual preferences and fantasies.

The psychological reports were used by the defence to formulate their legal arguments in front of Mr Justice Ognall in September 1994. The judge ruled that the correspondence and tape conversations which were the product of the undercover operation were inadmissible in evidence. As a consequence, the crown offered no evidence against Mr Stagg. He was immediately released from custody and the murder inquiry of Rachel Nickell was reopened. Nobody else has so far been charged with her murder.

Disputed confessions

An issue of considerable current public concern is that of false confessions. In recent years a significant contribution has been made by psychological expertise in determining the psychological vulnerabilities and interrogative circumstances which render a confession potentially invalid (Gudjonsson, 1992a, 1997c; Gudjonsson et al., 1993). The quashing of convictions by the Court of Appeal in a number of notorious cases, such as the 'Guildford Four' and the 'Birmingham Six', excited worldwide legal interest and are well discussed by Gudjonsson (1992a) and Gudjonsson and MacKeith (1997).

Psychological investigations into confessional evidence continues to lead to the acquittal of defendants in a continuing number of cases. Such evidence forms part of the rich research data on the reliability of testimony and suggestibility, which commenced with the work of Cattell (1895), Binet (1900) and Stern (1910). This work was taken up again in the USA by Buckhout (1974) and Loftus (1979), which resulted in growing acceptance in the courts of expert testimony concerning eyewitness testimony (Loftus, 1986). Loftus and her colleagues typically testify about the relevant research evidence rather than on their assessment of the individual case. This is referred to as the 'experimental approach' to human testimony, in contrast to the 'individual differences approach' of Gudjonsson and his colleagues in England (Schooler and Loftus, 1986). The 'individual differences approach' focuses on the psychological vulnerabilities or susceptibilities of the individual to giving erroneous accounts of events (Gudjonsson, 1992a); it is this vulnerability to the arrest situation and interrogative stress that lies at the root of many false confessions, although some false confessions are inspired by the wish to protect the real culprit (Sigurdsson and Gudjonsson, 1996).

Munsterberg (1908) was the first author to write about the psychological aspects of false confession, although the phenomenon of false confession was well recognised in the seventeenth century by the Spanish Inquisitor, Alonso de Salazar Frias (Henningsen, 1980, 1996). Munsterberg's view was that false confessions were very much a normal phenomenon which was triggered by unusual circumstances, although he did draw attention to melancholia as a condition in which false confessions were likely to arise. In the USA the work of Wrightsman and Kassin (1992), Ofshe (1989, 1992), and Ofshe and Leo (1997), along with the work of Gudjonsson (1992a) in the UK, focused on providing a theoretical model for understanding the psychology of false confession and demonstrated that false confessions do sometimes occur in serious criminal cases. It was not until the early 1980s, however, that psychological evidence, which disputed the validity of confession evidence, began to have some impact on the courts in the UK (Gudjonsson, 1992a) and the USA (Shapiro, 1990).

The major difference between England and Scotland with regard to confession evidence is that in Scotland the accused cannot be convicted solely on the basis of a confession (Gudjonsson, 1992a). In spite of the absence of a corroboration requirement, English law on confession evidence has changed fundamentally with the introduction of the Police and Criminal Evidence Act 1984 (PACE; Home Office, 1985), which came into effect in January 1986. PACE is accompanied by four Codes of Practice, which provide guidance to the police about procedure and the treatment of suspects (Home Office, 1995a). The Codes themselves only have legislative power in that a breach may result in evidence, including confession evidence, being ruled inadmissible by the judge after hearing legal submissions in the absence of the jury. PACE has not been revised since its implementation in 1986, but the Home Office has published an important revised version of the Codes of Practice which came into effect on 10 April 1995 (Home Office, 1995a). The most important change since the implementation of PACE is the modification of the right to silence. Following the implementation of the Criminal Justice and Public Order Act 1994, adverse inferences can be drawn by the court if a suspect chooses to remain silent when questioned by the police or if he or she chooses not give evidence in court. Psychologists are now increasingly being asked to assess cases where suspects exercised their right to silence while being questioned by the police and are at risk of having adverse inferences drawn by the court from their silence when the case goes to trial. Of particular importance is the greatly increased complexity of the current police caution (Shepherd *et al.*, 1995; Clare *et al.*, 1997). Many suspects detained at police stations are intellectually disadvantaged (Gudjonsson *et al.*, 1993) and may not have understood the legal implications of refusing to answer the questions put to them by the police (Gudjonsson, 1994b).

Offenders' attribution of blame for their crime

During the past decade a number of studies have looked at the attribution of blame by offenders and these have furthered our understanding of the ways in which offenders view their crime (Gudjonsson, 1984a; Gudjonsson and Singh, 1988, 1989). Offenders' perception of their offence in terms of blame is sometimes considered important in legal proceedings as well as being relevant to the offender's likely responsiveness to treatment. Of particular concern to the courts is the extent to which the offenders accept responsibility for their crime and experience genuine remorse for it, as well as the role of mental factors in the crime, such as depression, loss of control and distorted perceptions and thought processes.

Two scales have been constructed to measure offenders' attributions for their criminal acts and these can be useful when preparing court reports. These are known as the Gudjonsson Blame Attribution Inventory (BAI; Gudjonsson, 1984a; Gudjonsson and Singh, 1989) and Attribution of Blame Scale (ABS; Loza and Clements, 1991), respectively. These scales rely on self-report by the offender and aim to measure the offender's perceptions and understanding of his or her crime rather than actual causes. The BAI was devised in order to measure two types of attribution relevant to how offenders attribute blame for their criminal acts. First, 'external attribution', which measures the extent to which offenders report external justification for their crime (e.g., blaming the offence on provocation, social or environmental factors). Secondly, 'mental element attribution', which measures the extent to which offenders blame their crime on mental factors, such as depressed mood and a temporary loss of self-control. The BAI also measures the amount of guilt or remorse that offenders report feeling about the offence they have committed.

The Attribution of Blame Scale (ABS) of Loza and Clements (1991) is designed to measure the offender's general criminal attributions rather than attributions in relation to a specific crime. The advantage of this is that it directly reflects the offender's general attitudes within specific domains, irrespective of the nature of a specific crime. The disadvantage is that the ABS, unlike the BAI, cannot be used to measure the attitude of the offender to a specific crime he or she had committed.

Amnesia

In serious criminal cases defendants sometimes claim partial or complete amnesia for the criminal act. The claim of amnesia is highest in violent crimes, particularly in cases of homicide where it is typically claimed by between 25 and 45 per cent of offenders (Kopelman, 1995). The amnesia mainly occurs in two types of circumstance. First, when the offender was at the time of the crime severely intoxicated. Here there is often a history of alcoholism and alcoholic blackouts. Secondly, the offence occurs during extreme emotional arousal. Here the offence tends to be unpremeditated and the victim is often a lover, a spouse or a close friend.

Amnesia during or after the commission of a crime is not to be confused with normal forgetting in everyday life. It represents a pathological condition, which can be either *organic* or *psychogenic* in origin. Organic amnesia refers to memory loss which is caused by some damage, temporary or permanent, to brain functions. The organic causes include brain disease, head injury, epilepsy, drug toxicity and alcohol blackouts. Psychogenic amnesia occurs without brain pathology and is predominantly psychological in nature (e.g., due to emotional intensity, psychological trauma or stress). This type of amnesia includes 'fugue states' (i.e., loss of memory of one's personal identity, associated with a period of wandering) and situation-specific amnesia where the memory for specific behaviours is lost (e.g., about a violent crime).

What is not known is the proportion of psychogenic amnesias that are actually genuine. Some authors are very sceptical about the genuineness of psychogenic amnesia (e.g., Bradford and Smith, 1979; Bronks, 1987). Such scepticism was highlighted in the English landmark Podola case (1959). Schacter (1986) suggests some methods of differentiating between feigned and genuine amnesia, but these are without empirical support. One major problem is that amnesia may represent a continuum in levels of awareness in memory rather than falling at the extreme end of either being genuine or simulated (Kopelman, 1995).

Recovered memories

In recent years there has been much public interest in the phenomenon of 'recovered memories' of childhood sexual abuse (Loftus and Ketcham, 1994; Ofshe and Watters, 1994; Pendergrast, 1996). These cases allegedly involve the memories of sexual abuse in childhood being 'repressed' and later 'recovered' in adulthood after the accusing person has received therapy. The most common type of therapy which is reported by the families of the accuser is psychotherapy, followed by hypnotherapy (Gudjonsson, 1997d). These are different from those cases where the accused person had allegedly always remembered the abuse, but only chose to report it in adulthood, with or without therapy. The consequences of the accusations are often devastating to the families involved, with the majority (59 per cent) of the accusers and their families having no subsequent contact with one another (Gudjonsson, 1997d), almost one-third (29 per cent) of the accused persons had to seek therapy themselves because of the stress involved in the accusations, and criminal or civil proceedings were instigated in 13 per cent of cases (Gudjonsson, 1997b).

Gudjonsson (1997b, 1997d, 1997e) had studied 282 families who were members of the British False Memory Society (BFMS) by having them fill in a detailed questionnaire. The majority of the cases allegedly involved recovered memories (Gudjonsson, 1997d). In thirty-seven of the cases criminal proceedings were reported as having been instigated. These cases were followed up and a supplementary questionnaire was completed about the outcome of the cases (Gudjonsson, 1997b). In twenty-three of the cases a defendant was charged by the police, but three of the cases were subsequently discontinued by the Crown Prosecution Service. Twenty cases proceeded to court, and in eight of the cases there were convictions and lengthy prison sentences. One important finding emerged with regard to the nature of the accuser's memory. The involvement of the police and a subsequent conviction in court was significantly associated with the absence of alleged recovered memories concerning the childhood sexual abuse. Gudjonsson (1997b) concluded that the police, lawyers, judges and jurors seem reluctant to accept the testimony of accusers who claim recovered memories of sexual abuse and such cases are less likely to reach court. This finding indicates that alleged recovered memories of childhood sexual abuse are particularly problematic in evidential terms. In view of the nature of such cases, including the length of time since the sexual abuse allegedly happened, such cases are almost inevitably without corroboration. If the accusations are true they are difficult to prove and the judiciary is understandably reluctant to rely entirely on memories which have been allegedly 'repressed' and then suddenly appear years later, with or without the aid of therapy.

Conclusions

Psychology can contribute to criminal court proceedings in a number of different ways. In this chapter the contributions of psychologists to evidential problems in criminal law within the framework of the English legal system are discussed.

There are various criminal courts in the UK, and the requirements for psychological evidence occur in three stages of criminal proceedings, namely, pretrial, trial and sentencing. Fitness to plead, known in the USA as competency to stand trial, is discussed in some depth and differences between jurisdictions are noted. Evidence on competency, whether by special tests or general psychological assessment, is an important function of both psychology and psychiatry, since it is a cognitive issue which usually has a psychiatric causation. Trial issues involve the psychologist in providing evidence concerning the alleged illegal act (*actus reus*) and the criminal intention of the accused (*mens rea*). Certain defences are purely psychological, such as duress, suggestibility and absentmindedness, while others, such as diminished responsibility, have both cognitive and medical components. Psychologists now have a new statutory role in treating offenders. Admissibility of psychological testimony is the *raison d'être* of forensic psychology as defined here, and the limitations and developments are discussed with particular reference to the Raghip and Kane cases and the US Federal Rules of Evidence. Finally, special topics in criminological psychology which relate to the expert testimony given by psychologists are considered, including attribution of blame, amnesia, child abuse and molestation, disputed confessions and offender profiling. Expert testimony in the criminal courts represents a substantial part of forensic psychology's contribution, and while not encompassing quite such a full range of psychological problems as are met with in the civil courts, nevertheless contains more variety than is generally realised, and the consequences of the psychologists' evidence may make the difference between freedom and a life in prison, and in other jurisdictions perhaps of life itself.

10

THE ASSESSMENT AND THE TESTIMONY

A psychological framework

Introduction

Psychologists find themselves being required to testify in court in a variety of ways. Some psychologists are actively involved in court work, either full time or part time, while at the other extreme psychologists with no experience of court work are required to testify about a patient they treated previously. The BPS survey, discussed in Chapter 3, showed that the majority of British psychologists who had testified in court had testified only once or twice. In addition, British psychologists have had no training in the preparation of court reports and how to testify in court. For them testifying in court is often a stressful and intimidating experience. What is needed, in addition to formal training and workshops, is a framework and some general principles which guide psychologists through the different stages of the forensic involvement.

This chapter provides psychologists with a framework for conducting the assessment and prepares them for giving evidence in court. It identifies the essential components of the different stages of the expert's involvement, commencing with the initial referral and terminating with the expert's testimony in court. At each stage there are basic tasks and procedures that need to be worked through by the expert. These are discussed in detail and the potential pitfalls at each stage are highlighted. Haward (1981), Carson (1990), Cooke (1990a, 1990b) and Beaumont (1994) provide useful advice for UK psychologists about testifying in court. As far as psychological report writing is concerned, Ownby (1997) provides an excellent basic guide for practitioners, which has a small section on forensic psychology. Blau (1984), Weiner (1987), Singer and Nievod (1987), Shapiro (1990), Brodsky (1991), Pope et al. (1993), Geiselman (1995) and Valciukas (1995) provide valuable advice to USA psychologists about court report writing and presentation of evidence in court, which is of relevance to UK psychologists.

General advice

Preparing reports and testifying in court should be taken very seriously. Often there is a great deal at stake for the parties involved. Gudjonsson (1993) argues that poor psychological evidence falls into two overlapping categories. Firstly, *evidence which fails to inform*, and secondly, *evidence which is either misleading or incorrect*. He argues that on occasions poor expert evidence may result in a miscarriage of justice.

A recent study among five senior forensic psychiatrists in Sweden indicates an alarming discrepancy in their clinical decision making and opinions when assessing the same case material (Belfrage and Lidberg, 1996). The reasons for this disparity are not known, but the differences appeared to be largely random. This suggests that as far as forensic psychiatric assessments are concerned, diagnostic and treatment decisions are quite haphazard. In view of the potential legal implications of clinical decision making in forensic practice, this disparity raises important human rights issues.

No similar study has been conducted among forensic psychologists. Indeed, no systematic research has been conducted into the quality of expert psychological reports and oral evidence in court. The general quality of expert psychological reports therefore remains unknown. It is likely that the more the clinical decision-making practice is based on interpretations and opinions, rather than on factual data, the greater the disparity between experts.

Pope *et al.* (1993) offer some helpful advice to psychologists who are using the MMPI (or MMPI-2) in the forensic assessment. They identify and discuss the causes of poor quality evidence which they attribute to the following factors: lack of preparation, unfamiliarity with forensic settings and procedures, delays between the assessment and the presentation of the evidence in court, carelessness, impartiality and adversarial bias, the use of technical jargon, poor listening skills, distorted cognitive processes (such as hindsight bias, confirmation or inferential error), the use of sarcasm and jokes during testimony, 'know-it all' attitude, and the need to be the centre of attention.

The referral

The BPS survey (Gudjonsson, 1996a) shows that most UK psychologists are nowadays referred cases directly from solicitors rather than medical colleagues. When cases are referred indirectly from medical or other colleagues the psychologist should normally ask that the case be commissioned in the normal way through a solicitor. Sometimes clients, their family, or television programme producers contact the experts for assistance. If the expert is interested in taking on the case then he or she should request a formal letter of instruction from a solicitor. It is unwise to take on a case where there is no solicitor involved because the report may be used inappropriately and without the legal implications of the findings being carefully considered by a suitable lawyer. For example, experts who act on behalf of television programmes, and express their findings in public without sound legal advice from the client's solicitor, may cause damage to the client's case in future legal proceedings, as well as exposing themselves to a civil action in defamation.

The Law Society has produced guidelines for solicitors about instructing expert witnesses in civil and criminal cases (Law Society, 1996). It recommends that solicitors provide experts with clear written instructions, which should include the following:

a Basic information such as names, addresses, telephone numbers, dates of birth, and dates of incidents;

b The type of expertise which is called for;

c The purpose for requesting the report, and a description of the matter to be investigated;

d Questions to be addressed;

e The history of the matter, identifying any factual matters that may be in dispute;

f Details of any relevant documents (stating which, if any, the expert may refer to in their report in view of the possibility of discovery);

g Whether the expert will be expected to confer with the experts instructed by other parties with a view to reaching agreement on the issues or narrowing those in dispute;

h Whether prior authority to incur the estimated fees needs to be obtained by the solicitor before the instructions can be confirmed;

i In the case of medical reports: where the medical records are situated (including, where possible, the hospital number); whether or not the consent of the client/patient to an examination and disclosure of records has been given; and whether or not the records are to be obtained and provided by the solicitor;

j Whether this report is intended as advice to the client and/or solicitor or for use in court and if the latter, whether there is any agreement for the first version of the report to be marked draft and whether there are any matters requiring comments separately from the formal report;

k In cases concerning children, a note that the paramountcy of the child's welfare may override the legal professional privilege attaching to the report and that disclosure might be required; and confirmation that the court has given leave for the child to be examined.

In addition to the above the Law Society recommends that the solicitor and expert should agree in advance on the time frame within which the report is completed. If experts request clarification of instructions solicitors should respond promptly.

The primary objective of the Law Society's guidelines is to promote optimal or aspirational professional practice. Such clear and comprehensive instructions are of great assistance to experts, but unfortunately this optimal standard of instruction is not always exercised by solicitors. Sometimes the questions to be addressed in the report are not included in the letter of instruction and there may be no reference to the legal issues involved. When this happens the psychologist should go back to the solicitor and ask for more detailed instructions. The Crown Prosecution Service often give very limited instructions in their letter of referral. Typically, the relevant papers in the case are forwarded to the expert and what is requested is 'a report for the Crown' without any clear instruction about what the psychological and legal issues are. For this the psychologist will need to study the case papers, including the case summary, counsel's advice, and report from the defence psychologist, if these are available. The problem is that sometimes lawyers for the defence and the crown do not appear to know themselves exactly what contribution the psychologist may be able to make to the case and what questions should be addressed in the report. This problem is also commonly experienced among American psychologists (Pope *et al.* 1993).

Prior to undertaking an assessment the psychologist should ascertain what kind of an assessment is required and that he or she is properly qualified and competent to undertake the evaluation. It is important to check with the solicitor the date by which the report is needed and when the case is likely to go to court, in the event that the time schedule clashes with other commitments. The psychologist should understand the legal issues involved in the case and be aware of any ethical issues that may arise from the involvement in the case. *The letter of instructions determines the nature and focus of the assessment.* It is therefore very important that the psychologist fully understands the instructions given by the solicitor. The more narrowly focused the instructions the less flexibility the psychologist has in conducting the assessment. Solicitors sometimes ask for a very narrowly focused assessment, such as 'What is my client's intelligence level?' or 'How suggestible is my client?' The psychologist will need to know the context in which such a narrow assessment is being requested and the reason for it. Sometimes solicitors have little idea of the nature and complexity of the psychological evaluation and think that one or two psychometric tests will provide all the answers needed. This is a very simplistic view of the forensic assessment, but one that is commonly held by lawyers. In other cases solicitors deliberately narrow down the assessment because the client had been assessed comprehensively previously but the solicitor does not wish to disclose that report to the court (Gudjonsson, 1994a). The solicitor then instructs another psychologist and ensures that he or she focuses only on those tests that previously produced favourable results. The psychologist may be unaware of this kind of practice at the time of being instructed, but it should become apparent from the history taking of the client.

It is preferable that the solicitor provides the psychologist with questions concerning the legal issues and the psychologist then applies whatever method or psychological tests are appropriate to address the pertinent issues. For example, in cases of disputed confessions the relevant question might be: 'Was my client fit to be interviewed whilst in police detention?' or 'Is my client's confession to the police reliable (valid)?' Other legal issues might be: 'Is my client fit to plead and stand trial?', 'What was my client's mental state at the time of the commission of the crime?', 'What are the effects of the road traffic accident on my client's mental functioning?'

A common problem with forensic referrals is that the psychologist is consulted close to the trial date. When assessments have to be hurried the planning and preparation that are required for a comprehensive assessment may be unsatisfactory. This can undermine the value of the evaluation and testimony.

Fees should be agreed in advance with the referral agent and confirmed in writing. Estimates are normally provided, which include preparation time, assessment time, scoring tests, preparation of the report, and travel time. These are typically expressed in terms of hourly rates for clinical time and travel time, respectively. Rates for attendance at court should also be provided and agreed in advance, although these are normally paid directly by the court. It is important in legally aided cases that solicitors obtain proper authority for the expert's fees and that this authority is confirmed in writing prior to the commencement of the assessment.

On occasions experts may be referred cases by the Crown Prosecution Service that they had previously declined to take on for the defence due to other commitments at the time of the referral. This does not raise any problems unless the expert has discussed the case in detail previously with the defence solicitor, or unless he or she was in possession of compromising defence documents, which may raise ethical dilemmas and make the solicitor unhappy about the expert undertaking the assessment on behalf of the crown. Some experts are only able to take on a small proportion of the cases referred to them by the defence (Gudjonsson, 1996b). As a result some of these cases may be referred to them again at a later date by the Crown Prosecution Service, who would be unaware of the previous interactions between the expert and the defence. In one case a psychologist was sent papers in a criminal case by the defence along with a letter of instructions to act on behalf of the defence. The psychologist did not read the papers but returned them immediately to the defence with a letter explaining that he could not take on the case due to existing commitments. Several months later the case was referred to the same psychologist by the Crown Prosecution Service. Once the defence heard of this they objected to the expert becoming involved for the crown on the basis that he had had the opportunity of reading the defence papers. The fact that he had not read the papers made no difference to the solicitor's suspicions and another psychologist was instructed by the crown.

On occasions solicitors may discuss a defence case in detail with an expert in order to prevent him or her from being able to take the case on for the crown. One of us (Gudjonsson) has been approached on a number of occasions by American attorneys, some of whom, it later emerged, had deliberately obtained his co-operation under false pretences, either to prevent the US government from instructing him or so that they could use the expert's name and standing in order to bargain with the government about mitigation (i.e., claiming that they had the expert on their side and would call him to testify unless the government mitigated the charge or the sentence). According to Pope *et al.* (1993) this is not an uncommon practice among American attorneys.

The following are some key points to remember prior to undertaking the assessment:

1 Make sure that the instructions given are clear and adequate.
2 Make sure you understand the instructions and that you are qualified and competent to conduct the assessment.
3 Check that you have been provided with all the relevant documents in the case.
4 Make sure you understand the legal issues in the case and that you are familiar with the relevant law and legal terminology.
5 Make sure you are able to complete the assessment within the time allowed and that you will be available at the time of the trial in the event of your having to testify. Avoid taking on cases where there is insufficient time for a reasonably comprehensive assessment to be conducted.
6 Discuss and agree fee arrangement with the referral agent prior to under-taking the assessment. Provide a detailed estimate of fees and wait for the necessary authority to be granted by the relevant body (e.g. Legal Aid Board). The estimate should be agreed by the solicitor in writing.

The assessment

Prior to the commencement of the assessment the psychologist should check that the documents forwarded by the referral agent are complete and if additional material is required then this should be requested immediately. The material required will depend on the nature of the case and the issues addressed. Copies of audio or video tapes of police interviews should be requested if these are relevant to the issues being addressed. All relevant material should be carefully reviewed before the psychologist conducts the psychological evaluation. Informants, such as relatives and friends, as well as professional colleagues, may need to be consulted before the report can be completed. Here the client's consent, preferably in a written form, should be obtained in accordance with requirements of confidentiality (see Chapter 4).

Psychologists should be aware that sometimes solicitors do not forward relevant material because they do not want to alert the expert to its content. For example, previous psychological reports or the client's proof of evidence (i.e., his or her privileged statement to the solicitor) may contain information of which the solicitor does not want the expert to become aware. In other instances, solicitors may follow the Law Society's recommendation (see heading 'f' above) and notify the expert of the documents that they do not wish to be referred to in the report, or that they ask the psychologist to delete a reference to the documents after the report is completed (see Chapter 3). This practice of covering up knowledge of documents seen can cause serious ethical dilemmas for psychologists and possibly undermines their professional integrity (see Chapter 4). These matters need to be carefully thought through and resolved, preferably before undertaking the assessment.

Prior to meeting the client the psychologist has to plan and prepare for the assessment. After studying all the papers, and if necessary consulting with the solicitor about the instructions, the psychologist should have a sufficient overview of the case to organise the strategy for the assessment. By this time the psychologist should be clear about the questions being addressed in the assessment. In order to make it reasonably focused and effective, the psychologist should have formulated a model of understanding of the psychological issues involved and formulated various hypotheses that he or she wishes to test. The psychologist should by this time be able to differentiate the fundamental aspects of the case from the peripheral issues. The method of assessment should then be decided. When psychometric tests are used these should be relevant and appropriate to the questions being addressed in the expert's report as well as being reliable and valid. The tests chosen should also be appropriate for use with the person being assessed. For example, persons of low intelligence may not be able to complete questionnaires reliably, and those who are sufficiently bright but cannot read will have to have the questionnaires read out to them. Language problems and the effects of clients' different cultural backgrounds will also need to be considered when selecting and applying psychometric tests.

A comprehensive assessment typically involves a detailed interview with the client, which includes a mental state examination and relevant history taking, in addition to appropriate psychometric testing (see Chapter 6). The relative time taken up with each of these activities depends on the individual case. In some cases the psychometric testing is the primary focus of the assessment, whereas in other instances the clinical interview evaluation may be far more important. Psychometric testing should take place in conjunction with other information gathering, as considered appropriate in a given case.

Pope et al. (1993) point out that the expert's possible cognitive biases may influence the outcome of the psychological assessment. These include such factors as being influenced by 'premature cognitive commitment' (i.e. forming set opinions from first impressions and then clinging to them in spite of evidence to the contrary), 'confirmation bias' (i.e., the tendency to seek out information that is consistent with one's beliefs, theories and hypotheses), and 'hindsight bias' (i.e., knowledge of the 'known fact' influencing the opinion reached). Hindsight bias differs from acknowledged reappraisal of a situation with the benefit of hindsight in that the reappraisal is presented as the original view of the matter.

During the assessment various issues may arise which need to be assessed. For example, a defendant's performance on an IQ test may be below that expected from his or her educational and occupational background. This raises a number of possibilities which need to be specifically examined, such as, 'Is the defendant deliberately faking poor performance?', 'Has there been genuine intellectual deterioration, and if so what are the reasons for the deterioration?', 'Is the defendant's current mental state such that the present findings are not reliable?' The possibility of clients faking on psychometric tests is always something that needs to be considered during the forensic assessment.

There are, of course, a number of factors beside deliberate faking which may influence test performance, including understanding of the questions, tiredness, anxiety, agitation, depression, preoccupation, a chronic medical condition and lack of motivation. The psychologist should be fully alert to any conditions or situations which may affect the interpretation of the test results. Proper explanations of tests and the development of trust are also important factors in obtaining reliable test scores (Grossarth-Maticek et al., 1995).

Pope et al. (1993) strongly recommend that when the MMPI is used experts should 'Let the objective test results speak for themselves' (p. 190). That is, the expert should start with the actual scores and their meaning and avoid engaging in 'hunches and guesses'. This is a very sensible advice. However, test scores are not meaningful in isolation. Apart from their percentile rank, lawyers will want to know the meaning of the scores and how they can be applied to the legal issues in the case. This is often the most difficult part of the assessment. Clinically trained psychologists would normally be expected to be able to competently administer psychological tests, such as the WAIS-R, basic neuropsychological tests, and personality tests, but it is the relevance and weight of the scores which determines their importance within a given case. What do the test scores actually mean within the framework of the case? For example, exactly how does a defendant's low IQ score make his confession to the police unreliable (or 'invalid' in psychological terms)? How does an abnormal MMPI profile make a defendant unfit to plead and stand trial? This means that the expert has to be able to identify psychological problems and vulnerabilities, for example from an interview or by psychological testing, and then show their relevance to the legal issues being addressed. Lack of confidence and experience make some experts cling to test scores and they remain reluctant to offer interpretations to the court of what the scores actually mean within the context of the case.

During the first contact with the client the limitations of confidentiality regarding forensic assessments should be discussed. This is particularly important when the expert has been commissioned by the Crown Prosecution Service or the Social Services Department because any sensitive or incriminating material may be brought up in court and used against them. This should be made very clear to the client at the beginning of the assessment. Even when acting on behalf of the client's defence the report may be disclosed to the opposing side by the solicitor even if it contains some sensitive and unfavourable material.

It is important that psychologists keep detailed and accurate notes of their interviews with clients. These may have to be produced in evidence at a later date, perhaps after an interval of several years. Pope et al. (1993) recommend that psychologists should also keep detailed notes of the client's demeanour and physical appearance as well as any problems with language, vision, hearing and other physical defects.

Some of the key points concerning the assessment are:

1 Check that all the relevant background material is available.
2 Carefully review all the material and listen to police interview tapes when relevant.
3 Develop a good overview of the case.
4 Determine what the salient issues and questions are that require an assessment.
5 Make sure you are familiar with all the relevant and up-to-date research findings.
6 Plan the assessment and decide on the tests to be used. The tests chosen should be appropriate for the questions addressed in the report and to the client being assessed. Psychologists should be flexible in their approach to a case. The tests used should be reliable and valid. Avoid using only parts of tests or short forms with reduced reliability and validity.
7 Consult with informants as necessary, but ensure you have the client's written consent to do so.
8 At the beginning of the assessment inform the client of the limitations of confidentiality with regard to forensic evaluations.
9 Give yourself sufficient time to conduct the assessment. Remember that more than one appointment may be needed.
10 Beware of 'hindsight bias' and 'confirmation bias' during the assessment.
11 Make sure the assessment is thorough and complete.
12 Keep detailed and careful notes of the assessment. These may have to be produced in evidence.
13 Score the psychometric tests carefully. Double check the scoring.
14 Think carefully about how the findings from the assessment can be interpreted within the framework of the legal issues. This is often the most difficult part of the assessment.

The report

Once the expert has completed the assessment the preparation of the report begins. The report has to be written with the forensic context in mind, which means that the style, format and content have to be aimed at the non-psychologist reader. The presentation of the report is of major importance. It acts as a formal communication to the referral agent, and ultimately to the court. The lay-out of the report and its detail depend on a number of factors, including the nature of the case, the types of instruction given by the solicitor, and the preference and practice of the expert. Regardless of the legal and psychological issues addressed in the report, *clarity* and *simplicity* are fundamental to an effective report. The report is there to *inform* the lawyers, the judge and the jury about the client's psychological functions and behaviour, including his or her mental problems and deficits. It is important that the report is written in simple and easily understood language. Technical jargon should be avoided. Descriptions of the tests used, factual information, and opinions should be expressed simply and clearly. It is important to differentiate the factual evidence from interpretations and opinions. Carson (1990) strongly emphasises that expert witnesses should make their evidence as factual as possible. In his view, even though expert witnesses are entitled to give an opinion, in contrast to ordinary witnesses, opinions are much easier to discredit than factually based evidence during the cross-examination.

The Law Society (1996) recommends that solicitors check the expert's report upon receipt and ensure that it adequately provides the information requested. They list the kind of information they would expect to be in the report. Expert psychological reports should normally contain the following information (this list has incorporated the recommendations of the Law Society and expanded it with a particular reference to forensic psychological reports):

a   Basic details, such as the name of the client, his or her date of birth, age, where seen, dates of appointments, and total amount of time seen for assessment.

b   The name and address of the referral agent.

c   The purpose of the assessment as per letter of instruction.

d   Information about the method used in the investigation (e.g. interview, psychometric testing, behavioural observations, experimental procedures). The names of informants consulted and interviewed should be provided.

e   A list of documents and material provided by the referral agent or that obtained from other sources.

f   Details of information obtained from interview with the client.

g   Details of information obtained from other sources, including that of informants.

h   Brief description of the tests used. If short or abbreviated forms are used this should be stated.

i   Sufficient details of test scores for another psychologist to be able to evaluate the results.

j   Details of the client's demeanour and motivation during the assessment.

k   Discussion of the principal findings.

l   Conclusions and opinions. The inferences drawn and opinions reached should be reasoned.

m   The name, professional address, qualifications and affiliation of the examiner.

n   A table appended to the report in those cases where there is extensive raw data from psychometric tests which could be provided in this form when appropriate.

There is a disagreement in the literature about how much detail and raw data should be disclosed to lawyers about test scores. Binder and Thompson (1995) point out that attorneys in the USA often ask for raw data from neuropsychological and personality assessments. They point out two problems with this practice. First, lawyers are not qualified to interpret the raw scores themselves and commonly obtain the raw data only in order to obtain material for cross-examination, which may be against the client's interest. Secondly, the disclosure of raw data may threaten the validity of psychometric tests in future use. These two problems are also of considerable concern to some British psychologists (Tunstall *et al.*, 1982).

A similar problem exists when psychologists provide detailed descriptions of subtle psychological tests in their report. This practice may undermine the validity of some psychometric tests. The present authors recommend that psychologists should be very careful about disclosing raw test data and details of confidential test material in their report to non-psychologists. Psychologists should be fully aware of the implications and ethical issues involved (see Chapter 4).

The argument in favour of some disclosure about the tests used and raw scores is that it is very difficult for psychologists to evaluate another psychologist's test findings without a certain amount of detail being provided in the report. As Matarazzo (1995) reminds us, psychologists may vary considerably in their interpretation of test scores. Providing the actual raw scores, or the scaled score equivalents, makes it much easier for the psychologist to evaluate any differences in scores between assessments. Freides (1993) recommends that as a standard procedure a table with the test scores be routinely attached to the neuropsychological report. As an alternative procedure, depending upon the amount of test detail that is available and needed for evaluating the results, the basic test data can be provided in the body of the report under the heading, 'Present Test Results'.

It is recommended that psychological reports should be organised in sections. As far as the forensic evaluation is concerned this may include headings such as, Reason for Referral, Documents Seen (all documents and material provided by the referral agent should be specified), Background Information (the psychologist may wish to provide a brief account of the client's background and the case), Past Test Results (all known relevant past test results should be reported), Present Test Results (the assessment tools used should be listed and test results provided in tabular or narrative form), Behaviour During Assessment (behavioural observations during testing and interview of the client are often important in the overall evaluation of the case), Interview with Client, Interviews with Informants, Discussion, Conclusions and Recommendations (these should be focused on the pertinent issues listed in the Reason for Referral).

It is important that psychologists are aware of consistencies or inconsistencies in their data or across data sets. Consistencies corroborate and strengthen the findings and the expert's conclusions. Inconsistencies will need to be explained and they may be used in the cross-examination to attack the reliability and validity of the evaluation.

The report should be carefully checked for accuracy and clarity before it is forwarded to the referral agent. Minor factual or typographical errors are easy to make and overlook. They can cause an embarrassment to the expert when brought up during the cross-examination by the opposing side as a way of challenging his or her competence and thoroughness.

The findings of the assessment and the report should normally only be disclosed to the referral agent. In some instances defence solicitors will forward a copy of the report to their client. The report is a confidential document as far as the expert is concerned. It should not be disclosed to other parties without the consent of the client and his or her solicitor. When more than one expert is instructed for one side it may be desirable for these experts to consult in order to avoid undue overlap in their assessment. This does not generally create any problems, although such consultation may be brought up in cross-examination as a way of challenging the true independence of the experts from one another. Solicitors are much more reluctant to agree to prior contact and consultations among opposing experts, particularly when they may not wish to disclose the knowledge or the content of the report to the opposing side.

Once the report is completed the referral agent may provide the expert with feedback on the report and ask for certain changes to be made. Earlier in this chapter it was shown that one of the Law Society's recommendations is that experts may be asked to produce a draft of their report for the solicitor to comment on before the final version is completed and that certain matters requiring comments may be produced separately from the formal report. These recommendations of the Law Society are open to abuse by solicitors and can create a number of ethical difficulties for the psychologist (see Chapter 4). It is one thing for solicitors to correct factual errors in the report and request clarification of certain issues, but when they are instrumental in fundamentally influencing the content of the report in terms of relevant factual information and opinions it becomes a serious ethical issue which may well undermine the integrity of the expert and that of his or her profession. As is made clear in Chapter 4, psychologists should not comply with any request to alter reports which is likely to mislead the court. Solicitors can be very persuasive when requesting that the report be altered to make it more favourable to their client. Sometimes they are themselves under pressure from counsel to have the report favourably altered. After the solicitor has failed to persuade the psychologist to alter the report the client's counsel may try to do so, either on the telephone or during a pretrial conference.

Another strategy that solicitors sometimes use is to have the expert's report retyped, with unfavourable material deleted, in a form of a written statement made under Section 9 of the Criminal Justice Act 1967. This is a sworn Witness

Statement which requires the expert's signature to be witnessed. At the top of the statement it reads:

> This statement (consisting of pages each signed by me) is true to the best of my knowledge and belief and I make it knowing that, if it is tendered in evidence, I shall be liable to prosecution if I have wilfully stated in it anything which I know to be false or do not believe to be true.

Psychologists must check very carefully through reports that have been retyped by solicitors and compare it with the original report. Solicitors sometimes delete unfavourable material from the report and psychologists may sign the witness statement without being aware of alterations to the report. Reports written in the form of a Section 9 Witness Statement are commonly requested by the police and also sometimes by solicitors, because sworn Witness Statements are more readily accepted by the courts than signed reports and often save witnesses having to give evidence in person (i.e., such statements may be read out in court).

When provided with a report disclosed by the opposing side it may be necessary to provide a supplementary report. Check through the other expert's report carefully and provide an objective and dispassionate commentary on it. In some instances psychologists fail to include all relevant test scores in their report and when this happens the client's solicitor or the Crown Prosecution Service can formally request that these are provided. Psychologists should obtain the consent of the respective referral agents before they consult or discuss the case with the psychologist from the opposing side. This permission may be provided in the referral letter as indicated earlier in this chapter or it can be sought separately. Occasionally lawyers refuse to give their consent for experts to consult prior to their giving evidence in court. Proper consultation among experts is often desirable and saves court time.

Some of the key points to remember when preparing the report are:

1 Decide on the style, format and content of the report and how detailed it should be. Keep the report as brief as possible. The report represents a formal communication between the expert and the referral agent and the court.
2 The report should focus on characteristics that differentiate the client from his contemporaries.
3 Express factual information, findings from tests, and opinions clearly and without unnecessary technical jargon. Use clear structure, plain English, and ensure that facts and opinions are clearly separated. Clarity and simplicity are essential for effective communication. Paragraphs should be short and focused.
4 Give the factual basis for the inferences drawn and opinions given.

5 Be careful not to disclose so much information about psychometric tests in the report that a test's validity could be undermined in future use.

6 It is recommended that basic test scores be provided in the body of the report, or in a table appended to the report, in order for another psychologist to be able to properly evaluate the findings.

7 Look for and highlight consistencies across different sets of data. Major inconsistencies should be pointed out and explained, if possible.

8 Remember that clients are sometimes given a copy of the report by their solicitor.

9 Check that the report adequately provides the information requested by the referral agent.

10 Check carefully through the report for factual and typographical errors.

11 Do not disclose the report to any unauthorised persons.

12 Remember that your report may influence the outcome in the case and have serious consequences.

13 Do not conduct a biased assessment for the side instructing you because you wish to please the referral agent.

14 Remember that solicitors and barristers may place experts under considerable pressure to alter the report to make it more favourable to their client's defence. Consider the ethical issues involved and do not compromise your integrity or that of your profession.

15 Reports often have important consequences for the client and the case. The assessment and the report should be completed thoughtfully, comprehensively and conscientiously.

Pretrial preparation

Once the report is completed the referral agent may contact the expert and ask for a pretrial conference. This is a very important preparation for any live testimony. The purpose of this conference is to go through the expert's report in detail and make sure that counsel understands the expert's findings and the basis of his or her opinions. At the conference the solicitor and counsel may ask the expert some pertinent questions. Some barristers are well informed about psychological and psychiatric evidence and may be able to test the strength of the expert's opinions and his or her likely performance under cross-examination. Counsel will sometimes inform the psychologist of the type of questions that will be asked by him or her during the examination in chief and the likely strategy of the opposing counsel during the cross-examination.

Another advantage of a pretrial conference is for all relevant experts in the case for the party concerned to meet and discuss similarities and contradictions between experts. Haward (1981) describes how different experts testifying for one party may give totally contradictory evidence and discredit one another.

In the USA experts are commonly asked to produce a 'deposition testimony' prior to their testimony in court. This is a statement taken under oath in a non-courtroom setting (e.g., a lawyer's office) in the presence of a court reporter. It provides the opposing party with the opportunity of learning about the expert's background and expertise and what he or she is going to say in their live testimony (Singer and Nievod, 1987). What the expert says in the 'deposition' will be available to the judge and jury and can be used to challenge the live testimony when discrepancies occur. Experts should be very careful in what they say in their deposition and prepare for it as if they were undergoing live testimony in court.

Another major difference between expert evidence in the USA and the UK is that in the USA experts are often required to give the lawyers copies of all clinical notes they made during the evaluation, copies of any tape-recorded interviews with the client and raw test scores. These can be used to help cross-examine the expert witness.

A careful and thorough preparation for the testimony is essential. The trial or an appeal hearing may take place many months, and sometimes years, after the psychological evaluation. All the material in the case will need to be reviewed again and relevant police interview tapes should be listened to again, if at all practicable. The expert's report, test material and interview notes should be read in order to refresh the expert's memory about the evaluation.

Some of the key points to remember about the pretrial preparation are:

1   Good preparation for the testimony is essential.
2   When the expert is likely to testify it is important that he or she attends a pretrial conference with the lawyers who commissioned the report.
3   Prior to attending court the expert should carefully review all the documents and material in the case, and listen to police interview tapes if this is relevant and practicable.
4   The expert should read his or her report, clinical interview notes, and test scores.
5   Experts from opposing sides are increasingly encouraged to consult and try to agree on salient points prior to their live testimony. This must be done with the consent of all legal parties concerned.

Attending court

It is important to dress properly for court appearances; the legal profession is a conservative one and expects professional experts to match their stereotype. To arrive in T-shirt and trainers is not only seen as a mark of disrespect to 'the majesty of the law' and likely to receive adverse comment in the judge's summing-up, or opposing counsel's closing address to the jury, as in Anderson's case (1971) but also may have a very real effect upon the acceptability of the psychologist's testimony by the jury, who usually take some trouble to look 'presentable'. While scientific evidence should stand on its own merit, psychologists should understand the strength of personal quirks in decision making, and make an effort to prevent diminution of the impact of their testimony from this source. The social psychology literature on appearance and its effects has been successfully utilised by the retail trade and there are relevant lessons to be learnt from this source.

The expert witness should be punctual, and it is customary to reach court half an hour before commencement of the hearing, or at a time designated by the client's lawyer, in case counsel or solicitor wish to have a final word before entering court. On arrival, the psychologists should look at the notice board near the entrance, where the cases are listed, and where the number of the court hearing their particular case is shown. This is important, as some courts are housed in more than one building, each with its own entrance. London's Central Criminal Court, for example, has eighteen separate courts, some of which are located on the opposite side of the Old Bailey. Its civil equivalent, the High Court in the Strand, is a warren of court rooms, and some of the smaller court-rooms used for cases concerning children are not easy to find.

Another reason for consulting the list of hearings for the day is to determine the status of the judge hearing the case. Male Puisne judges are listed as Mr Justice (name), referred to as The Honourable Mr (name) and should be addressed as 'My Lord' (never M'lud!). Circuit judges appear as (name), J., referred to as Judge (name) and addressed as 'Your Honour'. Recorders, lower down the scale, are part-time judges, referred to as Mr (name), QC and addressed traditionally as 'Sir' (although nowadays they are more commonly addressed as 'Your Honour'). Women judges, still a small minority, are addressed by the equiv-alent title appropriate to their sex. If they are High Court judges they are addressed as 'My Lady', otherwise as 'Madam'. In the Magistrates' Court, a stipendiary magistrate sits alone and lay magistrates normally sit in threes, with the person in the middle acting as the 'Chairperson'; they are addressed as 'Your Worship(s)' or as 'Sir' or 'Madam' according to the gender of the magistrate who is chairing the proceedings. As in other walks of life, no one is offended if addressed as someone of somewhat higher status, but can resent being accorded lower status with its implicit denial of present achievement. It is however always best to address people by their correct title because addressing judges incorrectly in this way may be interpreted as inappropriate and sycophantic.

In Scotland all judges, irrespective of the nature of the court, are addressed as 'My Lord'. In the USA judges are addressed as 'Your Honour' or 'Judge'.

The testimony

Having acquired the necessary information from the court lists, the psychologists should go direct to the waiting area for the appropriate court, and seat them-selves conspicuously where they can both see and be seen by the solicitor and counsel when they arrive, or when they leave court, if the trial is already in progress. As an expert witness the psychologist is normally allowed to sit in court while other witnesses give their evidence and during legal arguments, although this is at the discretion of the judge. This provides the psychologist with familiarity with the court, which may relieve anxiety about testifying.

Witnesses have to follow a certain etiquette in court. When entering the witness box the expert should position himself or herself in such a way as to face the judge. They have to read the oath or to affirm. This should be done clearly and firmly. When asked questions by an advocate they should turn towards that advocate and before answering turn back towards the judge. All answers should be addressed to the judge and not to the advocate who asked the question. Unless invited to do so by the judge, all witnesses have to give their evidence standing. The acoustics are poor in many courtrooms and it is essential that witnesses speak sufficiently loudly to be clearly heard by the judge and jury. In addition, many witnesses speak too fast when giving their evidence. Most judges make detailed notes of the expert's testimony. It is useful to follow the judge's pen as he or she makes notes, because this will ensure that the expert is not speaking too fast for proper notes to be made.

Once the psychologist goes in the witness box he or she is offered the New Testament and required to take the standard oath, which reads: 'I swear by Almighty God, that the evidence I shall give will be the truth, the whole truth, and nothing but the truth.' If the witness is not a Christian then an alternative religious book may be used. If the witness objects to being sworn then he or she is permitted to affirm instead of taking the oath. The Affirmation reads: 'I (state name) solemnly and sincerely and truly declare and affirm that the evidence I shall give shall be the truth, the whole truth and nothing but the truth.'

As far as the evidence itself is concerned, there are three main phases to oral evidence. Firstly, there is the 'examination-in-chief' or 'direct examination' of witnesses. This is conducted by the side for whom the witness is appearing. Most commonly, the witness would be testifying for the side originally instructing him or her. Occasionally, an expert who was originally instructed by the Crown Prosecution Service may be asked to give evidence on behalf of the defence. In other words, he or she is called as a defence witness because the evidence is favourable to the defence. The purpose of this phase is to put forward the witness's testimony before the court. In the case of expert witnesses, this can be done by the witness being taken through his or her report. In general, leading questions are not permitted during the examination-in-chief.

The second phase, 'cross-examination', involves the witness being asked questions by the opposing counsel about the evidence presented during the examination-in-chief. Leading questions are allowed, and the purpose is to test the strength of the witness's evidence. This can be stressful and taxing for the expert who is appearing in adversarial proceedings. As Haward (1981) states:

> The cross-examination is the judicial way of testing the merits of the opposing arguments. At best it may be merely a polite probing for possible weaknesses or inconsistencies, an attempt to obtain some

acceptable degree of rapprochement between two apparently different sets of opinion. At worst the cross-examination can be a rude, emotional, overbearing and personal attack on the witness as well as a devious, subtle and biased critique of his methods, findings, conclusions and opinions: which end of this continuum any particular cross-examination falls will depend upon the personality, skill, and experience of the cross-examining counsel and the nature of the evidence given by the expert.

(p. 262)

The third phase, 're-examination', involves the advocate acting for the party for whom the witness is appearing asking questions that have arisen out of the cross-examination. This is sometimes necessary in order to correct a possible misconception which arose out of the cross-examination or for the expert's main points in the examination-in-chief to be reinforced.

The judge may interrupt the examination at any of the three phases in order to clarify the expert's testimony. He or she should ensure that expert witnesses are treated fairly and courteously by the legal advocates. However, this is not always the case and sometimes judges take a very active part in the questioning of expert witnesses (Tunstall et al., 1982).

Expert witnesses are often required to give evidence in court on more than one occasion. The evidence may be given in front of the judge only during a 'trial within a trial', then again in front of the jury, and if there is a retrial the process may be conducted all over again (Tunstall et al., 1982; Gudjonsson, 1992a). If there are inconsistencies between the expert's evidence on different occasions then this may be used against the witness during cross-examination (the legal advocates may have a transcript of the witness's previous testimony or detailed notes).

Experts are sometimes asked hypothetical questions by the advocates or the judge. These are questions which are based on mere supposition or hypotheses. They must bear some relationship to the evidence given by the expert, although they 'do not have to be tied rigidly to facts proved at the trial' (Robertson and Vignaux, 1995). According to Haward (1981) hypothetical questions have two purposes. Firstly, to supplement or reinforce information already obtained from the witness, and secondly, to counteract points made by the opposing side.

Carson (1990) points out that lawyers tend to dichotomise issues and questions and this is often difficult for psychologists to cope with. Lawyers like short replies, such as 'yes', 'no', 'possible', or 'probable', because it gives them more control over the questioning. If the psychologist is unable to answer the question satisfactorily in this way he or she can explain to the judge why that is the case. A short 'yes' or 'no' answer may misrepresent or oversimplify the psychologist's answer and this is not desirable and should be avoided.

One major difficulty with using psychometric test results in court, as Gudjonsson (1992b) has pointed out, is that the law is often forced by statute to forego discretion and deal in absolute terms on the all-or-nothing principle. Psychologists find to their dismay that the courts are using some arbitrary measure, such as an IQ score 70, above or below which offenders or suspects may be treated in markedly and unjustifiably, different ways. The judgment of the Court of Appeal on 5 December 1991, in Raghip's case (1991) has, to a certain extent, changed this rigid attitude of the courts to arbitrary IQ scores (see Chapter 9 for the legal implications of the judgment in the case).

The law uses its own terminology and its precise meaning may vary from one jurisdiction to another. It is important that the psychologist is familiar with the legal terminology where he or she is testifying. The use of terms such as 'insanity', 'diminished responsibility', 'fitness to plead', 'voluntariness', 'oppression', and 'reliability', have precise legal meanings, which may differ from what the psychologist assumes they mean.

Hypothetical questions can be an effective way of undermining the expert's findings and conclusions (Shapiro, 1990). The advocate may incorporate unfounded premises which are unacceptable to the expert in order to raise alternative hypotheses for the expert's findings. Robertson and Vignaux (1995) point out that such questions can be difficult to answer while the expert is under pressure in the witness box and without access to the necessary data. The best way of coping with such questions is for the expert to be aware of such tactics and to have carefully considered alternative hypotheses for the findings prior to entering the witness box. However, sometimes hypothetical questions are difficult to anticipate beforehand and the dichotomising approach by the courts to evidence can undermine the credibility of the expert's testimony as the following example illustrates:

Judge   If a Fellow of the Royal Society obtained an IQ of 60 on the test (WAIS-R) would you conclude that he suffered from a significant intellectual impairment?
Psychologist Yes, I would.
Judge   Any test that describes a Fellow of the Royal Society as intellectually impaired is useless.

Here the judge makes the unfounded assumption that a Fellow of the Royal Society might obtain an IQ score of 60 on the intelligence test administered. Even if that was the case there could be a number of explanations for this, which include the possibility of a marked intellectual deterioration due to organic (brain) pathology. Such comments by a trial judge in front of the jury are likely to seriously undermine the credibility of the expert's evidence, but would have had less effect if the psychologist had insisted on qualifying his answer before returning to the counsel's questioning.

Some of the key points to remember during the presentation of oral evidence are as follows:

1   Witnesses have to follow a certain etiquette in court. The expert witness should be fully familiar with these details.
2   Expert evidence involves three distinct phases, referred to as 'examination-in-chief', 'cross-examination' and 're-examination', respectively. Expert witnesses should be properly prepared for all three phases. Their function is to assist the judge and jury in understanding the psychological issues in the case.
3   Presentation is of crucial importance during oral evidence. The expert must be suitably dressed, their evidence must be clearly and simply presented, and their answers should be short and straight to the point. The expert should not become emotionally involved in cases.
4   Courts deal in absolute (dichotomous) terms on the all-or-nothing principle, which often causes difficulties for psychologists.
5   Expert witnesses may have to testify on more than one occasion in a case. Inconsistencies in their evidence may be used against them during cross-examination.

Conclusions

The forensic assessment consists of a sequence of stages. At each stage there are set tasks and procedures that need to be understood and completed. The chapter began by describing the initial contact between the psychologist and the referral agent. The initial contact may involve a two-way interaction between the lawyer and the psychologist and the outcome influences the nature of the instruction given by the referral agent. Sometimes psychologists have to advise lawyers about the appropriate question that they should be asking the psychologist to address. The instructions given by the lawyer define the nature and scope of the forensic assessment. Once the psychological evaluation is completed the findings are sometimes presented in a written report or presented as a Section 9 Witness Statement. It may then form the basis for negotiations between the two opposing sides. When the report is strongly in favour of the defence the Crown Prosecution Service may decide not to proceed with the case. If the report is not agreed by the opposing side then the expert will have to testify in court.

It is important that psychologists understand the legal as well as the clinical issues pertaining to the case they are assessing. In addition, they must be familiar with legal terminology. The use of language is particularly important in forensic work. The precise meaning of words used by lawyers must be clearly understood by the forensic psychologist. The legal use of the words is often different to psychological usage and may vary between different legal jurisdictions.

Good preparation at each stage is vital. Prior to commencing the assessment psychologists should have a good overview of the case and the fundamental issues involved. They should select assessment procedures and psychometric tests that are relevant to solving the legal issues. Inexperienced psychologists may become lost in peripheral issues and detail and fail to focus on the fundamental issues. Interpreting test results satisfactorily within the framework of the legal issues is often one of the most difficult parts of the assessment.

Cases often require a great deal of thinking and effort. Even if psychologists are experienced in the assessment of cases, each case must be carefully considered on its own merit. There is no short cut or compromise to a good forensic evaluation.

The presentation of the written report and oral evidence in court are of vital importance. The results of the assessment must therefore be presented clearly, simply and honestly. The purpose of the evidence is to inform the judge and jury in a clear, credible and effective way about the client's relevant psychological status.

11

CONCLUSIONS

Forensic psychology in a nutshell

This final chapter briefly draws together the main threads of the subject as answers to the six questions represented by Kipling's 'honest serving men' and then focuses on contemporary problems in forensic psychology.

WHY forensic psychology? The profession has developed this speciality from a mixture of motives. The original pioneers probably entered court partly from the civilised person's natural desire to secure justice for a fellow citizen (it is noteworthy that all the early cases were in support of an individual rather than the state) and partly to extend their own professional expertise in applying psychology's new corpus of scientific knowledge. While such motives may still apply, the psychology profession, growing exponentially since the mid-century, is anxious to explore areas of interest likely to become new specialities and sub-specialities, extend its frontiers of knowledge, and especially develop new career structures to absorb its ever-growing army of graduates.

WHAT is forensic psychology? In Europe, and in the UK especially, forensic psychology is generally seen as the application of psychological skills and knowledge to the search for expert evidence relative to problems posed by a particular case. In the USA, a more embracing definition is used, in which forensic psychology is seen as embracing the whole gamut of psycholegal issues, including particular evidence as such, but more concerned with research into the background of general problems of legal procedure, law enforcement, criminology, penology, witness testimony, and so on. In England this has been called psychological jurisprudence and in Scotland it could be termed psycholegalism, analogous to the Scottish medicolegalism.

WHEN did forensic psychology originate? While psychology, as part of philosophy, has influenced the development of law since primitive times, it was not until it embraced science in the early nineteenth century that it became capable of producing evidence that met the law's admissibility criteria in respect of validity, reliability and cogency that it could be accepted in court. Forensic psychology, within the restricted definition adopted in this book, was primarily an entrepreneurial product of graduates from Wundt's Psychological Laboratory in Leipzig. Europe was the birthplace of forensic psychology, dating from Schrenck-Notzing's testimony in a Bavarian court in 1896. As Wundt's students travelled to America, forensic psychology blossomed there at the turn of the century, and later became world-wide via European colonial and American overseas influence.

However, between the early 1920s and late 1940s psychologists in the USA did not regularly appear as expert witnesses in the courts. In the UK, forensic psychology had a much slower start and it appears that it was not until 1958 that psychologists began to give evidence in court. Prior to that time psychological findings were invariably incorporated into the evidence of psychiatrists, prison doctors and school medical officers.

WHO are forensic psychology's clients? In terms of contract law it is the person or organisation to whom the psychologist contracts, or is under contract, to provide the forensic service. It may be the expert's employer, as when an educational psychologist testifies in a juvenile case on behalf of his local education authority, or a clinician goes before a Mental Health Review Tribunal in respect of one of his hospital's patients. It may be the corporate entity in whom the psychologist shares a partnership, and which handles the administrative side of a profitable forensic business. It may be one of the parties involved, such as the accused, prosecutor or the plaintiff seeking assistance with their case, or even a close relative in, say, a case of alleged testamentary incompetency, or an individual anticipating future police action and seeking treatment as a possible defence. It may be the local police division, seeking help by hypnosis, offender-profiling, etc., in a specific investigation. It may be with some protest group or organisation, such as 'Justice', seeking to remedy an injustice. All such contracting parties have occurred in the past. Apart from those cases undertaken as part of one's contract of employment, the most efficient and satisfactory contracts are those made directly with the legal advisor of the supplicating party: only in this way can the psychologist obtain the full details of both sides of the case, and have access to any relevant legal advice that may be needed in respect of case precedents, possible sanctions, permissible mitigating factors and so on, which are important in planning the nature and scope of the psychological investigation. It also ensures that the lawyer's own firm will be responsible for the fees and agreed expenses; other clients may decamp, refuse or be unable to pay, and seeking redress through the courts may cost more than is eventually gained.

WHERE should the psychological investigation take place? Ideally in the psychologist's own consulting rooms, where all test material, equipment and reference books are to hand. Increasingly, psychologists are undertaking private forensic work through the medium of partnerships, often in the form of a limited liability company, which makes the contracts, provides second opinions on reports, and usually facilities such as equipment, consulting rooms and waiting area, receptionist and secretarial back-up. Such services can often be located in convenient locations in cities, may cost less than the overheads paid to an employing authority, and have certain tax advantages in the way fees are withdrawn from the profits. In major criminal cases the accused being investigated is often in prison, and the assessment venue is often noisy or otherwise unsuitable: the minimum requirement should be a legal interview room, but it is better to seek the prison medical officer's permission to use a room in the prison hospital where more time and better facilities are available for the assessment, including access to the inmate's medical notes. Prison visits can be organised directly through the hospital wing of the prison rather than through legal visits, although this varies from one prison to another. Sometimes a domiciliary visit is requested, usually when the plaintiff is disabled from an accident. If the examinee is of the opposite sex to the psychologist, care should be taken that a third party is present in a neighbouring room at the time, not only as a chaperon, but to ensure that domestic distractions such as children, pets, tradesmen and other visitors do not interrupt the session. In evaluating the assessment data, allowance should be made for the effect the different environments will have on the test results. In some cases laboratory or field experiments will be indicated, which may take the psychologist into novel situations and environments.

HOW should the psychologist respond to the referral agent's request for assistance? Firstly by identifying the precise problem that needs solving; the solicitor's referral letter is often couched in the most general terms because a psychological factor has been recognised but the client has little idea exactly how it can best be examined. The psychologist must first look at its relevance, for it may be more appropriately dealt with by a colleague in a different speciality or even a different profession. There may be more than one problem teased out from the initial enquiry, some of which should be referred elsewhere – to a neurologist or psychiatrist, for instance. Psychologists, having decided that the remaining problems lie within their own speciality, must then decide whether the solution lies within their professional competence. If so, the means of obtaining the solution is then planned. In most cases this will involve a detailed and comprehensive assessment of some relevant factor of the accused or plaintiff, such as cognitive efficiency, competency or mental deterioration; post-traumatic stress, level and orientation of sexual arousal, and so on. Diagnosis, questions of insanity and diminished responsibility involve the psychologist from time to time, but the judiciary have mixed views on whether these questions fall exclusively within the purview of psychiatry. The means of determining and measuring these factors must be carefully considered in terms of validity and reliability, selecting a variety of techniques which can provide inter-test confirmation of critical findings. The psychological armamentarium from which such tests and techniques are selected will include cognitive and personality tests, including tests of intellectual abilities and suggestibility and other especially relevant factors, such as perception and visual acuity, as well as psychophysiological testing, monitoring and recording instruments. In some cases, there will be no individual assessment required, the psychologist analysing other evidence, such as documents or crime scenes, or carrying out a literature search or laboratory or field experiments to obtain behavioural or psychosocial norms with which the behaviour in dispute can be compared.

The most basic and essential requirements for a competent and credible psychological evaluation are good *preparation* at each stage (i.e., assessment of client, report writing, and presentation of evidence in court), clear *focus* on the relevant and essential issues, *clarity* in terms of communications to the referral agent and the court, and *impartiality*.

Contemporary problems in forensic psychology practice

This section draws together, restates and, where necessary, expands some of the professional problems which have been mentioned earlier. They represent issues which appear to have been previously inadequately addressed, if at all, and which deserve further discussion and subsequent action within the profession as a whole.

Forensic psychologists are still exploring the limits of their speciality, and are likely to continue until a comprehensive definition can be generally agreed. Within any one jurisdiction both narrow and wide definitions of forensic psychology exist, each of which has practical implications, both for the forensic practice and for the profession of psychology as a whole. This is not to say that psychologists should deliberately exclude themselves from certain activities merely because they fall outside the definition of forensic psychology which they hold: it does mean that their professional function, in legal casework, for example, is conducted under the forensic label, while other psycholegal activities outside their forensic definition (unless the latter is all-inclusive) are conducted as part of applied psychology related to the psychologist's basic speciality.

A second problem arises from the first: exactly what is meant by the term 'forensic psychologist'? Are they well-qualified and experienced experts, called in when necessary and appropriate to apply the expertise of their own speciality, to the evidence in some particular case, as the present authors maintain? Or are they members of a full-time speciality, qualified in general psychology, and trained to act as expert witnesses, as the present appellation of 'chartered forensic psychologist' and the introduction of postgraduate training courses in the subject would suggest?

These questions raise a third problem. Modern scientific psychology encompasses such a breadth and depth of knowledge, that its original and traditional specialities, such as clinical, educational, social, occupational, and so on, can no longer contain the many diverse fields of specialised knowledge and techniques that have developed in recent decades. In consequence, numerous sub-specialities and 'groups of special interest', such as health psychology, neuropsychology, witness psychology, child psychology, prison psychology, feminine psychology, etc. are coming into existence. The question then is: do chartered forensic psychologists hold themselves out as experts on any and all psychological problems, itself a professional impossibility? Or are they experts in a basic speciality confining their activity to forensic problems arising within that speciality? If so, how are lawyers supposed to distinguish between the former, who know little about a lot, and the latter, who know a lot about a little? And if both are using the same 'forensic psychologist' label, how will lawyers know whether the speciality of the latter is appropriate to their client's immediate needs? The medical profession solved this problem before it arose; there are no forensic 'doctors', but there are forensic psychiatrists and forensic pathologists. These two well-known and established medical specialities have a medicolegal role which is clearly perceived and understood by lawyers, yet their professional allegiance and career structure is still within their primary medical speciality. It offers just what the legal profession wants; a high level of professional expertise together with courtroom experience. In a less well-defined way, this is how psychology has developed its forensic activity, its practitioners performing expert applications of their basic speciality, mostly clinical or educational, to forensic problems. This function is appropriately called 'forensic psychology' but the practitioners themselves have until now regarded themselves as members of their basic division in psychology.

The foregoing discussion raises yet another problem arising from the definition of 'forensic psychology'. The new speciality of forensic psychology now being created will require its own professional group, such as a division or section, to act as a forum for its deliberations, and to co-ordinate and regulate the practice of the speciality. At present this is done by the BPS's Division of Criminological and Legal Psychology, which has adopted the broader definition of forensic psychology. If a wide definition of forensic psychology is chosen, the corresponding speciality group would overlap and possibly embrace existing professional or special interest groups, such as criminology, legal psychology and similar sub-divisions of the psycholegal field. If a narrow definition is accepted, then the interests and activities of the forensic division would be equally narrow, but would still overlap some aspects of existing groups. Central to these four problems arising from the basic speciality definition is the question of how the legal profession will be able to recognise the kind of expert who is professionally competent to solve the psychological problem(s) arising in a particular case. Only recently have most lawyers been able to understand the essential differences between a psychologist and a psychiatrist, and not all do so today. Few realise that different specialities exist within psychology, or understand their boundaries. Even psychologists themselves sometimes have difficulties in accurately differentiating one professional field from another (educational and child psychology, for example). The current variations in labelling interests and applications as forensic only adds to the confusion. Forensic psychology, whatever we mean by that, owes its existence to, and is dependent upon, the legal profession, and there is an urgent need to make the former user-friendly and to consider and reduce the current communication problem, much of which appears to have arisen from the psychologist's semantic and terminological vagaries of recent years.

Chapter 2 introduced the defence of insanity, which has been a central medi-colegal issue for centuries. This is a purely legal term, the definition of which has changed with time, particularly in the USA, but which, in its present UK formulation within the M'Naghten Rules, embraces somewhat contradictory medical, philosophical and psychological concepts. These are, namely, those of disease, mind and knowing. Clearly, the concept of *disease*, which is a physical entity or process, is logically incompatible with the metaphysical concept of *mind*, which is a purely abstract notion or theory-based idea, while the cognitive concept of *knowing* certain conduct to be *wrong* begs questions about the meanings ascribed to both terms in the context of criminal law. Psychologists, in conjunction with psychiatrists, have been called to give expert evidence on the issue of insanity, and find themselves in the heteroclitical position of presenting scientific evidence to support legal concepts. The combined efforts of American lawyers and psychiatrists have failed to find a completely satisfactory solution to this dilemma, although some of the newer formulations derived from or replacing the M'Naghten Rules have worked better. However, what brings consistency of medical evidence, leaning heavily on the Diagnostic Statistical Manual, rarely explains the real-life problem, which is how well the offenders understood the nature of their own conduct and could control their actions. Insanity is not iden-tical with psychiatric illness, and some jurisdictions accept a purely psychogenic causation, such as the insane jealousy of the Othello syndrome. Law reform moves forward slowly but constantly, and psychology, with its now recognised position within the concept of insanity, should surely be working towards rational and practical improvements in this area. A significant move towards a less definite line drawn judicially between normal and disabling intelligence followed expert psychological testimony on this problem (see Chapter 10), but changes in precedential law should not have to wait until an appropriate case calls in a particularly well-qualified and experienced expert, or is publicly contro-versial enough to launch an official enquiry, as in the Confait case (Fisher, 1977). Other legal concepts, on which psychologists give expert testimony, such as *diminished responsibility*, *automatism*, *fitness to plead*, *voluntariness*, *reliability* and *fitness for interview*, would also benefit from redefining to better scientific stan-dards, and both law and psychology would gain from a programme of inter-professional discussions designed to bring recommendations for semantic improvements in these concepts before the legislators so that the relevant statutes can be amended in due course.

While the qualitative nature of legal terms and concepts produces problems for the expert witness, the quantitative aspect is not without problems. In crim-inal law, in contradistinction to civil law, the courts work on the all-or-nothing principle in a world of black and white, although recent judgments in the Court of Appeal indicate greater flexibility towards the admissibility of expert psycho-logical evidence. The accused is either guilty or not guilty, sane or insane, responsibility-diminished or not; the victim one of murder or manslaughter (depending upon intention or the time elapsing between injury and death), the guilt beyond reasonable doubt or not, and so on. There is no judgment in between. Exceptionally, grades may be introduced but are then compartmentalised – actual or grievous bodily harm; driving without due care and attention or dangerous driving; or the alternatives may be extended, as in the not proven verdict of the Scottish courts. In real life, human behaviour is analogue rather than digital, and any pigeonholing must inevitably be arbitrary. So where, how and by whom are these arbitrary lines to be drawn? How consistently are they followed, both intra- and inter-judicially? What degree of reasonable doubt must the evidence go beyond in order to satisfy a jury, and what happens when they all hold different notions of what that degree should be? Questions like these are essentially psychological, and one would expect psychologists to be considering them and suggesting some practical answers.

During the past decade there has been a very rapid increase in the demand for psychological expertise in both civil and criminal cases. The reasons for this increased demand are due to better recognition among the legal profession about the unique contributions that psychologists can make to judicial proceedings, greater independence from medical colleagues, and the broadening of the criteria for admissibility of expert psychological evidence in the courts due to the pioneering work of psychologists in recent years.

There is an insufficient number of suitably qualified experts available to cope with the demand and as a result sometimes inexperienced, ill-prepared and unsupervised psychologists are commissioned to prepare reports and appear before the courts. There are different principles and models of training in psychology, some of which are discussed in detail by Melton (1987) in relation to the development of forensic psychology in the USA. The BPS is currently developing accreditation criteria for postgraduate training in forensic, criminological and legal psychology. This is an important development which we fully support.

In the past, postgraduate training in clinical psychology accompanied by specialised forensic expertise and experience undoubtedly have been the best basic prerequisites for becoming a forensic psychologist. Certainly the very substantial overlap in the offending and mentally disordered populations, as well as the frequency of forensic problems involving states of mind affecting *mens rea*, competencies, sequelae of accidents justifying compensation, and the many clinical problems arising in family law indicate that clinical psychology is the most useful foundation on which to build forensic skills. However, if the profession is going to make the chartered forensic psychologist a general practitioner, it will be essential to provide some basic training in the other specialities which have also made significant contributions to forensic practice, such as educational, occupational, child and social psychology.

As far as the UK is concerned, during the past few years there has been rapid growth in postgraduate training courses in forensic psychology and related fields, conforming to the BPS's principles of continuing professional development described by Lindley (1997). These courses provide a good academic base from which psychologists can develop specialised expertise. There are also nowadays several specialised and reputable workshops available for developing courtroom skills. These are often helpful and give the psychologist greater confidence in presenting evidence in court.

To date, existing postgraduate courses do not appear to provide the necessary *practical skills* required to become a competent forensic psychologist. We would like to see courses in clinical and forensic psychology provide extensive workshops on the professional, ethical and practical aspects involved in the preparation of court reports and presentation of oral evidence in court, as well as providing opportunities for observations of experienced experts at work. This would include psychologists practising defending a report against a critical class of peers or experienced cross-examiners. It is also important that psychologists who are entering forensic psychology practice are closely supervised by senior colleagues. This is already happening in forensic psychiatry as in the case of senior registrars whose work is supervised by their consultants.

Another area of great current concern is the need for impartiality. Partial and biased evidence, whether in a written or oral form, is very damaging to the expert concerned as well as to the profession as a whole. The inherent nature of an adversarial criminal justice system, where each side instructs their own expert, makes the expert potentially susceptible to bias and to manipulation by lawyers to produce a favourable report. The same holds true for civil proceedings, although here there appears to be a move towards court-appointed experts (Woolf, 1996).

The future of forensic psychology

What does the future hold for forensic psychology? Undoubtedly, the improved recognition among the judiciary of the unique contributions of psychology to criminal and civil proceedings will continue, as well as the increased independence of psychologists from their medical colleagues. Indeed, there is growing reliance in the courts on the use of expert psychological testimony. This is good for the psychology profession, but there is danger that in future too much emphasis could be placed on the importance of psychological vulnerabilities and mental disorder. As Gudjonsson and MacKeith (1997) point out, in the current climate there is temptation for the defence to attempt to discover some kinds of psychological vulnerabilities and then overgeneralise from the limited findings in order to provide a defence argument. This could result in guilty defendants, who otherwise would have been properly convicted, being acquitted by the courts. The fact of the matter is that expert testimony is susceptible to misuse and abuse both in criminal and civil cases. Experts must be objective, impartial and scrupulous in their work. We would not like to see a situation where many trials were largely determined by expert witnesses, irrespective of the nature of the case.

The use of computers and the Internet have made access to information easier. This has many advantages for the forensic psychologist and for lawyers. Unfortunately, easy access to the psychological literature, and also possibly to confidential test material, increases the likelihood that such material will be collected and abused by defendants and unscrupulous lawyers. Not only does lack of test confidentiality undermine the validity of many psychological tests, it undermines the whole concept of justice. This means that psychologists may periodically have to develop new and alternative tests and techniques, as well as improving ways of detecting malingering when it occurs.

CASES CITED

Anderson (1971). R v. Anderson and others, 3 All ER 1152.

Arnold (1724). R v. Arnold, 16 State Trials 695.

Ashford (1819). Ashford v. Thornton, 1 Barnewall and Alderson 905.

Beaney (1978). R v. Beaney, 1 WLR 770.

Bruce (1966). Bruce v. Dyer, 58 DLR 2nd 211, 216.

Byrne (1960). 2 QB 396; 3 WLR 440.

Calderon (1990). Calderon v. Spencer and Hughes, *American Journal of Forensic Psychology*, 8, (1) 69–74.

Chief Constable of Devon and Cornwall (1982). R v. Chief Constable of Devon and Cornwall, 8 QB 458, 471.

Daubert (1993). The Daubert v. Merrell Dow Pharamacuticals Inc. 61 LW 4805, 113 S. Ct. 2786.

Dusky (1960). 362 US 402.

Dyson (1831). 7 C & P 305.

English Exporters (1973). English Exporters v. Eldonwell, 2 WLR 435.

Francis (1874). R v. Francis LR 2 CCR 128.

Frye (1923). Frye v. U.S. 293 Fed. 1013.

Graham (1982). 1 WLR 294; 1 Sll ER 801.

Hadfield (1800). R v. Hadfield, 27 State Trials (New Series) 1281.

Hawley (1964). Police v. Morton and Pick, Bakewell. Magistrates' Court, 21 January 1964.

Howe (1909). Howe v. Bishop, 2 KB 390.

Ingram (1975). Crim LR 457, CA.

Kane (1997). *The Times*, 21 June, p. 6, *Daily Telegraph* 21 June, p. 13.

Kenny (1994). Crim LR 284.

Meering (1919). Meering v. Grahame White Aviation Company, 122 LT 44.

Meyers (1965). R v. Meyers, A.C. 1001.

M'Naghten (1843). R v. M'Naghten, 10 Cl.& F. 200.

Morris (1978). Morris v. Stratford-on-Avon R.D.C. 1 WLR 1059.

Penguin Books (1961). R v. Penguin Books, Crim. LR 176.

Pitchard (1836). 7 C & P 303.

Podola (1959). 3 All ER 418.

Quinn (1962). R v. Quinn, 2 QB 245.

Raghip (1991). R v. Silcott, Braithwaite and Raghip. *The Independent*, 6 December.

Ramona (1989). Ramona v. Ramona, in Appelbaum, P.S and Zoltek-Jick, C.(1996) 'Psychotherapists' duties to third parties', *American Journal of Psychiatry*, *153*, 457–465.

Scane (1959). Scane v. Ainger. Queen's Bench Division, High Court of Justice, 8 December 1959, in Haward (1960) *Bulletin of the British Psychological Society*, *41*, 76 (Abstract).

Sim (1936). Sim v. Stretch, 2 All ER 1237.

Simpson v. Simpson (1992). 1 Family Law Reports 601.

Spicer (1977). Spicer v. Holt, AC 987, 1000.

Stagg (1994). R v. Stagg, Central Criminal Court, London, 14 September.

Staniforth (1975). R v. Staniforth, 2 WLR 849.

Tarasoff (1976). Tarasoff v. Regents of UCLA, 118 Cal.Rep. 129.

Torney (1996). Belfast Crown Court, 15 February.

Turner (1960). Turner v. Thorne, 21 DLR 2nd 211, 216.

Turner (1975). R v. Turner, 60. Cr.App.R.80. CA.

Wilkinson (1897). Wilkinson v. Downton, 2 QB 57.

Willis (1882). Willis v. Bernard, 8 Bing 376.

REFERENCES

Allam, J., Middleton, D., and Browne, K. (1997). 'Different clients, different needs? Practice issues in community-based treatment for sex offenders'. *Criminal Behaviour and Mental Health*, 7, 69–84.

Allport, G. W. (1931). 'What is a trait of personality?' *Journal of Abnormal and Social Psychology*, 25, 368–372.

—— (1937). *Personality: A Psychological Interpretation*. New York: Holt, Rinehart & Winston.

Anastasi, A. and Urbina, S. (1996). *Psychological Testing*. 6th edn New Jersey: Prentice-Hall, Inc.

Appelbaum, P.S. and Zoltek-Jick, C. (1996). 'Psychotherapist's duties to third parties'. *American Journal of Psychiatry*, 157, 457–465.

Arcaya, J. M. (1987). 'Role conflicts in coercive assessments: evaluations and recommendations'. *Professional Psychology: Research and Practice*, 18, 422–428.

Bagby, R. H., Nicholson, R. A., Rogers, R. and Nussbaum, D. (1992). 'Domains of competency to stand trial'. *Law and Human Behavior*, 16, 491–507.

Bailey, R. W. (1968). *Annotated Bibliography of Statistical Stylistics*. Ann Arbor: University of Michigan.

Baker, E. (1997). 'The introduction of supervision registers in England and Wales: a risk communications analysis'. *Journal of Forensic Psychiatry*, 8, 15–35.

Baker, J. H. (1979). *Introduction to English Legal History*. 2nd edn London: Butterworths.

Ball, C. (1981). 'Use and significance of school reports in juvenile courts', *British Journal of Social Work*, 11, 474–483.

Barclay, G. C. (1995). *The Criminal Justice System in England and Wales 1995*. London: Home Office.

Barker, A., Gunn, J., Hamilton, J., and Stanley, S. (1993). 'The courts and bodies overseeing and administering the law in the United Kingdom (and Ireland)'. In J. Gunn and P. J. Taylor (eds), *Forensic Psychiatry. Clinical, Legal and Ethical Issues*. Oxford: Butterworth Heinemann, pp. 167–209.

Barker, D. and Padfield, C. (1996) *Law*. 9th edn Oxford: Butterworths.

Barnes, C.(1970). *Report of the Commission on Obscenity and Pornography*. New York: Random House.

Barry, M., Gudjonsson, G., Gunn, J., Hall, D., d'Orban, P., Stanley, S. and Taylor, P. J. (1993). 'The mentally disordered offender in non-medical setting'. In J Gunn and P. J. Taylor (eds), *Forensic Psychiatry. Clinical, Legal and Ethical Issues*. Oxford: Butterworth Heinemann, pp. 732-793.

Bartko, J. J. and Carpenter, W. T. (1976). 'On the methods and theory of reliability'. *Journal of Nervous and Mental Diseases*, 163, 307–317.

Bartlett, F. C. (1932). *Remembering*. Cambridge: Cambridge University Press.

Bartol, C. R. and Bartol, A. M. (1987). 'History of forensic psychology'. In I. B. Weinder and A. K. Hess (eds), *Handbook of Forensic Psychology*. New York: John Wiley & Sons, pp. 3–21.

Beaumont, J. G. (1994). 'Expert witness'. *The Psychologist*, 7 (11), 511–512.

Beck, A. T. and Steer, R. A. (1987). *Beck Depression Inventory*. New York: The Psychological Corporation. Harcourt Brace Jovanovich, Inc.

Beck, A. T. and Steer, R. A. (1991). *Beck Scale for Suicide Ideation*. New York: The Psychological Corporation. Harcourt Brace Jovanovich, Inc.

Beck, J. C. (ed.) (1990). *Confidentiality vs. Duty to Protect*. Washington, DC: American Psychiatric Press.

Belfrage, H. and Lidberg, L. (1996). 'Forensic psychiatric assessments in practice: a blind study of different forensic psychiatrists' assessments of the same case'. *Criminal Behaviour and Mental Health*, 6, 331–337.

Ben-Veniste, R. (1970). 'Pornography and sex crime: the Danish experience'. In *The Report of the Commission on Obscenity and Pornography*. New York: Bantam Books. pp. 272–274.

Berry, D. T. R. (1995). 'Detecting distortions in forensic evaluations with the MMPI-2'. In Y. S. Ben-Porath, J. R. Graham, G. C. N. Hall, R. D. Hirschman, and M. S. Zaragoza (eds), *Forensic applications of the MMPI-2*. London: Sage Publications, pp. 81–102.

Binder, L. M. and Thompson, L. L. (1995). 'The ethics code and neuropsychological assessment practice'. *Archives of Clinical Neuropsychology*, 10, 27–46.

Binet, A. (1900). *La Suggestibilité*. Paris: Schleicher.

Binet, A. and Simon, T. (1905). 'Methodes nouvelles pour le diagnostic du nouveau intellectuel des abnormaux'. *Année Psychologie*, 11, 191–244.

Blackburn, R. (1996). 'What is forensic psychology?'. *Legal and Criminological Psychology*, 1, 3–16.

Blau, T. H. (1984). *The Psychologist as an Expert Witness*. New York: John Wiley & Sons.

Bluglass, R. (1990a). 'The Mental Health Act 1993'. In R. Bluglass and P. Bowden (eds), *Principles and Practice of Forensic Psychiatry*. London: Churchill Livingstone, pp. 1,173–1,187.

—— (1990b). 'Shoplifting'. In R. Bluglass and P. Bowden (eds), *Principles and Practice of Forensic Psychiatry*. London: Churchill Livingstone, pp. 1173–1187.

Bluglass, R. and Bowden, P. (eds) (1990). *Principles and Practice of Forensic Psychiatry*. London: Churchill Livingstone.

Bond, T., Bridge, J., Mallender, P. and Rayson, J. (1997). *Blackstone's Guide to the Family Law Act 1996*. London: Blackstone Press.

Bradford, J. and Smith, S.M. (1979) 'Amnesia and homicide: the Padola case and a study of thirty cases'. *Bulletin of the American Academic of Psychiatry and the Law*, 7, 219–231.

Bradley, R.H., Caldwell, B.M., Brisky, J., Magee, M. and Whiteside, L. (1992). 'The HOME Inventory'. *Research in Developmental Disability*, 13, 313–333.

Brandt, J. (1988). 'Malingered amnesia'. In R. Rogers (ed.), *Clinical assessment of malingering and deception*. London: Guilford Press, pp. 65–83.

Brent, D. A., Perper, J. A., Moritz, G. et al. (1993) 'The validity of diagnosis obtained through psychological autopsy procedures in adolescent suicide victims: use of family history'. Acta Psychiatrica Scandinavica, 87 (2) 118–122.

Bridge, J., Bridge, S. and Luke, S. (1990). Blackstone's Guide to the Children Act 1989. London: Blackstone Press Limited.

Bring, J. and Aitken, C. (1996). 'United States v. Shonubi and the use of statistics in court'. Expert Evidence, 4, 134–142.

Briscoe, O., Carson, D., d'Orban, P., Grubin, D., Gunn, J., Mullen, P., Stanley, S. and Taylor, P. J. (1993). 'The law, adult mental disorder, and the psychiatrist in England and Wales'. In J. Gunn and P. J. Taylor (eds), Forensic Psychiatry. Clinical, Legal and Ethical Issues. London: Butterworth-Heinemann Ltd, pp. 21–117.

British Psychological Society (1995a). 'Code of conduct'. The Psychologist, 8, 452–453.

—— (1995b). 'Professional liability insurance', The Psychologist, 8, 82–85.

—— (1997). Ethical Guidelines on Forensic Psychology 1997. Division of Criminological and Legal Psychology. Leicester: British Psychological Society.

Britton, P. (1997). The jigsaw man. London: Bantam Press.

Brodsky, S. L. (1991). Testifying in Court: Guidelines and Maxims for the Expert Witness. Washington, DC: American Psychological Association.

Bromley, E. (1981). 'Confidentiality'. Bulletin of the British Psychological Society, 34, 468–469.

Bronks, I. G. (1987) 'Amnesia: organic and psychogenic'. British Journal of Psychiatry, 151, 414–415.

Brown, B. (1985). 'The involvement of psychologists in sentencing'. Bulletin of the British Psychological Society, 38, 180–182.

Brown, J. L. (1988) 'Inexpert experts'. Adoption and Fostering, 12, 4.

Brown, M., King, E. and Barraclough, B. (1995). 'Nine suicide pacts', British Journal of Psychiatry, 167, 448–451.

Bryan, W. J. (1962). Legal Aspects of Hypnosis. Springfield,Ill.: Thomas.

Buckhout, R. (1974). 'Eyewitness testimony'. Scientific American, 231 (6), 23–31.

Burt, C. (1962). 'Sir Francis Galton and his contribution to psychology'. British Journal of Statistical Psychology, 15, 1–49.

Butcher, J. N. (1996). International Adaptations of the MMPI-2. Research and Clinical Applications. London: University of Minnesota Press.

Camargo, R. J. (1997). 'Factor cluster and discriminative analysis of data on sexually active clergy: molesters of youth identified', American Journal Of Forensic Psychology, 15 (2) 5–24.

Canter, D. (1992). 'An evaluation of the "Cusum" Stylistic Analysis of Confessions' Expert Evidence, 1, 93–99.

—— (1994). Criminal Shadows. London: Harper Collins.

Canter, M. B., Bennett, B. E., Jones, S. E. and Nagy, T. F. (1994). Ethics for Psychologists: A Commentary on the APA Ethics Code. Washington: American Psychological Association.

Carr, A. P. (1992). Anthony and Berryman's Magistrates' Court Guide, London: Butterworth.

Carson, D. (1990). Professionals and the Courts. A Handbook for Expert Witnesses. Birmingham: Venture Press.

—— (1993). 'Recent legal developments: expert scientific evidence – admissibility – whether must be "generally accepted" – Frye – Federal Rules of Evidence'. *Expert Evidence*, 2, 78–88.

Carter-Ruck, P. S., Walker, R. and Starte, H. N. A. (1992). *Carter-Ruck on Libel and Slander*. London: Butterworths.

Castell, J. H. F. (1966). *The Court Work of Educational and Clinical Psychologists (EDPP)* British Psychological Society.

Cattell, J. M. (1895). 'Measurements on the accuracy of recollections'. *Science*, 2, 761–766.

Chiswick, D. (1990). 'Fitness to stand trial and plead, mutism and deafness'. In R. Bluglass and P. Bowden (eds), *Principles and Practice of Forensic Psychiatry*. London: Churchill Livingstone, pp. 171–178.

Churchill, R. R. and Love, A. V. (1988). *Law of the Sea*, Manchester: Manchester University Press.

Clare, I. C. H. (1993). 'Issues in the assessment and treatment of male sex offenders with mild learning disabilities'. *Sexual and Marital Therapy*, 8, 167–180.

Clare, I. and Gudjonsson, G. H. (1992). *Devising and piloting a new 'Notice to Detained Persons'*. Royal Commission on Criminal Justice. London: HMSO.

Clare, I. C. H., Gudjonsson, G. H. and Harrati, P. (1997). 'The current police caution in England and Wales: how easy it is to understand'. *Journal of Community and Applied Social Psychology*, in press.

Clark, D. F., Britton, P., Cooke, D. J., Hall, J. N. and Litton, R. A. (1987). 'Insurance and legal advice for psychologists'. *Bulletin of the British Psychological Society*, 40, 324–327.

Cohen, A., Dolan, B. and Eastman, N. (1996). 'Research on the supervision registers: inconsistencies in local research ethics committee responses'. *Journal of Forensic Psychiatry*, 7, 413–419.

Cohen, J. (1961). 'A study of suicide pacts', *Medico-Legal Journal*, 29, 144–151.

Colman, A. M. and MacKay, R. D. (1995). 'Psychological evidence in court. Legal developments in England and the United States'. *Psychology, Crime and Law*, 1, 261–268.

Colnerud, G. (1997). 'Ethical dilemmas of psychologists – a Swedish example in an international perspective'. *European Psychologist*, 2 (2), 164–170.

Cooke, D. (1980). *The Role of the Forensic Psychologist*. Springfield, Illinois: Charles C. Thomas.

—— (1990a). 'Being an "expert" in Court'. *The Psychologist*, 3, 216–221.

—— (1990b). 'Do I feel lucky? Survival in the witness box'. *Neuropsychology*, 4, 271–285.

Cooke, D. J., Forth, A. E., Newman, J. and Hare, R. D. (eds) (1996). *International Perspectives on Psychopathy. Issues in Criminological and Legal Psychology*, No. 24. Leicester: British Psychological Society.

Copson, G. (1995). *Coals to Newcastle? Police Use of Offender Profiling*. London: Home Office Police Dept.

Cornell, D. G. (1987). 'Role conflict in forensic clinical psychology: Reply to Arcaya'. *Professional Psychology: Research and Practice*, 18, 429–432.

Coulthard, M. (1994). 'On the use of Corpora in the analysis of forensic texts'. *Forensic Linguistics*, 1, (1) 27–44.

CPTU (1992). *Investigative Interviewing. A Guide to Interviewing*. London: Home Office, Central Planning and Training Unit.

Crighton, D. and Towl, G. J. (1997). 'Self-inflicted death in prisoners in England and Wales'. In Towl, G. J.(ed.), *Suicide and Self-injury in Prison*. Leicester: British Psychological Society.

Cromberg, H. F. M. (1994). 'Law as a Branch of Applied Psychology'. *Psychology, Crime and Law*, *1*, 1–9.

Cronbach, L. J. (1984). *Essentials of Psychological Testing*. 4th edn New York: Harper-Collins.

Crystal, D. (1987). *Cambridge Encyclopaedia of Language, Section 15*. (Statistical Structure of Language), Cambridge: Cambridge University Press.

Culver, C. M. and Gert, B. (1990). 'The inadequacy of incompetency'. *Millbank Quarterly*, *68*, 619.

Cunningham, C. (1964). 'Forensic psychology'. *Bulletin of the British Psychological Society*, *17*, 7–12.

Curzon, L. B. (1986). *A Dictionary of Law*. 2nd edn. London: Pitman Publishing Ltd.

Dahlstrom, W. G., Welsh, G. S., and Dahlstrom, L. (1972). *An MMPI Handbook* (Vol. 1). Minnesota: University of Minnesota Press.

Darbyshire, P. (1992). *English Legal System in a Nutshell*. 2nd edn. London: Sweet and Maxwell.

Davies, G. M. (1983). 'The legal importance of psychological research in eyewitness testimony: British and American experiences'. *Journal of the Forensic Science Society*, *24*, 165–175.

Davis, A., Witterbrood, K. and Jackson, J. L. (1997). 'Predicting the criminal antecedents of a stranger rapist from his offence behaviour'. *Science & Justice*, *37*, 161–170.

Davis, T. (1994). 'ESDA and the analysis of contested contemporaneous notes of police interviews'. *Forensic Linguistics*, *1*, 71–80.

Department of Health (1994a). *Guidance on the discharge of mentally disordered people and their continuing care in the community*. NHS Executive HSG(94)27. London: Department of Health.

—— (1994b). *Introduction of Supervision Registers for Mentally Ill People*. Circular HSG(94)5. London: Department of Health.

Doll, E. A. (1965). *Vineland Social Maturity Scale*. Minneapolis: American Guidance Service.

Douglas, J. and Olshaker, M. (1996). *Mindhunter*. London: Heinemann.

East, Sir Norwood (1955). *Sex Offenders*. London: Delisle.

Edmondson, J. (1995). 'The psychologist as expert witness'. *Forensic Update*, *42*, 28–32.

Edmunds, R. (1993). 'Mental capacity to make property transfers: evidentiary aspects'. *Journal of Forensic Psychiatry*, *4* (2), 315–323.

Eigen, J. P. and Andoll, G. (1983). 'Historical developments in psychiatric forensic evidence', *International Journal of Law and Psychiatry*, *6*, 423–429.

Eysenck, H. J. and Eysenck, S. B. G. (1991). *Manual of the Eysenck Personality Scales (EPS Adult)*. London: Hodder & Stoughton.

Eysenck, H. and Gudjonsson, G. H. (1989). *The Causes and Cures of Criminality*. New York and London: Plenum Press.

Eysenck, H. J. and Nias, D. K. B. (1978). *Sex, Violence and the Media*. London: Maurice Temple Smith.

Fagillon, I. (1976). 'The problem of reliable hearsay evidence'. *Law Court Review*, *92*, 26.

Farr, J. and Jenkins, J. (1949). 'Tables for use with the Flesch Readability Formula', *Journal of Applied Psychology*, 33, 275–278.

Finch, J. D. (1984). *Aspects of Law Affecting the Paramedical Profession*. London: Faber.

Fisher, H. (1977). *Report of an Inquiry by the Hon. Sir Henry Fisher into the circumstances leading to the trial of three persons on charges arising out of the deaths of Maxwell Confait and the fire at 27 Doggett Road, London, SE6*. H. M. S. O., London.

Fisher, R. P. and Geiselman, R. E. (1992). *Memory-enhancing techniques for investigative interviewing: The cognitive interview*. Springfield, Ill.: Thomas.

Fitzgerald, E. (1987). 'Psychologists and the law of evidence: admissibility and confidentiality'. In G. Gudjonsson and J. Drinkwater (eds), *Psychological Evidence in Court*. Issues in Criminological and Legal Psychology, No. 11. Leicester: British Psychological Society, pp. 39–48.

Flesch, R. (1943). *Marks of Readable Style: A Study in Adult Education*. New York: Bur. of Publ., Teachers Coll., Columbia University.

—— (1946). *The Art of Plain Talk*. New York: Harper.

—— (1948). 'A new readability yardstick'. *Journal of Applied Psychology*, 32 (3), 221–233.

Flynn, J. R. (1987). 'Massive IQ gains in 14 nations: what IQ tests really measure'. *Psychological Bulletin*, 101, 171–191.

Freedman, M., Stuss, D. T. and Gordon, M. (1991). 'Assessment of competency', *Annals of Internal Medicine*, 115, 203.

Freides, D. (1993). 'Proposed standard of professional practice: neuropsychological reports display all quantitative data'. *The Clinical Neuropsychologist*, 7, 234–235.

Fryer, D. (1993). 'Occupational intelligence standards'. *School and Society*, 16, 273–278.

Gale, A. (ed.) (1988). *The Polygraph Test: Lies, Truth and Science*. London: Sage.

Gazono, C and Meloy, R. (1994). *Rorschach Assessment of Aggressive and Psychopathic Personalities*. Hillsdale, New Jersey: Erlbaum.

Geiselman, R. E. (1995). *Eyewitness Expert Testimony: Handbook for the Forensic Psychiatrist, Psychologist and Attorney*. Baboa Island, CA: ACFP Press.

Gibson, H. B. (1995). 'A further case of the misuse of hypnosis in a police investigation'. *Contemporary Hypnosis*, 12, 81–86.

Gilbert, G. M. (1948). *Nuremburg Diary*. London: Eyre and Spottiswoode.

Goldman-Eisler, S. (1976). 'Psycholinguistics'. In S. Kraus (ed.), *Encyclopedic Handbook of Medical Psychology*. London: Butterworth, pp. 421–426.

Goldstein, R. L. (1987). 'The psychiatrist's role in the retrospective determination of suicide'. *Journal of Forensic Sciences*, 32 (2), 489–495.

Gostin, L., Rassaby, E. and Buchan, A. (1984). *Mental Health Tribunal Procedure*. London: Oyez-Longman.

Gough, H. G. (1960). 'Theory and measurement of socialisation'. *Journal of Consulting and Clinical Psychology*, 24, 23–30.

Grainger, A. (1991). 'Mental incapacity: the medical or legal view?' *Law Society's Gazette*, 20, 17–20.

Gray, J. S. (1946). *Psychology in Human Affairs*. London: McGraw-Hill, pp. 140–174.

Greiffenstein, M. F., Baker, W. J. and Gola, T. (1994). 'Validation of malingered amnesia measures with a large clinical sample'. *Psychological Assessment*, 6, 218–224.

Grisso, T. (1986a). *Evaluating Competencies. Forensic Assessments and Instruments*. New York: Plenum Press.

—— (1986b). 'Psychological assessment in legal contexts'. In W. J. Curran, A. L. McGary and S. A. Shah (eds), *Forensic psychiatry and psychology*. New York, Philadelphia: F. A. Davis Company, pp. 103–128.

—— (1993). 'The differences between forensic psychiatry and forensic psychology'. *Bulletin of the American Academy of Psychiatry and Law*, *21*, 133–145.

Grossarth-Maticek, R., Eysenck, H. J. and Boyle, G. J. (1995). 'Method of test administration as a factor in test validity: the use of a personality questionnaire in the prediction of cancer and coronary heart disease'. *Behaviour Research and Therapy*, *33*, 705–710.

Grubin, D. (1996). *Fitness to Plead in England and Wales*. Hove, East Sussex: Psychology Press.

Gudjonsson, G. H. (1979). 'The use of electrodermal responses in a case of amnesia (a case report)'. *Medicine, Science and the Law*, *19*, 138–140.

—— (1984a). 'Attribution of blame for criminal acts and its relationship with personality'. *Personality and Individual Differences*, *5*, 53–58.

—— (1984b). 'A new scale of interrogative suggestibility'. *Personality and Individual Differences*, *5*, 303–314.

—— (1985). 'Psychological evidence in court: results from the BPS survey'. *Bulletin of the British Psychological Society*, *38*, 327–330.

—— (1987). 'The significance of depression in the mechanism of compulsive shoplifting'. *Medicine, Science and the Law*, *27*, 171–176.

—— (1988). 'The faking of deficit and psychiatric symptoms'. *Newsletter of the Division of Criminological and Legal Psychology*. Leicester: British Psychological Society. No. 23, 9–11.

—— (1989). 'Compliance in an interrogation situation: a new scale'. *Personality and Individual Differences*, *10*, 535–540.

—— (1990a). 'The relationship of intellectual skills to suggestibility, compliance and acquiescence'. *Personality and Individual Differences*, *11*, 227–231.

—— (1990b). 'Self-deception and other- deception in forensic assessment'. *Personality and Individual Differences*, *11*, 219–225.

—— (1991). 'The "Notice to Detained Persons", PACE codes, and reading ease'. *Applied Cognitive Psychology*, *5*, 89–95.

—— (1992a). *The Psychology of Interrogation, Confessions and Testimony*. Chichester: John Wiley & Sons.

—— (1992b). 'The admissibility of expert psychological and psychiatric evidence in England and Wales'. *Criminal Behaviour and Mental Health*, *2*, 245–252.

—— (1993). 'The implications of poor psychological evidence in court'. *Expert Evidence*, *3*, 120–124.

—— (1994a). 'Confessions made to the expert witness: some professional issues'. *Journal of Forensic Psychiatry*, *5*, 237–247.

—— (1994b). 'Psychological vulnerability: suspects at risk'. In D. Morgan and G. Stephenson (eds), *Suspicion and Silence. The Right to Silence in Criminal Investigation*. London: Blackstone Press Ltd, 91–106.

—— (1995a). 'The Standard Progressive Matrices: methodological problems associated with the administration of the 1992 adult standardisation'. *Personality and Individual Differences*, *18*, 441–442.

—— (1995b). 'Alleged false confession, voluntariness and "free will": Testifying against the Israeli General Security Service (GSS)'. *Criminal Behaviour and Mental Health*, 5, 95–105.

—— (1996a). 'Psychological evidence in court. Results from the 1995 survey'. *The Psychologist*, 5, 213-217.

—— (1996b). 'Forensic psychology in England: one practitioner's experience and viewpoint'. *Journal of Criminological and Legal Psychology*, 1, 131–142.

—— (1996c). 'Psychology and the law'. In C. R. Hollin (ed.), *Working with Offenders. Psychological Practice in Offender Rehabilitation*. Chichester: John Wiley & Sons, pp. 40–59.

—— (1997a). *The Gudjonsson Suggestibility Scales Manual*. Hove, East Sussex: Psychology Press.

—— (1997b). 'Members of the British False Memory Society: the legal consequences of the accusations for the families'. *Journal of Forensic Psychiatry*, 8, 348–356.

—— (1997c). 'The Police and Criminal Evidence Act (PACE) and confessions'. *British Journal of Hospital Medicine*, 57, 445–447.

—— (1997d). 'Accusations by adults of childhood sexual abuse: A survey of the members of the British False Memory Society (BFMS)'. *Applied Cognitive Psychology*, 11, 3–18.

—— (1997e). 'The members of the BFMS, the accusers and their siblings'. *The Psychologist*, 10, 111–115.

Gudjonsson, G. H., Clare, I., Rutter, S. and Pearse, J. (1993). *Persons at Risk During Interviews in Police Custody: The Identification of Vulnerabilities*. Royal Commission on Criminal Justice. London: HMSO.

Gudjonsson, G. H. and Copson, G. (1997). 'The role of the expert in criminal investigations'. In J. L. Jackson and D. A. Bekerian (eds), *Offender Profiling. Theory, Research and Practice*. Chichester: John Wiley & Sons.

Gudjonsson, G. H. and Gunn, J. (1982). 'The competence and reliability of a witness in a criminal court'. *British Journal of Psychiatry*, 141, 624–627.

Gudjonsson, G. H. and Haward, L. R. C. (1982). 'Case report – hysterical amnesia as an alternative to suicide'. *Medicine, Science and the Law*, 22, 68–72.

Gudjonsson, G. H. and MacKeith, J. (1997). *Disputed Confessions and the Criminal Justice System*. Maudsley Discussion Paper No. 2. London: Institute of Psychiatry.

Gudjonsson, G. H., Rutter, S. C. and Clare, I. C. H. (1995). 'The relationship between suggestibility and anxiety among suspects detained at police stations'. *Psychological Medicine*, 25, 875–878.

Gudjonsson, G. H. and Sartory, G. (1983). 'Blood-injury phobia: a "reasonable excuse" for failing to give a specimen in a case of suspected drunken driving'. *Journal of the Forensic Science Society*, 23, 197–201.

Gudjonsson, G. H. and Shackleton, H. (1986). 'The pattern of scores on Raven's Matrices during "faking bad" and "non-faking" performance. *The British Journal of Clinical Psychology*, 25, 35–41.

Gudjonsson, G. H. and Singh, K. K. (1988). 'Attribution of blame for criminal acts and its relationship with type of offence'. *Medicine Science and the Law*, 28, 301–303.

—— (1989). 'The revised Gudjonsson Blame Attribution Inventory'. *Personality and Individual Differences*, 10, 67–70.

Gunn, J. (1991). 'The trial of psychiatry: insanity in the twentieth century'. In K. Herbst and J. Gunn (eds), *Mentally Disordered Offender*. Oxford: Butterworth Heinemann.

Gunn, J. and Taylor, P. J. (eds) (1993). *Forensic Psychiatry, Clinical, Legal and Ethical Issues.* Oxford: Butterworth Heinemann.

Gunning, R. (1945) 'Gunning finds papers too hard to read'. *Editor and Publisher*, 19 May.

Guthkelch, A. N. (1980). 'Post-traumatic amnesia, post-concussional symptoms and accident neurosis'. *European Neurology*, 19, 91–102.

Haas, L. and Malouf, J. (1989). *Keeping up Good Work: A Practitioner's Guide to Mental Health Ethics.* Sarasota, FL: Professional Resource Exchange.

Hale, M. (1980). *Human Science and Social Order: Hugo Munsterberg and Origins of Applied Psychology.* Philadelphia: Temple University Press.

Hale, W. W., Dingemans, P., Wekking, E. and Cornelissen, E. (1993). 'Depression and assessment of intellectual functioning'. *Journal of Clinical Psychology*, 49, 773–776.

Hamilton, J. (1990). 'Manslaughter: assessment for the court'. In R. Bluglass and P. Bowden (eds), *Principles and Practice of Forensic Psychiatry.* London: Churchill Livingstone, pp. 205–214.

Hardcastle, R. A. (1997). 'CUSUM: a credible method for the determination of authorship.' *Science & Justice*, 37, 129–138.

Harding, T. (1993). 'A contemporary survey of medico-legal systems'. In J. Gunn and P. J. Taylor (eds), *Forensic Psychiatry: Clinical, Legal and Ethical Issues.* London: Butterworth-Heinemann, pp. 118–166.

Hare, R. D. (1982). 'Psychopathy and the personality dimensions of psychoticism, extraversion and neuroticism'. *Personality and Individual Differences*, 3, 35–42.

Harnett, P. (1995). 'The contribution of clinical psychologists to family law proceedings in England'. *Journal of Forensic Psychiatry*, 6, 173–183.

Hathaway, S. R. and McKinley, J. C. (1989). *MMPI-2. Manual for Administration and Scoring.* Minneapolis, Minnesota: University of Minnesota Press.

Haward, L. R. C. (1953). 'Forensic psychology.' *Lector Medicus, 1* (10) 2–3. (Society of Honorary Medical Librarians, BM/Hospital, London, WC1).

—— (1958). 'Judd's Golden Jubilee', *Bulletin of the British Psychological Society*, 36, 19–20.

—— (1959). 'The psychologist in a court of law'. *Bulletin of the British Psychological Society*, 39, 1–8.

—— (1961). 'Forensic psychology. some problems and proposals'. *Bulletin of the British Psychological Society*, 14, 1–5.

—— (1963). 'Reliability of corroborated police evidence in a case flagrante delicto', *Journal of the Forensic Science Society*, 3, 71–78.

—— (1964). 'Thematic apperception analysis as a forensic technique', *Journal of the Forensic Science Society*, 4 (4), 209–216.

—— (1965). 'Hearsay and psychological reports'. *Bulletin of the British Psychological Society*, 18, 21–26.

—— (1969). 'The use of specially devised thematic apperception cards in aviation psychology'. *Flight Safety* (Pergamon Press), 3 (2), 12–14.

—— (1975a). 'Obscenity and the forensic psychologist'. *New Behaviour*, 2, 4–6.

—— (1975b). 'The admissibility of psychological evidence in obscenity cases', *Bulletin of the British Psychological Society*, 28, 466–469.

—— (1981). *Forensic Psychology.* London: Batsford.

—— (1982). 'Pornography and forensic psychology'. In Yaffe, M. and Nelson, E. C.(eds) *The Influence of Pornography on Behaviour.* London: Academic Press.

—— (1983). 'Professional responsibility'. In A. Liddel (ed.), *The Practice of Clinical Psychology in Great Britain*. Chichester: Wiley.

—— (1997). 'Document-making analysis as expert evidence', *Police Journal*, 70, 154–158.

Hawton, K. and Catalan, J (eds) (1982). *Attempted Suicide*. Oxford: Oxford University Press.

Hays, P. (1964). *New Horizons in Psychiatry*. Harmondsworth: Penguin, pp.30–33.

Heilbrun, K. (1992). 'The role of psychological testing in forensic assessment'. *Law and Human Behavior*, 16, 257–272.

Henningsen, G. (1980). *The Witches' Advocate: Basque Witchcraft and the Spanish Inquisition (1609–1614)*. Reno, NV: University of Nevada Press.

—— (1996). 'The child witch syndrome: satanic child abuse of today and child witche trials of yesterday'. *Journal of Forensic Psychiatry*, 7, 581–593.

Heuston, R. F. V. and Buckley, R. A. (1992). *Salmon and Heuston on Law of Torts*. London: Sweet and Maxwell.

Hill, G. (1987). 'Defence subs on the up and up', *Doctor*, 10 December, p.8.

Hirson, A. and Howard, D. M. (1994). 'Spectrographic analysis of cockpit voice recorder tape'. *Forensic Linguistics*, 1 (1), 59–70.

Hodgkinson, H. M. (1973). 'Mental impairment in the elderly'. *Journal of the Royal College of Physicians*, 7, 305–317.

Holmes, R. M. and Holmes, S. T. (1996). *Profiling Violent Crimes. An Investigative Tool*. London: Sage Publications.

Home Office (1985). *Police and Criminal Evidence Act 1984*. London: HMSO.

—— (1995a). *Police and Criminal Evidence Act 1984. Codes of Practice, revised edition*. London: HMSO.

—— (1995b). *The Criminal Justice and Public Order Act 1994*. London: HMSO.

Honeycombe, G. (1984). *The murders of the Black Museum 1870–1970*. London: Arrow Books Limited.

Horowitz, S. W., Lamb, M. E., Esplin, P. W., Boychuk, T. D., Krispin, O. and Reiter-Lavery, L. (1997). 'Reliability of criteria-based content analysis of child witness statements'. *Legal and Criminological Psychology*, 2, 11–21.

Jackson, J. and Doran, S. (1992). 'Diplock and the presumption against jury trial: a critique'. *Criminal Law Review*, 755–766.

Jobes, D. A., Berman, A. L. and Josselson, A. R. (1986). 'The impact of psychological autopsies on medical examiners' determination of manner of death'. *Journal of Forensic Sciences*, 31 (1) 177–189.

Judd, C. H. (1908). *Laboratory Equipment for Psychological Experiments*. London: Fisher Unwin.

Kapardis, A. (1977) *Psychology and Law*. Cambridge: Cambridge University Press.

Kaplan, J. P. (1994). 'Review'. *Forensic Linguistics*, 1, 94–105.

Kassin, S. M. and Wrightsman, L. S. (1985). 'Confession evidence'. In S. M. Kassin and L. S. Wrightsman (eds), *The Psychology of Evidence and Trial Procedures*. London: Sage Publications, pp 67–94.

Kaufman, A. (1978). 'Medico-legal aspects of head injuries: intellectual improvment and clinical-psychological assessment'. *Medicine, Science and Law*, 18, 56–62.

Keith-Spiegel, P. and Koocher, G. (1985). *Ethics in Psychology*. New York: Random House.

Klein, P. (1992). *Handbook of Psychological Testing*. London: Routledge.

—— (1995). 'Personality tests'. In S. E. Hampson and A. C. Colman (eds), *Individual Differences and Personality*. London: Longman, pp. 77–98.

Kohlberg, L. (1976). 'Moral stages and moralization: the cognitive-developmental approach'. In T. Lickona (ed.), *Moral Development and Behavior: Theory, Research and Social Issues*. New York: Holt, Rinehart and Winston.

Kohlberg, L. and Candee, D. (1984). 'The relationship of moral judgement to moral action'. In W. Kurtines and J. Gewirtz (eds), *Morality, Moral Behavior, and Moral Development*. New York: John Wiley & Sons.

Kopelman, M. D. (1987). 'Crime and amnesia: a review'. *Behavioral Sciences and the Law*, 5, 323–342.

—— (1995). 'The assessment of psychogenic amnesia'. In Baddeley *et al.* (eds), *Handbook of Memory Disorders*. John Chichester: Wiley & Sons, pp. 427–448.

Kuenzel, H. (1994). 'On the problem of speaker identification by victims and witnesses'. *Forensic Linguistics*, 1 (1), 45–58.

La Follete, M. and Purdie, R. (1996). *A Guide to the Family Law Act (1996)*. London: Butterworths.

Laming, J. R. L. (1987). 'Just Noticeable Difference'. In Gregory, R. L. (ed.), *Oxford Companion to the Mind*. Oxford: Oxford University Press.

Lande, R. G. and Armitage, D. T. (eds) (1997). *Principles and Practice of Military Forensic Psychiatry*. Springfield: Charles C. Thomas.

Lane, D. A. (1987). 'Psychological evidence in the juvenile court'. In G. Gudjonsson and J. Drinkwater (eds), *Psychological Evidence in Court*. Issues in Criminological and Legal Psychology, No. 11. Leicester: British Psychological Society, pp. 20–28.

Lang, R. A. (1993). 'Neuropsychological deficits in sexual offenders: implications for treatment'. *Sexual and Marital Therapy*, 8, 181–200.

Laurence, J.-R. and Perry, C. W. (1988). *Hypnosis, Will, and Memory: A Psycho-Legal History*. New York: Guilford Press.

Law Society (1996). *Volume 1: Fast Track, Housing, Multi-party Actions, Expert Evidence, Cost. Responses by the Law Society Civil Litigation and Courts and Legal Services Committees*. London: The Law Society.

Leng, R. (1990). '*Mens rea* and the defences to a criminal charge'. In R. Bluglass and P. Bowden (eds), *Principles and Practice of Forensic Psychiatry*. London: Churchill Livingstone, pp. 237–250.

Leng, R. and Taylor, R. (1996). *Blackstone's Guide to the Criminal Procedure and Investigations Act 1996*. London: Blackstone Press Limited.

Levi, J. N. (1994). 'Language as evidence'. *Forensic Linguistics*.1 (1), 1–26.

Levi, J. N. and Walker, A. G. (1990). *Language and the Judicial Process*. London: Plenum.

Lezak, M. D. (1995). *Neuropsychological Assessment*. 3rd edn Oxford: Oxford University Press.

Liebling, H., Chipchase, H. and Velangi, R.(1997). 'Why do women self-harm in Ashworth Maximum Security Hospital?' *Issues in Criminological and Legal Psychology*, No. 27. Leicester: British Psychological Society.

Lindley, P. A. (1997). 'Continuing professional development in the British Psychological Society: the differing needs of the professional and the professional body'. *European Psychologist*, 2 (1), 11–17.

Lindsay, G. (1996). 'Psychology as an ethical discipline and profession'. *European Psychologist*, 1, 79–88.

Lindsay, G. and Colley, A. (1995). 'Ethical dilemmas of members of the British Psychological Society'. *The Psychologist*, 8, 448–453.

Lloyd-Bostock, S. (1996). 'The jury in the United Kingdom: juries and jury reseach in context'. In G. Davies, S. Lloyd-Bostock, M. McMurran and C. Wilson (eds), *Psychology, Law, and Criminal Justice*. New York: Walter de Gruyter & Co., pp. 349–359.

Lockhart, W. B. (1970). *Report of the Commission on Obscenity and Pornography*. Washington, DC: US Government Printing Office.

Loftus, E. F. (1979). *Eyewitness Testimony*. Cambridge: Harvard University Press.

—— (1985). 'The experimental psychologist as advocate or impartial educator'. *Law and Human Behaviour*, 10 (1/2), 63–78.

—— (1986). 'Ten years in the life of an expert witness'. *Law and Human Behavior*, 10, 241–263.

Loftus, E. F. and Ketcham, K. (1991). *Witness for the Defense*. New York: St Martin's Press.

—— (1994). *The Myth of Repressed Memory*. New York: St Martin's Press.

Lorge, T. and Blau, R. D. (1942). 'Broad occupational groupings by estimated abilities'. *Occupation*, 21, 288–295.

Loza, W. and Clements, P. (1991). 'Incarcerated alcoholics' and rapists' attributions of blame for criminal acts'. *Canadian Journal of Behavioural Science*, 23, 76–83.

Mackay, R. D. and Coleman, A. M. (1991). 'Excluding expert evidence: a tale of ordinary folk and common experience'. *Criminal Law Review*, 797–864.

Markesinis, B. S. and Deakin, S. F. (1994). *Tort Law*. 3rd edn Oxford: Clarendon Press.

Marston, W. M. (1917). 'Systolic blood pressure symptoms of deception'. *Journal of Experimental Psychology*, 2, 117–163.

Martell, D. A. (1992). 'Forensic neuropsychology and the criminal law'. *Law and Human Behavior*, 16, 313–336.

Matazarro, J. D. (1990). 'Psychological assessment versus psychological testing', *American Journal of Psychology*, 45, 999–1017.

Matarazzo, R. G. (1995). 'The ethical neuropsychologist. Psychological report standards in neuropsychology'. *The Clinical Neuropsychologist*, 9, 249–250.

McCary, J. L. (1956). 'The psychologist as expert witness in court', *American Psychologist*, 11, 8–13.

McConkey, K. M. and Sheehan, P. W. (1995). *Hypnosis, Memory, and Behavior in Criminal Investigation*. London: The Guilford Press.

McKinlay, W. W., Brooks, D. N. and Bond, B. M. R. (1983). 'Post-concussional symptoms, financial compensation and outcome of severe blunt head injury'. *Journal of Neurology, Neurosurgery and Psychiatry*, 46, 1,084–1,091.

McPherson, J. (1990). 'The forensic aspects of psychiatry in the armed forces'. In R. Bluglass and P. Bowden (eds), *Principles and Practice of Forensic Psychiatry*. London: Churchill Livingstone, 1,387–1,396.

Meehl, P.E. (1954). *Clinical Versus Statistical Predictions*. Minneapolis: University of Minnesota Press.

Meir, N. C. (1945). *Military Psychology*, New York:Harper.

Melton, G. B. (1987).'Training in psychology and law'. In I. B. Weiner and A. K. Hess (eds), *Handbook of Forensic Psychology*. New York: John Wiley and Sons, pp. 681–697.

Milne, R. and Bull, R. (1996). 'Interviewing children with mild learning disability with the cognitive interview'. In N. K. Clark and G. M. Stephenson (eds), *Investigative and*

Forensic Decision Making. Issues in Criminological and Legal Psychology. No. 26. Leicester: British Psychological Society.

Milner, J. S. (1986). *Child Abuse Potential Inventory: Manual.* 3rd Edition, Webster, N.C: Psytec Corporation.

Milsom, S. F. C. (1969). *Historical Foundations of Common Law.* London: Butterworths.

Mitchell, B. (1997). 'Diminished responsibility manslaughter'. *Journal of Forensic Psychiatry, 8,* 101–117.

Mitchell, S. and Richardson, P. J. (1985). *Archbold. Pleading, Evidence and Practice in Criminal Cases.* 42nd edn London: Sweet and Maxwell.

Monahan, J. (1981). *Predicting Violent Behavior: An Assessment of Clinical Techniques.* Beverly Hills: Sage Publications.

—— (1984). 'The prediction of violent behavior: toward a secondary generation of theory and policy'. *American Journal of Psychiatry, 141,* 10–15.

—— (1988). 'Risk assessment of violence among the mentally disordered: generating useful knowledge'. *International Journal of Law and Psychiatry, 11,* 249–257.

Montgomery, J. (1997). *Health Care Law.* Oxford: Oxford University Press.

Morris, A. and Gelsthorpe, L. (1993). 'Juveniles – Laws and facilities in the United Kingdom'. In J. Gunn and P J. Taylor (eds), *Forensic Psychiatry. Clinical, Legal and Ethical Issues.* Oxford: Butterworth Heinemann, pp. 210–251.

Morton, A. Q. (1978). *Literary Detection.* London: Bowker.

Morton, A. Q. and Michaelson, S. (1990). 'The Qsum plot'. Internal Report CSR-3–90. University of Edinburgh: Department of Computer Science.

Munsterberg, H. (1908). *In the Witness Stand.* New York: McClure.

—— (1909). *Psychology and Crime.* London: Unwin.

Murphy, G. H. and Clare, I. C. H. (1995). 'Adult's capacity to make decisions affecting the person: psychologists' contribution'. In R. Bull and D. Carson (eds), *Handbook of Psychology in Legal Contexts.* Chichester: John Wiley & Sons, pp. 97–128.

NACRO (1984). *School Reports in Juvenile Courts,* London: National Association for the Care and Resettlement of Offenders.

Nash, B. (1982). 'The psychologist as expert witness: a solicitors view'. In J. Shapland (ed.) *Lawyers and Psychologists: The Way Forward.* Leicester: British Psychological Society.

Newman, C. (1983). 'Psychometric tests examined in open court'. *Bulletin of the British Psychological Society, 36,* 296.

Nietzel, M. T. and Dillahay, R. C. (1986). *Psychological Consultation in the Courtroom.* Oxford: Pergamon Press.

Nilbett, B. and Boreham, J. (1976). 'Cluster analysis in court'. *Criminal Law Review,* 175–180.

Novaco, R. W. (1975). *Anger Control: The Development and Evaluation of an Experimental Treatment.* Lexington, Mass.: Heath.

Ofshe, R. (1989). 'Coerced confessions: the logic of seemingly irrational action'. *Cultic Studies Journal, 6,* 1–15.

—— (1992). 'Inadvertant hypnosis during interrogation: false confessions due to dissociative state: misidentified multiple personality disorder and the satanic cult hypothesis'. *International Journal of Clinical and Experimental Hypnosis, 40,* 125–156.

Ofshe, R. J. and Leo, R. A. (1997). 'The social psychology of police interrogation. The theory and classification of true and false confessions'. *Studies in Law, Politics and Society, 16,* 189–151.

Ofshe, R. and Watters, E. (1994). *Making Monsters. False Memories, Psychotherapy, and Sexual Hysteria.* London: Charles Scribner's Sons.

Ormerod, D. C. (1996). 'The evidential implications of psychological profiling'. *Criminal Law Review*, 863–877.

Ownby, R. L. (1997). *Psychological Reports. A Guide to Report Writing in Professional Psychology.* Chichester: John Wiley & Sons.

Palmer, T. (1971). *The Trials of OZ*, Manchester: Blond and Briggs.

Pankratz, L. (1988). 'Malingering on intellectual and neuropsychological measures'. In R. Rogers (ed.) *Clinical Assessment of Malingering and Deception.* London: Guilford Press, pp. 169–192.

Parker, H. (1987). 'The use of expert reports in juvenile and magistrates' courts'. In G. Gudjonsson and J. Drinkwater (eds), *Psychological Evidence in Court.* Issues in Criminological and Legal Psychology, No. 11. Leicester: British Psychological Society, pp. 15–19.

Peay, J. (1996). *Inquiries into Homicide.* London: Duckworth.

Pendergrast, M. (1996). *Victims of Memory.* London: HarperCollins.

Perr, I. N. (1981). 'Wills, testamentary capacity, and undue influence', *Bulletin of the American Academy of Psychiatry and Law*, 9, 15–22.

Petch, E. and Bradley, C. (1997). 'Learning the lessons from homicide inquiries: adding insult to injury.' *The Journal of Forensic Psychiatry*, 8, 161–184.

Pfeifer, J. E. and Brigham, J. C. (1993). 'Ethical concerns of nonclinical forensic witnesses and consultants'. *Ethics and Behavior*, 3, 329–343.

Piaget, J. (1932). *The Moral Judgement of the Child.* London: Routledge and Kegan Paul.

Pollock, P. H. (1996). 'A cautionary note on the determination of malingering in offenders'. *Psychology, Crime and Law*, 3, 97–110.

Pope, H. S., Butcher, J. N. and Seelen, J. (1993). *The MMPI, MMPI-2 and MMPI-A in Court. A Practical Guide for Expert Witnesses and Attorneys.* Washington, DC: American Psychological Association.

Pope, K. S. and Vetter, V. A. (1992). 'Ethical dilemmas encountered by members of the American Psychological Association'. *American Psychologist*, 47, 397–411.

Prestige, C. (1997). 'Disciplinary board'. In *Annual Report 1996–1997.* Leicester: British Psychological Society.

Professional Affairs Board (1995). 'Professional liability insurance'. *The Psychologist*, 8 (2), 82–85.

—— (1997). 'Disclosure of raw test scores in legal cases'. *The Psychologist*, 10 (4), 180.

Prokop, O. (1974). 'Judgment in a case involving parapsychology'. *Kriminalische und forensische Wissenschaft*, 14, 105–108.

Randall, C. (1997). 'Judges free man jailed over IRA funeral murders'. *The Daily Telegraph*, 21 June, p. 13.

Raymond, S. G. and Bornstein, S. J. (1991). 'Europsychiatres et Europsychologues: du nationalisme social a la politique sociale en Europe'. *Annales de Psychiatrie* 6 (2), 136–139.

Reason, J. and Lucas, D. (1984). 'Absentmindedness in shops: its incidence, correlates and consequences'. *British Journal of Clinical Psychology*, 23, 121–131.

Redmond, F. C. (1987). 'Testamentary capacity'. *Bulletin of the American Academy of Psychiatry and Law*, 15, 241–256.

Reiser, M. (1980). *Handbook of Investigative Hypnosis.* Los Angeles: LEHI Publishing.

Rembar, C. (1969). *The End of Obscenity*. London: Deutsch.

Resnick, P. J. (1988a). 'Malingered psychosis'. In Y. S. Ben-Porath, J. R. Graham, G. C. N. Hall, R. D. Hirschman and M. S. Zaragoza (eds), *Forensic Applications of the MMPI-2*. London: Sage Publications, pp. 34–53.

—— (1988b). 'Malingering of posttraumatic disorders'. In Y. S. Ben-Porath, J. R. Graham, G. C. N. Hall, R. D. Hirschman and M. S. Zaragoza (eds), *Forensic Applications of the MMPI-2*. London: Sage Publications, pp. 84–103.

Ressler, R. K. and Schachtman, T. (1992). *Whoever Fights Monsters*. St. Martin's Paperbacks: New York.

Retterstol, N. (1993). *Suicide. A European Perspective*. Cambridge: Cambridge University

Robertson, B. and Vignaux, G. A. (1995). *Interpreting Evidence. Evaluating Forensic Science in the Courtroom*. Chichester: John Wiley & Sons.

Robertson, G., Pearson, R. and Gibb, R. (1996). 'The entry of mentally disordered people to the criminal justice system'. *British Journal of Psychiatry*, 169, 171–180.

Rogers, R. (1988). *Clinical Assessment of Malingering and Deception*. London: Guilford Press.

—— (1990). 'Development of a new classifactory model of malingering'. *Bulletin of the American Academy of Psychiatry and Law*, 18, 323–333.

Rogers, R., Bagby, R. M. and Dickens, S. E. (1992). *The Structured Interview of Reported Symptoms*. Odessa, FL: Psychological Assessment Resources, Inc.

Royal College of Psychiatrists (1997). 'Nine-point programme of action'. *College News*, Issue 2, July.

Sackeim, H. M. and Gur, R. C. (1979). 'Self-deception, other-deception and self-reported psychopathology'. *Journal of Consulting and Clinical Psychology*, 47, 213–215.

Sadoff, R. L. (1988). 'Ethical issues in forensic psychiatry'. *Psychiatric Annals*, 18, 320–323.

Sakhova, T. V. (1986). 'Legal-psychological expertise in civil legal procedure', *Psikolicheskii Zhurnal*, 7 (4), 55–61.

Salter, A. (1988). *Treating Child Sex Offenders and Victims. A Practical Guide*. London: Sage Publications.

Sawyer, J. (1966). 'Measurement and prediction, clinical and statistical'. *Psychological Bulletin*, 66, 178–200.

Schacter, D. L. (1986). 'Feelings-of-knowing ratings distinguish between genuine and simulated forgetting'. *Journal of Experimental Psychology: Learning, Memory and Cognition*, 12, 30–41.

Schinka, J. A. and Borum, R. (1993). 'Readability of adult psychopathology inventories'. *Psychological Assessment*, 5, 384–386.

Schooler, J. W. and Loftus, E. F. (1986). 'Individual differences and experimentation: complementary approaches to interrogative suggestibility'. *Social Behaviour*, 1, 105–112.

Schrenck-Notzing, A. (1897). *Über Suggestion und Erinnerungsfälschung in Berthold Prozess*. Leipzig: Barth.

Schwitzgebel, R. L. and Schwitzgebel R. K. (1980). *Law and Psychological Practice*. Chichester: Wiley.

Shapiro, D. L. (1990). *Forensic Psychological Assessment. An Integrative Approach*. London: Allyn and Bacon.

Shepherd, E. W., Mortimer, A. K. and Mobasheri, R. (1995). 'The police caution: comprehension and perceptions in the general population'. *Expert Evidence. The International Digest of Human Behaviour, Science and Law*, 4, 60–67.

228

Sheppard, D. (1995). *Learning the Lessons*. 1st edn London: Zito Trust.

—— (1996). *Learning the Lessons*. 2nd edn London: Zito Trust.

Shipley, W. C. (1940). 'A self-administered scale for measuring intellectual impairment and deterioration', *Journal of Psychology*, 9, 371–377.

Shuman, D. W. (1993). 'The use of empathy in forensic examinations'. *Ethics and Behavior*, 3, 289–302.

Shuy, R. (1993). *Language Crimes*. Cambridge: Blackwell.

Sigurdsson, E., Gudjonsson, G. H., Kolbeinsson, H. and Petursson, H., (1994). 'The effects of ECT and depression on confabulation, memory processing, and suggestibility'. *Nordic Journal of Psychiatry*, 48, 443–451.

Sigurdsson, J. F. and Gudjonsson, G. H. (1996). 'Psychological characteristics of "false confessors". A study among Icelandic prison inmates and juvenile offenders.' *Personality and Individual Differences*, 20, 321–329.

Singer, M. T. and Nievod, A. (1987). 'Consulting and testifying in court'. In I. B. Weinder and A. K. Hess (eds), *Handbook of Forensic Psychology*. New York: John Wiley & Sons, pp. 529–554.

Smith, J. D., Tracy, J. I. and Murray, M. J. (1993). 'Depression and category learning'. *Journal of Experimental Psychology: General*, 122, 331–346.

Spar, J. E. and Garb, A. S. (1992). 'Assessing competence to make a will', *American Journal of Psychiatry*, 149, 169–174.

Spielberger, C. D. (1983). *State-Trait Anxiety Inventory. STAI (Form Y)*. Palo Alto, CA: Consulting Psychologists Press, Inc.

Spillman, J. and Spillman, J. (1993). 'The rise and fall of Hugo Munsterberg', *Journal of the History of the Behavioural Sciences*, 29, 322–338.

Steller, M. and Boychuk, T. (1992). 'Children as witnesses in sex abuse cases: investigative interview and assessment techniques'. In H. Dent and R. Flin (eds), *Children as Witnesses*. Chichester: John Wiley & Sons, pp. 47–71.

Steller, M. and Koehnken, G. (1990). 'Criteria-Based Statement Analysis'. In D. R. Raskin (ed.), *Psychological Methods in Criminal Investigation and Evidence*. New York: Springer, pp. 217–246.

Stephenson, G. H. (1992). *The Psychology of Criminal Justice*. Oxford: Blackwell.

Stern, L. W. (1910). 'Abstracts of lectures on testimony', *American Journal of Psychology*, 21, 273–282.

Stone, A. A. (1993). 'Post-traumatic stress disorder and the law: critical review of the new frontier'. *Bulletin of the American Academy of Psychiatry and Law*, 21, 23–36.

Svartvik, J. (1967). *The Evans Statements*. Gothenberg: Acta Universitas.

Taylor, A. J. W. (1979). 'Forensic psychology: principles, practice and training'. In W. A. M. Black and A. J. W. Taylor (eds), *Deviant Behaviour*. Auckland: Heinemann, pp. 3–8.

Taylor of Gosforth, Lord (1995). 'The Lund Lecture'. *Medicine, Science and the Law, 35*, 3–8.

Taylor, P. J. and Kopelman, M. D. (1984). 'Amnesia for criminal offences'. *Psychological Medicine*, 14, 581–588.

Terman, L. M. and Merrill, M. A. (1937). *Measuring Intelligence*. Boston: Houghton Mifflin.

Theilgaard, A. (1996). 'A clinical psychological perspective'. In C. Cordess and M. Cox (eds), *Forensic Psychotherapy. Crime, Psychodynmics and the Offender Patient*. London: Jessica Kingsley Publishers, pp. 47–62.

Thelen, M. H., Rodriquez, M. D. and Sprengelmeyer, P. (1994). 'Psychologists' beliefs concerning confidentiality with suicide, homicide and child abuse', *American Journal of Psychotherapy*, *48* (3), 363–379.

Timsit, M. (1992). 'La place du Rorschach dans l'expertise en matiére criminelle' (English abstract). *Psychologie-Medicale*, *24*, (11), 1186–1199.

Totty, R. N., Hardcastle, R. A., and Pearson, J. (1987). 'Forensic linguistics: the determination of authorship from habits of style'. *Journal of the Forensic Science Society*, *27*, 13–28.

Towl, G. (ed.) (1996). *Suicide and Self-injury in Prisons*. Leicester: British Psychological Society.

Towl, G. J. and Crichton, D. A. (1996). *Handbook of Psychology for Forensic Practitioners*. London: Routledge.

Trankell, A. (1972). *Reliability of Evidence*. Stockholm: Beckmans.

—— (1982). 'The scope of psychological expertise contributions to the evaluation of witness evidence'. In A. Trankell (ed.), *Reconstructing the Past. The Roles of Psychologists in Criminal Trials*. Deventer, The Netherlands: Kluwer, pp. 11–25.

Tunstall, O., Gudjonsson, G., Eysenck, H. and Haward, L. (1982). 'Professional issues arising from psychological evidence presented in court'. *Bulletin of the British Psychological Society*, *35*, 329–331.

Udolf, R. (1983). *Forensic Hypnosis*. Lexington, Mass.: Heath.

Undeutsch, U. (1982). 'Statement Reality Analysis'. In Trankell, A. (ed.), *Reconstructing the Past*. Deventer, Netherlands: Kluwer.

—— (1989). 'The development of Statement Reality Analysis'. In J. C. Yuille (ed.) *Credibility Assessment*. Deventer, Netherlands: Kluwer, pp. 101–119.

Valciukas, J. A. (1995). *Forensic Neuropsychology. Conceptual Foundations and Clinical Practice*. London: The Haworth Press, Inc.

Wagstaff, G. F. (1988). 'A response to the comments of Gibson, Haward, and Orne', *British Journal of Experimental and Clinical Hypnosis*, *5* (1), 45–49.

Walker, N. (1968). *Crime and Insanity in England: Historical Perspectives*. Edinburgh: Edinburgh University Press.

Ward, E. S. (1978). 'On a point of evidence', *Bulletin of the British Psychological Society*, *31*, 8–10.

Wasik, M. and Taylor, R. (1995). *Blackstone's Guide to the Criminal Justice & Public Order Act 1994*. London: Blackstone Press Limited.

Webster, C., Harris, G., Rice, M., Cormier, C. and Quinsey, V. (1994). *The Violence Prediction Scheme: Assessing Dangerousness in High Risk Men*. Toronto: Centre of Criminology, University of Toronto.

Wechsler, D. (1955). *The Wechsler Intelligence Scale for Children*, New York: Psychological Corporation.

—— (1974). *Manual for the Wechsler Intelligence Scale for Children – Revised*. New York: Psychological Corporation.

—— (1981). *Manual for the Wechsler Intelligence Scale for Adults – Revised*. New York: Psychological Corporation.

Weiner, I. B. (1987). 'Writing forensic reports'. In I. B. Weiner and A. K. Hess (eds), *Handbook of Forensic Psychology*. New York: John Wiley & Sons, pp. 511–528.

—— (1995). 'Psychometric issues in forensic applications of the MMPI-2'. In Y. S. Ben-Porath, J. R. Graham, G. C. N. Hall, R. D. Hirschman and M. S. Zaragoza (eds), *Forensic Applications of the MMPI-2*. London: Sage Publications, pp. 48–81.

Winkler, J. D., Kanouse, D. E., and Ware, J. E. (1982). 'Controlling for acquiescence response set in score development'. *Journal of Applied Psychology*, 67, 555–561.

Winter, D. G. (1996). *Personality. Analysis of interpretation of lives*. London: McGraw-Hill Companies, Inc.

Woolf, Lord (1996). *Access to Justice. Final Report to the Lord Chancellor on the Civil Justice System in England and Wales*. London: HMSO.

Wrightsman, L. S. and Kassin, S. M. (1992). *Confessions in the Courtroom*. London: Sage Publications.

INDEX

abilities, definition 81–2
'abnormality of mind' 167
ABS *see* Attribution of Blame Scale
absentmindedness, as defence 166–7
abuse: alcohol/drugs 91, 147; children 116, 117–19, 179–80; recovered memories 179–80
accident inquiries 148, 151
acquiescence, psychological testing 96
actuarial role, forensic psychologists 72–3, 78
actus reus 164–5
administrative law 145–51, 153
admiralty law *see* maritime law
admissibility: evidence by hypnosis 21; general requirements for 15–18, 169–73, 180–1; offender profiling 174, 175–6
advisory role, forensic psychologists 73–5, 78
age *see* mental age
airline accidents 113–14, 151
Aitken, C. 73
alcohol abuse 91, 147
American Psychological Association (APA) 37, 39–42, 44–5
amnesia 97–8, 178–9
anxiety 94–5, 103
anxiety-reduction hypnosis 21
APA *see* American Psychological Association
appearance, attending court 196–7
Arcaya, J. M. 51
armed forces 13–14
Army Tests 13
assault, tortious 60
assessment 185–90, 193, 200–1; codes of

conduct 40, 43; diminished responsibility 167–8; ethical dilemmas 45; financial competency 137–9, 140; fitness to plead 163–4; forensic psychologists' role 68–70, 78; forensic psychology/forensic psychiatry contrast 76; general advice 182–3; impartiality 56–7; mental states 91–6; psychological surveys 26, 34–5; risk 25, 142–3, 168; suicide risk 142–3; taking on cases 205–6; *see also* profiling; psychological testing
attention, psychological testing 93–4
Attribution of Blame Scale (ABS) 178
auditory material, analysis 103, 111–14
autopsies *see* psychological autopsies

BAI *see* Blame Attribution Inventory
Baker, J. H. 6
Barker, D. 141
battery, tort 60
'battle of the experts' 33, 74
bespoke assessment 137–9
Best Evidence Rule 17–18
bias: assessments 187–8; codes of conduct 45; eagerness to please 52–7; reports 30–1, 51, 193–4, 210; statistical evidence 126; *see also* response bias
Binder, L. M. 192, 199
Binet-type psychometrics 12–13
Blackburn, R. 3
Blame Attribution Inventory (BAI) 178
Boreham, J. 104
boundaries, ethical dilemmas 45, 46
Boychuk, T. 118
BPS *see* British Psychological Society
Bradley, C. 150